A Survey of Sierra Leonean English

Momodu Turay

Sierra Leonean Writers Series

A Survey of Sierra Leonean English

Copyright © 2017 by Momodu Turay

ISBN 978-99-88-8698-0-9

All rights reserved. No part of this book may be reproduced in any form or by any electronic or mechanical means except by reviewers for the public press without written permission from the publishers.

First published June 2017
Reprinted with slight revisions April 2023
Reprinted with additional revisions July 2025

Sierra Leonean Writers Series (SLWS)
Warima/Freetown
UNIMTECH, Kissy Dockyard, Freetown, Sierra Leone
Publisher: Prof. Osman Sankoh (Mallam O.)
publisher@slwritersseries.org
www.slwritersseries.org

DEDICATION

This work is dedicated to the journalists, lecturers and students of English in Sierra Leone who have amply demonstrated that there is an English variety in the country which we can proudly describe as ours.

ACKNOWLEDGEMENTS

It has been arduous to complete this book and I must therefore thank all those who have assisted me in diverse ways.

I would first like to thank Allah without whose unmerited favours this study would have been a mirage.

I am also indebted to Mr. Ajayi Coomber and Professor Magnus John whose assistance, guidance and direction have influenced the form and content of this presumably enviable study. Their eagle-eyed supervision during my doctoral studies was evident by inter alia their ability to identify the most awkward snag and find an almost instant solution.

My thanks are also due to my colleagues in the Language Studies Department for their encouragement. I am in particular indebted to Mrs.Elizabeth Kamara, the indefatigable Head of the English Unit and Mr. Kenneth Olushola Osho, the former Head of Department, , and Messers Joseph Lamin Kamara and Osman Kamara (once our former students, now very much more).

I wish to further thank my special friends - former teachers who have now become directors, managers, registrars and engineers - for the moral support they rendered me during the trying times of this study.

To my caring wife, Salamatu Samura, my siblings, the late Abdulai Turay, the late Mahmud Turay, and the late Aminata Turay; and to my nephew, the late Mustapha Turay, thank you very much for the support you gave me.

Finally, I am solely responsible for the shortcomings in this book.

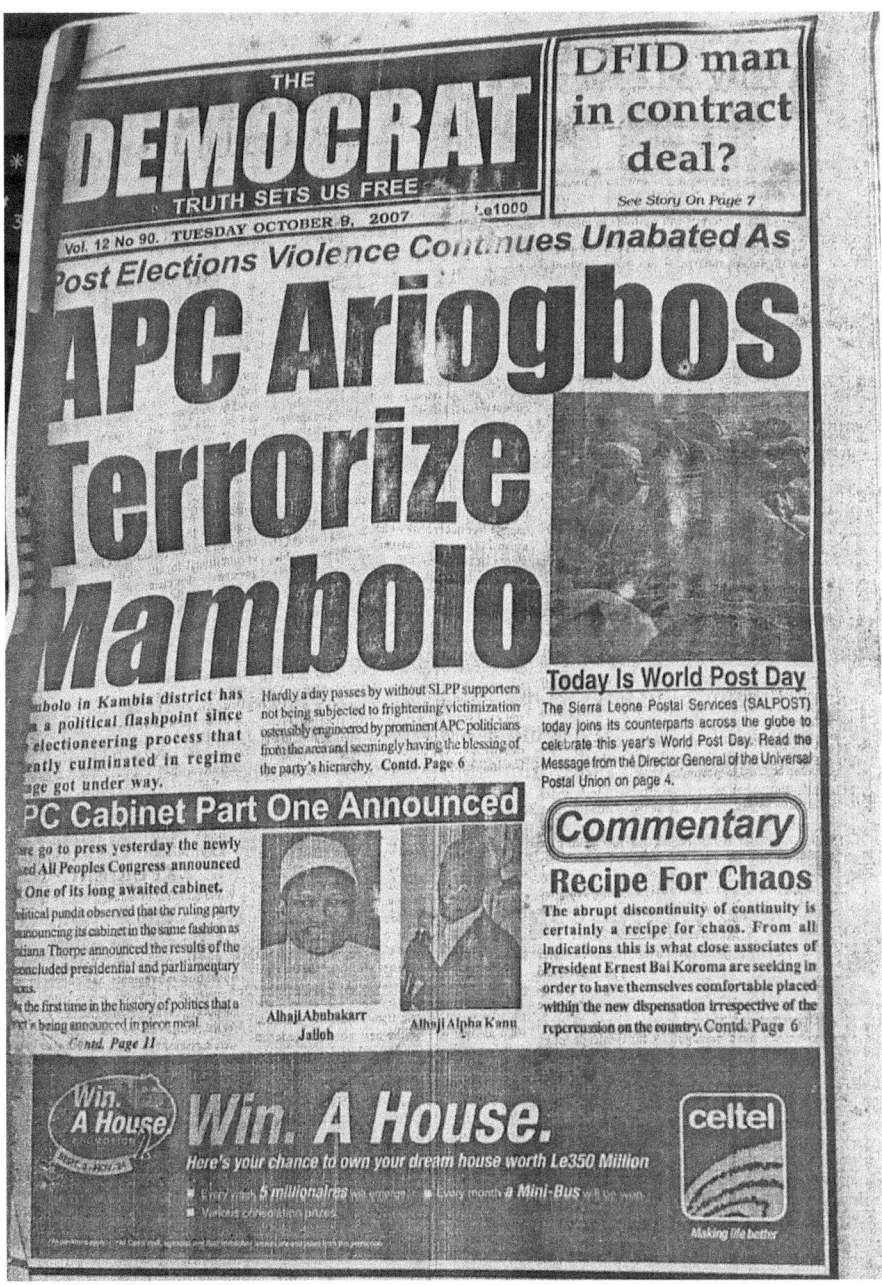

A Survey of Sierra Leonean English   *Momodu Turay*

> M.L. Bangura went on to state that he bears no grudge for Ernest Koroma but says the latter's failure and total refusal to implement the 2004 orders of the Supreme Court of Sierra Leone. He told the public through the media that if

A Survey of Sierra Leonean English   *Momodu Turay*

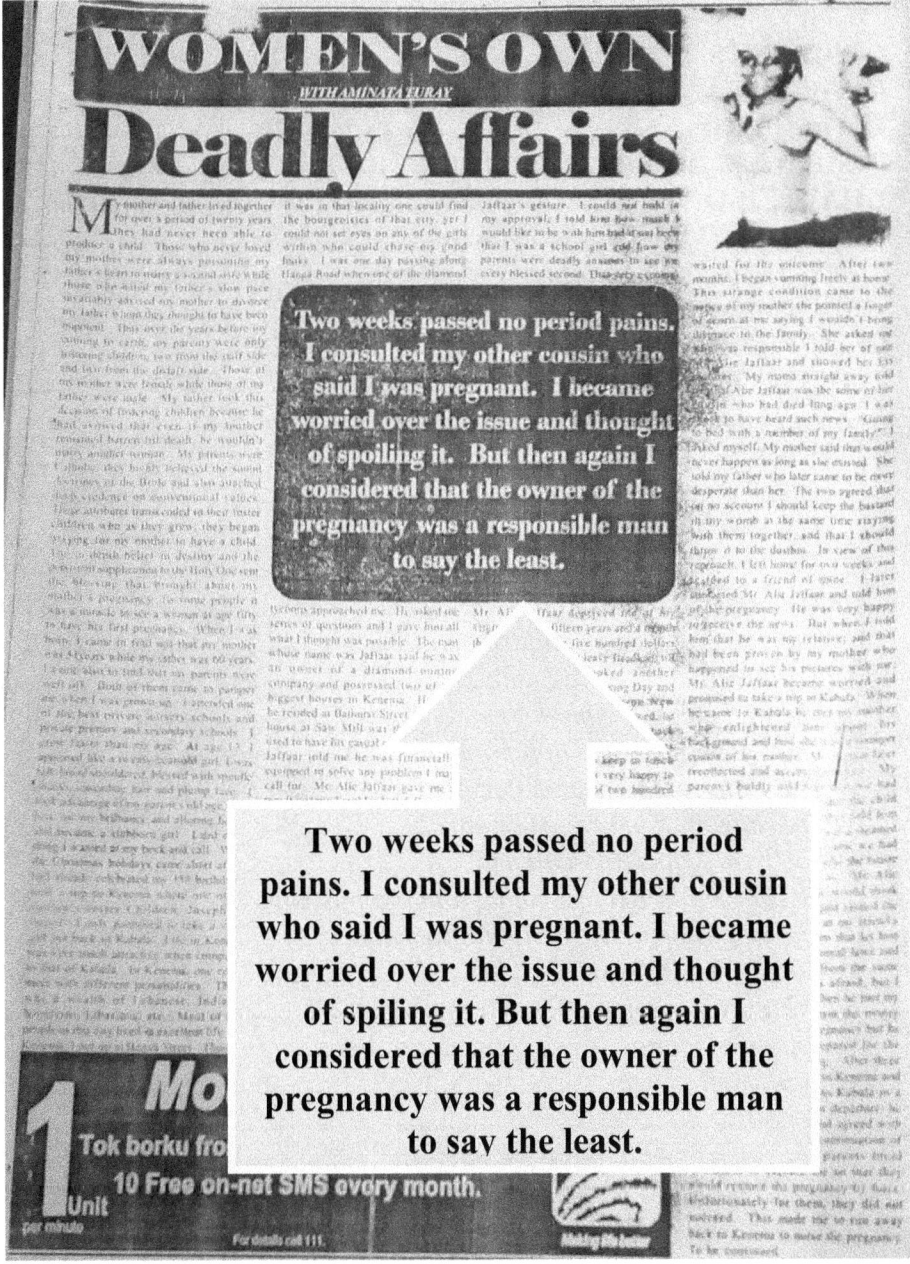

CONTENTS

CONTENTS..viii
List of Tables xvii
List of Graphs xviii
PREFACE...xx
CHAPTER ONE..22
INTRODUCTION 22
  Sierra Leone: A Socio-Linguistic Profile 22
  The Status of English 24
CHAPTER TWO..27
THE FEATURES OF SIERRA LEONEAN ENGLISH..............27
  The Phonological Peculiarities in the English of Educated Sierra Leoneans 27
    The Segmental Features..27
    The Vowel Related Peculiarity..27
    The Merging of Vowels 27
    The Substitution of Vowels..29
    Spelling-Induced Peculiarity 31
    Nasalisation 32
    The Merging of Diphthongs...33
    The Substitution of Diphthongs 33
    The Consonant-Related Peculiarity 34
    The Substitution of Consonants 34
    Spelling-Induced Peculiarity 35
    The Omission of the Linking and the Intrusive 'R'.................36
    The Omission of the Syllabic Consonants 37
    Consonant Deletion 38
    The Suprasegmental Features 38
    Syllable Timing 38
    Downdrift...39
    Tonality..42
    The Lack of Attitudinal Intonation..42
    The Lack of the Contrastive Stress 44
  The Lexical Peculiarities in the English of Educated Sierra Leoneans 46
    Collocation..46
    Collocation in Native English..46
    First Language Induced Collocation 47

Culturally Induced Collocation 48
Word Modification 48
The Extension of Word Meaning 49
The Restriction of Word Meaning 50
The Change of Word Meaning 51
Idiomaticity 51
Native English Idiom 51
Local Idiom 52
Innovation 53
Aboriginal Words 54
The Grammatical Peculiarities in the English of Educated Sierra Leoneans 54
    Noun 55
    Pronoun 56
    Verb 57
    Concord 57
    Infinitive/Participle 58
    Tense and Aspect 59
    Determiner 61
    Different Determiner 61
    Article Inclusion 63
    Article Omission 63
    Adjective 64
    Preposition 65
    Prepositional Usage 65
    Prepositional Inclusion 66
    Prepositional Omission 66
    Word Class 67
    Syntax 68
    Imbalance 68
    Repetition 69
    Structural Omission 71
    Comparison 71
    Content and Function Words 71
    Structural Differences 72
    Pronoun 72
    Pronoun in Compound Subject/Object 72
    Pronoun Copying 73

   The Placement of the Modifier 73
   Universal Tag 75
   Reduplication 75
   Responses to Negative Yes/No Questions/Statements 75
   The Discoursal Peculiarities in the English of Educated Sierra Leoneans 76
      Form of Address 76
      Proverb and Riddle 77
      Phatic Communion 78
      Style 79
   Conclusion 80
CHAPTER THREE.. 81
THE EXISTENCE OF THE HIGHLIGHTED FEATURES IN OTHER ENGLISH VARIETIES 81
   Introduction 81
   The Phonological Features in other English Varieties 81
      The Segmental Features in other English Varieties...................... 81
      Vowel Merging.. 81
      Vowel Substitution 82
      Spelling-Induced Peculiarity 83
      Nasalisation 84
      The Substitution of Consonants 85
      The Omission of the Linking and the Intrusive 'R' 86
      The Omission of the Syllabic Consonants 87
      Consonant Deletion 87
      The Suprasegmental Features in other English Varieties............ 88
      Syllable Timing 89
      Downdrift.. 89
      Tonality 90
      The Lack of Attitudinal Intonation... 90
      The Lack of the Contrastive Stress 91
   The Existence of the Lexical Features in other English Varieties... 92
      The Collocation-Related Peculiarity in other English Varieties.. 92
      Native English Collocation Peculiarity 92
      First Language-Induced Collocation 94
      Culturally-Induced Collocation... 94
      Word Modification Peculiarity in other English Varieties 95
      The Extension of the Meanings of Words 95

The Restriction of the Meanings of Words 95
The Change of the Meanings of Words 96
Idiom-Related Peculiarity in other English Varieties.................. 96
The Modification of Native English Idioms 97
The Use of Local Idioms 98
Innovation-Related Peculiarity in other English Varieties........... 99
Aboriginal-Related Peculiarity in other English Varieties........... 99
The Existence of the Grammatical Features in other English Varieties   100
   The Noun-Related Peculiarity in other English Varieties 101
   The Pronoun-Related Peculiarity in other English Varieties 101
   The Verb-Related Peculiarity in other English Varieties 102
   Concordial Use.. 103
   Infinitive/Participle 104
   Tense and Aspect 105
   The Determiner-Related Peculiarity in other English Varieties. 106
   Determiner Usage Related Peculiarity 106
   Determiner Inclusion-Related Peculiarity 107
   Determiner Omission-Related Peculiarity 109
   The Adjective-Related Peculiarity in other English Varieties ... 110
   Preposition-Related Peculiarity in other English Varieties........ 110
   Prepositional Usage-Related Peculiarity.................... 110
   Prepositional Inclusion-Related Peculiarity 112
   Prepositional Omission-Related Peculiarity 112
   Word Class-Related Peculiarity in other English Varieties 113
   Syntax-Related Peculiarity in other English Varieties 114
   Imbalance-Related Peculiarity 114
   Repetition-Related Peculiarity 115
   Structural Omission-Related Peculiarity in other English Varieties... 116
   The Omission of the Comparative Word 116
   The Omission of Function and Content Words 117
   Structural Difference-Related Peculiarity................... 118
   Pronoun in Compound Subject/Object....................... 118
   Pronoun Copying-Related Peculiarity 119
   The Modifier Placement-Related Peculiarity............. 119
   Universal Tag-Related Peculiarity 120
   Reduplication-Related Peculiarity 121

    Responses to Negative Yes/No Question/ Statement-Related
    Peculiarity 122
   The Discoursal Features in other English Varieties 122
    Form of Address-Related Peculiarity in   other English Varieties
                                      122
    Proverb And Riddle-Related Peculiarity in other English Varieties
    123
    Phatic Communion-Related Peculiarity in other English Varieties
    125
   Style-Related Peculiarity in other English Varieties 126
  Conclusion 127
CHAPTER FOUR..**128**
**THE CAUSES OF THE FEATURES OF THE SIERRA
LEONEAN ENGLISH VARIETY** **128**
  Introduction 128
  The Causes of the Phonological Features 128
    The Causes of the Segmental Features 128
    The Causes of the Vowel-Related Peculiarity 128
    The Vowel Merging-Related Peculiarity 128
    The Vowel Substitution-Related Peculiarity 129
    The Spelling-Induced Peculiarity 130
    The Nasalisation-Related Peculiarity 130
    The Diphthong Merging-Related Peculiarity 131
    The Diphthong Substitution-Related Peculiarity 131
    The Causes of the Consonant-Related Peculiarity 131
    The Consonant Substitution-Related Peculiarity 131
    The Spelling-Induced Peculiarity 132
    The Linking and the Intrusive 'R'-Related Peculiarity 133
    The Omission of the Syllabic Consonants 133
    The Omission of Consonants 133
    The Causes of the Suprasegmental Features 134
    The Syllable Timing Related Peculiarity 134
    The Downdrift-Related Peculiarity 134
    The Tonal-Related Peculiarity 135
    The Lack of Attitudinal Intonation-Related Peculiarity 135
    The Lack of the Contrastive Stress-Related Peculiarity 136
    Conclusion 137
  The Causes of the Lexical Peculiarities 138

The Causes Of The Collocation-Related   Peculiarity..............138
The Native English Collocation-Related Peculiarity 138
The First Language-Induced Collocation Peculiarity 138
The Culturally-Induced Collocation Peculiarity........................139
The Causes of the Word Modification-Related Peculiarity 139
The Extension of the Word Meaning-Related Peculiarity.........139
The Restriction of the Word Meaning Related Peculiarity 140
The Meaning Change-Related Peculiarity 140
The Causes of the Idiom-Related Peculiarity.............................141
The Modification of the Native English Idiom-Related Peculiarity 141
The First Language-Induced Idiom..141
The Causes of the Innovation-Related Peculiarity.....................141
The Causes of the Aboriginal-Related Peculiarity.....................142
Conclusion..142
The Causes of the Grammatical Related Peculiarity 143
The Causes of the Noun-Related Peculiarity 143
The Causes of the Pronoun-Related Peculiarity.........................144
The Causes of the Verb-Related Peculiarity 145
The Concordial-Related Peculiarity 145
The Infinitive/Participle-Related Peculiarity 146
The Tense/Aspect-Related Peculiarity..147
The Causes of the Determiner-Related Peculiarity 149
The Determiner Usage Related Peculiarity 149
The Determiner Inclusion-Related Peculiarity 150
The Determiner Omission-Related Peculiarity 150
The Cause(s) of the Adjective-Related Peculiarity 151
The Cause(s) of the Prepositional-Related Peculiarity...............151
The Prepositional Usage-Related Peculiarity...........................151
The Prepositional Inclusion-Related Peculiarity 153
The Prepositional Omission-Related Peculiarity.......................153
The Cause(s) of the Word Class-Related Peculiarity.................153
The Causes of the Syntax-Related Peculiarity 154
The Imbalance-Related Peculiarity..154
The Repetition-Related Peculiarity 154
The Causes of the Structural Omission-Related Peculiarity.......155
The Omission of the Comparative Word-Related Peculiarity....155

The Omission of the Content and Function Word-Related Peculiarity... 155
The Structural Difference-Related Peculiarity 156
The Order of Pronoun-Related Peculiarity 156
The Pronoun Inclusion-Related Peculiarity 156
The Placement of the Modifier-Related Peculiarity 157
The Universal Tag-Related Peculiarity 157
The Reduplication-Related Peculiarity 158
The Responses to Negative Yes/No Question/Statement-Related Peculiarity... 158
Conclusion 159
The Causes of the Discoursal-Related Preculiarity 159
The Form of Address-Related Peculiarity 159
The Proverb/Riddle-Related Peculiarity 160
The Phatic Communion-Related Peculiarity 160
The Style-Related Peculiarity 161
Conclusion 161
Summary 161
CHAPTER FIVE **163**
TESTS AND TEST RESULTS **163**
Introduction 163
The Phonological Peculiarities 163
Test on the Acceptability Level Relating to the Examples of the Vowel-Related Peculiarity.. 163
The Results of the Responses Relating to the Examples of the Vowel-Related Peculiarity.. 167
Test on the Acceptability Level Relating to the Examples of the Consonant-Related Peculiarity 169
The Results of the Responses Relating to the Examples of the Consonant-Related Peculiarity 170
Test on the Acceptability Level Relating to the Examples of the Suprasegmental Peculiarity 173
The Results of the Responses Relating to the Examples of the Suprasegmental-Related Peculiarity... 176
The Lexical Peculiarities 178
Test on the Acceptability Level Relating to the Examples of the Collocation-Related Peculiarity 178

The Results of the Responses Relating to the Examples of the
Collocation-Related Peculiarity 180
Test on the Acceptability Level Relating to the Examples of the
Word Modification-Related Peculiarity 182
The Results of the Responses Relating to the Examples of the
Word Modification-Related Peculiarity 184
Test on the Acceptability Level Relating to the Examples of the
Idiom-Related Peculiarity..186
The Results of the Responses Relating to the Examples of the
Idiom-Related Peculiarity..186
Test on the Acceptability Level Relating to the Examples of the
Innovation-Related Peculiarity..189
The Results of the Responses Relating to Examples of the
Innovation-Related Peculiarity..189
Test on the Acceptability Level Relating to the Examples of the
Aboriginal-Related Peculiarity..191
The Results of the Responses Relating to the Examples of the
Aboriginal-Related Peculiarity..192
The Grammatical Peculiarities 194
Test on the Acceptability Level Relating to the Examples of the
Noun-Related Peculiarity 194
The Results of the Responses Relating to the Examples of the
Noun-Related Peculiarity 195
Test on the Acceptability Level Relating to the Examples of the
Pronoun-Related Peculiarity..197
The Results of the Responses Relating to the Examples of the
Pronoun-Related Peculiarity..198
Test on the Acceptability Level Relating to the Examples of the
Verb-Related Peculiarity 200
The Results of the Responses Relating to the Examples of the
Verb-Related Peculiarity 202
Test on the Acceptability Level Relating to the Examples of the
Determiner Related-Peculiarity...204
The Results of the Responses Relating to the Examples of the
Determiner-Related Peculiarity...206
Test on the Acceptability Level Relating to the Examples of the
Adjective-Related Peculiarity..208

The Results of the Responses Relating to the Examples of the
Adjective-Related Peculiarity 208
Test on the Acceptability Level Relating to the Examples of the
Preposition-Related Peculiarity 210
The Results of the Responses Relating to the Examples of the
Preposition-Related Peculiarity 212
Test on the Acceptability Level Relating to the Examples of the
Word Class-Related Peculiarity... 213
The Results of the Responses Relating to the Examples of the
Word Class-Related Peculiarity... 214
Test on the Acceptability Level Relating to the Examples of the
Syntax-Related Peculiarity 216
The Results of the Responses Relating to the Examples of the
Syntax-Related Peculiarity 220
Conclusion 223
CHAPTER SIX.. 224
SUMMARY, CONCLUSIONS, RECOMMENDATIONS AND THE FUTURE OF ENGLISH AND ITS IMPLICATIONS FOR THE SIERRA LEONEAN VARIETY... 224
Introduction 224
Summary 224
Conclusions... 227
Recommendations for Further Research 228
The Future of English and Its Implications for the Sierra Leonean Variety.. 229
INDEX... 272

List of Tables

Table 1: Summary of the responses to the vowel-related peculiarity in the four institution _____ 168

Table 2: Summary of the responses relating to the examples of the consonant-related peculiarity in the four institutions _____ 171

Table 3: Summary of the responses relating to the examples of the suprasegmental-related peculiarity in the four institutions _____ 177

Table 4: Summary of the responses relating to the examples of the collocation-related peculiarity in the four institutions _____ 181

Table 5: Summary of the responses relating to the examples of the word modification-related peculiarity in the four institutions _____ 184

Table 6: Summary of the responses relating to the examples of the idiom-related peculiarity in the four institutions _____ 187

Table 7: Summary of the responses relating to the examples of the innovation-related peculiarity in the four institutions _____ 190

Table 8: Summary of the responses relating to the examples of the aboriginal-related peculiarity in the four institutions _____ 193

Table 9: Summary of the responses relating to the examples of the noun-related peculiarity in the four institutions _____ 196

Table 10: Summary of the responses relating to the examples of the pronoun-related peculiarity in the four institutions _____ 198

Table 11: Summary of the responses relating to the examples of the verb-related peculiarity in the four institutions _____ 203

Table 12: Summary of the responses relating to the examples of the determiner-related peculiarity in the four institutions _____ 206

Table 13: Summary of the responses relating to the examples of the adjective-related peculiarity in the four institutions _____ 209

Table 14: Summary of the responses relating to the examples of the preposition-related peculiarity in the four institutions _____ 212

Table 15: Summary of the responses relating to the examples of the word class-related peculiarity in the four institutions _____ 215

Table 16: Summary of the responses relating to the examples of the syntax-related peculiarity in the four institutions _____ 221

Table 17: Summary of the responses relating to the total peculiarities in the four institutions _____ 226

List of Graphs

Graph 1: Summary of the responses relating to the examples of the vowel-related peculiarity 167
Graph 2: Summary of the responses relating to the examples of the vowel-related peculiarity in the four institutions 168
Graph 3: Summary of the responses relating to the examples of the consonant-related peculiarity 172
Graph 4: Summary of the responses to the consonant-related peculiarity in the four institutions 172
Graph 5: Summary of the responses to the suprasegmental-related peculiarity 177
Graph 6: Summary of the responses to the suprasegmental-related peculiarity in the four institutions 178
Graph 7: Summary of the responses relating to the examples of the collocation-related peculiarity 181
Graph 8: Summary of the responses relating to the examples of the collocation-related peculiarity in the four institutions 182
Graph 9: Summary of the responses relating to the examples of the word modification-related peculiarity 185
Graph 10: Summary of the responses to the word modification-related peculiarity in the four institutions 185
Graph 11: Summary of the responses relating to the examples of the idiom-related peculiarity 188
Graph 12: Summary of the responses relating to the examples of the idiom-related peculiarity in the four institutions 188
Graph 13: Summary of the responses relating to the examples of the innovation-related peculiarity 190
Graph 14: Summary of the responses relating to the examples of the innovation-related peculiarity in the four institutions 191
Graph 15: Summary of the responses relating to the examples of the aboriginal-related peculiarity 193
Graph 16: Summary of the responses relating to the examples of the aboriginal-related peculiarity in the four institutions 194
Graph 17: Summary of the responses to the noun-related peculiarity 196
Graph 18: Summary of the responses relating to the examples of the noun-related peculiarity in the four institutions 197
Graph 19: Summary of the responses relating to the examples of the pronoun-related peculiarity 199
Graph 20: Summary of the responses relating to the examples of the pronoun-related peculiarity in the four Institutions 199
Graph 21: Summary of the responses relating to the examples of the verb-related peculiarity 203

Graph 22: Summary of the responses relating to the examples of the verb-related peculiarity in the four institutions... 204
Graph 23: Summary of the responses relating to the examples of the determiner-related peculiarity.. 207
Graph 24: Summary of the responses relating to the examples of the determiner-related peculiarity in the four institutions 207
Graph 25: Summary of the responses relating to the examples of the adjective-related peculiarity.. 209
Graph 26: Summary of the responses relating to the examples of the adjective-related peculiarity in the four institutions 210
Graph 27: Summary of the responses relating to the examples of the preposition-related peculiarity.. 213
Graph 28: Summary of the responses relating to the examples of the preposition-related peculiarity in the four institutions 213
Graph 29: Summary of the responses relating to the examples of the word class-related peculiarity.. 215
Graph 30: Summary of the responses relating to the examples of the word class-related peculiarity in the four institutions 216
Graph 31: Summary of the responses relating to the examples of the syntax-related peculiarity 222
Graph 32: Summary of the responses relating to the examples of the syntax-related peculiarity in the four institutions... 222
Graph 33: Summary of the responses relating to the total peculiarities 226
Graph 34: Summary of the responses to the total peculiarities in the four institutions 227

PREFACE

This work was originally submitted as a thesis for the degree of Doctor of Philosophy (Ph.D.) from the University of Sierra Leone in 2010, with the title: Towards the Nativisation of the English Language in Sierra Leone: A Case Study of the Print and Electronic Media.

For that exercise, I collected spoken and written data from local newspapers and from radio and television programmes, which involved educated Sierra Leonean users of the English language. The newspapers covered were 'Standard Times', 'The New Citizen', 'Concord Times', 'Kalleone', 'The Exclusive', 'The Spectator', 'The African Champion', 'New Vision', 'Unity', 'Independent Observer', 'Premier News', 'Sierra Express Media', 'For di People', 'Awoko', 'Awareness Times', 'We Yone', 'Positive Change', 'The Democrat', 'Salone Times', 'Junior Salone Times', 'The Pool' and 'Peep Magazine'. The electronic media were 'The Sierra Leone Broadcasting Service' (both radio and television), 'Radio Mount Aureol' and 'Kalleone Radio.'

In order to test the acceptability or otherwise of the features observed from the primary data, I chose lecturers of English and Final Year students offering English in tertiary institutions across the country; namely, Northern Polytechnic Institute (NP), Eastern Polytechnic Institute (EP), Njala University (NU) and Milton Margai College of Education and Technology (MMCET), who gave their candid opinions on the issues (see Chapter 5-Tests and Test Results).

It would appear that the source of the primary data is not adequate enough for the purpose of generalization. However, there is a consensus among linguistic scholars that the observed features are predominant in areas other than the media.

Following the submission of the thesis, I felt that the attention of the wider public should be drawn to the features which characterize Sierra Leonean English, especially resulting from nativisation and which hitherto had been considered as errors-thus the production of this <u>Survey</u>.

Momodu Turay

FOREWORD

It has long been recognized that when a language is transplanted, it does not remain the same; it is no longer the exclusive property of the mother country. This is evident in the distinction that is made, for example, between Latin American Spanish and Castilian Spanish. The same is true of the English language. Apart from native speakers with different varieties, there are non-native speakers' varieties. Nowadays we talk of Nigerian English, Ghanaian English, Indian English, Sri Lankan English and so on. With English as the official language of Sierra Leone, it is inevitable that a variety will emerge with its stamp of Sierra Leoneanness.

In his <u>A Survey of Sierra Leonean English,</u> Dr. Momodu Turay has assiduously and painstakingly highlighted the relevant features which characterize this variety.

It is hoped that native speakers and non-native speakers alike will be enlightened by this discourse and will realize that the Sierra Leonean does not have to sound like a British when he speaks English. The English language is one of the languages of Sierra Leone.

M. E. Ajayi Coomber
Linguistics Consultant

CHAPTER ONE

INTRODUCTION

Sierra Leone: A Socio-Linguistic Profile
Like all the countries in West Africa, Sierra Leone is a multilingual nation with no less than sixteen indigenous languages. Although none of these languages has been declared as an official language or even a national language, yet there are four among them that are more prominent than the others. They are Mende (whose native speakers are mainly found in the southern and eastern provinces); Krio (whose native speakers are mostly located in the Western Area); Temne and Limba (both of which have their native speakers mainly in the northern province). Krio serves as the lingua franca and is thus "used for inter-ethnic communication by as much as 95 percent of the population" (Oyétádé and Fashole-Luke, 2007:128).

The English language has further contributed to the multilingual nature of the country. It was first introduced by the British who traded with the coastal Sierra Leoneans by the end of the 16th century. This development was followed by the establishment of the Sierra Leone Colony in 1787 for liberated slaves. This move triggered the coming of the British colonial administration and Christian missionaries, mostly from England. In view of this development, school children were encouraged to study the Bible and it thus became the pupils' first contact with the English language. The status of the language reached its climax when the government declared it as an official language by imposing it as 'the sole language of administration, the church, commerce and education' (Fyle and Jones, 1980: XVIII).

Today, English is learnt as a second language in the country. In this regard, it is required for certain official, social, commercial or educational activities within the country. English is also a medium of instruction in schools and other formal institutions. Smart (1973) (cited by Palmer 1996:3) for example, highlights the importance of English in relation to formal education when he observes that:

> Obviously, English is a special subject in the curriculum of a school. It is a tool subject. No other subject is as essential for an understanding of other subjects (Smart, 1973: 9).

Moreover, English is a top requirement of those seeking jobs in the country, and it is often the language in which most of the business between and within government agencies is being conducted. It is also used for communication at national and international levels. This perhaps therefore, partly explains why the 1991 Constitution on which the country operates recognises competence in English as a pre-requiste for election as member of parliament. It states that a person is qualified for the post if he "… is able to speak and read the English language with a degree of proficiency sufficient to enable him to take an active part in the proceedings of parliament" (Act No. 6 of 1991 Constitution of the Sierra Leone, Section 75, Sub Section d, p. 64). Significantly, this pre-requisite also holds for election as president (Act No. 6 of the 1991 Constitution of Sierra Leone, Section 75, Sub Section d, p. 42). So widespread is its use and so essential is it as a tool of everyday life that it has become part and parcel of a substantial number of people that are evenly distributed across the regions. Lastly, as in most countries where English operates as a second language, it serves in Sierra Leone as a status marker and it is used as a yardstick to assess one's level of exposure to western civilisation. This is why certain western ceremonies like drinking toasts, paying tributes and some informal occasions are done in English not only because it is normal but also because it is prestigious. As Spencer states:

> It is normally through English that an individual breaks the bonds of West African traditional life and enters into some kind of relationship with the Westernised sectors of the society (Spencer: 1971:4).

On the whole, English continues to enjoy the pride of place in the country as it performs functions that are pivotal for the day-to-day practical task of governing the country. Pemagbi (1989) does not therefore exaggerate when he contends that:

> Even though English is not native to Sierra Leone, its functions are as crucial to the country's survival as they are to where it is used as a mother tongue (Pemagbi, 1989: 20).

It is worth noting here that Sierra Leoneans have been exposed not only to Southern British English (hereafter SBE), but also to other varieties of the language – native and non-native – through expatriate teachers, missionaries and other workers, the print and electronic media, et cetera.

The Status of English
It is becoming evident from the usage of English in Sierra Leone that a different variety of English has evolved. In proposing a national language policy for Sierra Leone, Fyle (1975) recommends the concurrent use of both the Sierra Leonean and the British varieties of English. The former variety, he suggests, should be used for local identity while the latter is to be used for wider international communication. However, Fyle merely suggests the use of the national variety without illustrating its features.

Pemagbi's study (1989) provides a glossary of words and expressions that have become pervasive among educated Sierra Leoneans for a considerable period. Also, Conteh-Morgan (1997) examines the evolving English variety in the country on the general consensus among linguists and language educators that 'the language as used in Sierra Leone exhibits certain patterns which are becoming entrenched...' (Conteh-Morgan, 1997:52). Finally, Maryns (2000) investigates the phonological features of Sierra Leonean refugees in Guinea between 1997 – 1998.

This study describes and explains the characteristics of the Sierra Leonean variety of English. According to the researcher's findings, apart from these three researches which specifically look into Sierra

Leonean English usage, all other discussions in relation to this variety are subsumed into the broad category of West African English (see Spencer (1971) and Bokamba (1991). Little research has therefore yet been conducted on the Sierra Leonean variety. This is unlike what is happening in non-native countries like Ghana, Nigeria, Singapore, India and so on, and this explains why Sierra Leone is said to occupy one of the "relatively blank areas on the map of English sociolinguistic research" (Conteh-Morgan, 1997:52 quoting Schmied, 1991). The irony is that Sierra Leone used to play a leading role in terms of English usage in West Africa. Holm, for example, observes that 'the Sierra Leoneans were particularly influential in shaping West African English as it developed in the 19th century (Holm, 1989:411). Similarly, Mazrui (1975) contends that '... the impact of Sierra Leone on West Africa as a whole was perhaps more in the spread of the English language than of Krio (Mazrui, 1975:41). The question then is why does the country now lag behind Nigeria and Ghana in relation to investigations into non-native English usage? Conteh-Morgan (1997) attempts to account for this phenomenon. In the first place, a significant number of educated Sierra Leoneans, she contends, wrongly perceive the English language as their native language. This perception can be traced to that of the returned slaves from Britain who, without any African language to their credit, considered the English language as theirs. It is this view that most of their descendants – the Krios – still share today. Secondly, there is the lack of a strong tradition of creative writing in the country which would have enabled Sierra Leonean writers to come to terms with the existential realities in the country (Contch-Morgan, 1997: 52-53). Consequently, many Sierra Leoneans particularly non-English teachers and non-linguists have failed to distinguish between what could have been features of a legitimate national variety from actual errors. And those who venture to regard them as peculiar features do so with timidity. The question that was persistently asked during the course of this research was:

> What are the nature and causes of the phonological, lexical, grammatical and discoursal features of Sierra Leonean English usage?

This study therefore seeks to describe and explain the characteristics of the Sierra Leonean variety with a view to sensitising Sierra Leoneans and the world at large about this phenomenon so that we could be at par with countries like Kenya, Ghana, Nigeria, Pakistan and so on.

CHAPTER TWO

THE FEATURES OF SIERRA LEONEAN ENGLISH

This chapter deals with the linguistic features of Sierra Leonean English usage. It investigates the peculiarities of educated Sierra Leoneans across the following language levels: phonology, lexis, grammar and discourse. The term 'educated Sierra Leonean' is used here to refer to a person with some kind of formal exposure to English that enables him to feel confident enough to express himself in the print and electronic media or to express his attitude towards given English words or structures. In this study, native English is used to refer to Received Pronunciation (RP) and the SBE.

The Phonological Peculiarities in the English of Educated Sierra Leoneans

The peculiarities in this section fall into two broad categories which are the segmental and the suprasegmental features of English. The segmental features generally comprise vowel and consonant related peculiarities. The suprasegmental features involve the use of syllable-timing, downdrift, tonality, stress and intonation.

The Segmental Features

This section describes the vowel- and consonant-related peculiarities.

The Vowel Related Peculiarity

The peculiarities in this section involve the merging and the substitution of vowels, spelling-induced peculiarities, nasalisation, the merging and the substitution of diphthongs.

The Merging of Vowels

A good number of the vowels in RP tend to be merged by educated Sierra Leoneans. For example, the distinction made in native English between the front close vowel /i/ and the centralised front half-close vowel /I/ appears to be uncommon in the Sierra Leonean English usage. This is what the following examples illustrate:

1a) 'still' pronounced as /stil/ for
1b) /stɪl/
2a) 'result' pronounced as /rizɔlt/ for
2b) /rɪzʌlt/
3a) 'qualify' rendered as / kwɔlifai / for
3b) / kwDlIfai /
4a) 'disseminate' pronounced as / disɛminet / for
4b) / dIsɛmIneIt /
5a) 'effective' pronounced as / ifɛktiv / for
5b) / ifɛktiv /

Similarly, the distinction in native English between the back open / D / and the back half-open / ɔ / vowels is not reflected in the speech of educated Sierra Leoneans. The tendency is to merge both phonemes into the back half-open vowel / ɔ /. This is evident in:

6a) 'profit' rendered as / prɔfit / for
6b) / prDfIt /
7a) 'quality' pronounced as / kwɔliti / for
7b) / kwDləti /
8a) 'baton' rendered as / batɔn / for
8b) / bætDn /
9a) 'economy' produced as / ɛkɔnɔmi / for
9b) / IkDnəmi /
10a) 'tolerate' pronounced as / tɔlaret / for
10b) / tDləreIt /

There is also the tendency for both the front open vowel /æ/ (see 11a – 14a) and the RP central back open vowel / α / (see 15a – 20a) to be merged as the central open vowel / a / as in the following:

11a) 'transparent' pronounced as / transpɛrɛnt / for
11b) / trænspærənt /
(12a) 'clandestine' produced as / klandɛstain / for
(12b) / klændɛstIn /
(13a) 'battle' produced as / batul / for
(13b) / bætəl /
(14a) 'language' rendered as / langwedʒ / for
(14b) / læŋgwIdʒ /
15a) 'half' produced as / haf / for

15b) / hɑf /
(16a) 'rather' rendered as / rada / for
(16b) / rɑðə /
(17a) 'hat' pronounced as / hat / for
(17b) / hɑt /
(18a) 'sharp' produced as / ʃap / for
(18b) / ʃɑp /
(19a) 'class' pronounced as / klas / for
(19b) / klɑs /
(20a) 'clerk' produced as / klak / for
(20b) / klɑk /

In addition, the distinction made in native English between the back close /U/ and the centralised back half-close /ʊ/ vowels is not made by most educated Sierra Leoneans. In other words, Sierra Leoneans are prone to merging both phonemes into the back close vowel / U /. This is seen in:

(21a) 'good' produced as / gud / for
(21b) / gʊd /
22a) 'full' pronounced as / ful / for
22b) / fʊl /
23a) 'woman' pronounced as / wuman / for
23b) / wʊmən /
24a) 'book' produced as / buk / for
24b) / bʊk /
25a) 'congratulate' pronounced as / kɔngratulet / for
25b) / kəngrætʃʊleIt /

The Substitution of Vowels

This peculiarity–type involves the use of a phoneme as a replacement for another phoneme. For example, Sierra Leoneans are inclined to replace the native English central half open vowel / ʌ / by the back half-open vowel /ɔ/. This is what the following examples show:

26a) 'much' produced as / mɔtʃ / for
26b) / m ʌ tʃ /
27a) 'run' rendered as / rɔn / for
27b) / rʌn /

28a) 'other' pronounced as / ɔda / for
28b) / ʌðə /
29a) 'troublesome' rendered as / trɔbulsɔm / for
29b) / trʌbəlsəm /
30a) 'won' pronounced as / wɔn / for
(30b) / wʌn /
(31a) 'wonder' produced as / wɔnda / for
(31b) / wʌndə /

Similarly, there is the tendency to substitute the central half-close vowel / 3 / either with the central open /a/ (as seen in 32a – 35a) or with the back half-open / ɔ / (as shown in 36a – 40a) vowels:
(32a) 'earn' produced as / an / for
(32b) / ɜn /
(33a) 'earth' pronounced as / at / for
(33b) / ɜθ /
(34a) 'expert' produced as / ɛkspat / for
(34b) / ɛkspɜt /
(35a) 'early' produced as / ali / for
(35b) /ɜli/
(36a) 'first' produced as / fɔst / for
(36b) /fɜst/
(37a) 'turn' rendered as /tɔn / for
(37b) /tɜn/
(38a) 'journey' produced as / dʒɔni / for
(38b) / dʒ ɜn i /
(39a) 'occur' produced as / ɔkɔ/ for
(39b) / əkɜ /
(40a) 'church' rendered as / tʃɔtʃ/ for
(40b) / tʃɜtʃ /

The above tendency has led to the emergence of a few homophones which do not exist in native English. Such homophones include:
(a) 'curb' /kɜb/ and 'cob' /kDb/ are both pronounced as /k ɔb/
(b) 'work' / wɜk / and 'walk' /wɔk / are both pronounced as /wɔk /

(c) 'born' / b ɔn / and 'burn' / bɜn / are both produced as / b ɔn /
(d) 'curse' / k ɜ s / and 'course' / kɔs / are both rendered as / k ɔ s /
(e) 'hurt' / h ɜ t / and 'hot' / hDt / are both produced as / h ɔt /

Finally, there is the tendency to substitute the mid central vowel /ə/ with the central open vowel /a /. This can be seen in:
(41a) 'stomach' produced as /stomak/ for
(41b) /stʌmək /
(42a) 'water' rendered as /wɔta / for
(42b) /wɔtə/
(43a) 'among' pronounced as /amɔng / for
(43b) /əmʌŋ/
(44a) 'tolerate' pronounced as / tɔlaret / for
(44b) /tDləreIt /

Spelling-Induced Peculiarity

This sub-category deals with peculiarities that are related to English spellings. In Sierra Leone, there is the tendency to pronounce English words according to their spellings. In native English, however, there are many inconsistences between the spellings of English words and their pronunciations. These account for some vowel-related and as we shall see in pp 35-36 some consonant-related peculiarities. Examples of the vowel-related peculiarities include:
(45a) 'journal' pronounced as /dʒɔna l / for
(45b) /dʒɔnəl/
(46a) 'democracy' produced as / dɛmokrasi / for
(46b) /dImDkrəsi/
(47a) 'malaria' rendered as / maleria / for
(47b) /məlɛəriə/
(48a) 'police' produced as /polis/ for
(48b) /pəlɪs/
(49a) 'primary' produced as / praimari / for
(49b) /praIməri/
(50a) 'monday' rendered as / mɔnde / for
(50b) /mʌndI/

(51a) 'climate' pronounced as / klaimet / for
(51b) / klaImIt /
(52a) 'transparent' produced as / transperɛnt / for
(52b) / trænspærənt /
(53a) 'impasse' rendered as / impɑs / for
(53b) / æmpɑs /
(54a) 'doctor' rendered as / dɔktɔ / for
(54b) / dDktə /
(55a) 'southern' produced as / sautan / for
(55b) / sʌðən /
(56a) 'funeral' pronounced as / fjuniral /
(56b) / fjunrəl /
(57a) 'medicine' produced as / mɛdisin /
(57b) / mɛdsIn /
(58a) 'extraordinary' rendered as /ɛkstraɔdinari/ for
(58b) /IkstrɔdənƏri/
(59a) 'basically' rendered as /besikali/ for
(59b) /beIsIkli/

Nasalisation

The vowel-related peculiarities also show instances of nasalisation. That is, Sierra Leoneans are predisposed to nasalising English vowels with the nasal consonants disappearing in the process. This is illustrated in:

(60a) 'reading' pronounced as /ridĩ/ for
(60b) /rIdIŋ/
(61a) 'income' pronounced as /ĩ kɔm/ for
(61b) /IŋkʌM/
(62a) 'understand' produced as / ɔ̃dastan / for
(62b) /ʌndəstænd /
(63a) 'emphasise' pronounced as /ɛ̃fa'saiz / for
(63b) /ɛmfəsaiz/
(64a) 'substandard' produced as / sɔbstãdad / for
(64b) / səbstændəd /

The Merging of Diphthongs
As with the pure vowels, diphthongs that are distinct in native English tend to be merged. For example, the front half-open centering /ɛə/ and the front half-close centering /Iə/ diphthongs are normally merged into the latter. This has often led to the neutralisation of the phonemic distinction in native English between certain words thereby creating 'new' homophones that are unfamiliar to the native English speaker. For example,

65a) 'spare' is pronounced as /spia/ for
65b) /spɛə/
 'spare' is made homophonous with 'spear'
66a) 'dare' is pronounced as /dia/ for
66b) /dɛə /
 'dare' is made homophonous with 'dear'
(67a) 'chairman' is rendered as / tʃiaman / for
(67b) /tʃɛəmən /
 'chair' is made homophonous with 'cheer'
68a) 'fair' is produced as / fia / for
(68b) /fɛə/
 ('fair' is made homophonous with 'fear')

The Substitution of Diphthongs
Like the native English monophthongs, Sierra Leoneans also have the tendency to substitute English diphthongs. For example, the front –closing diphthong /eI/ tends to be substituted with the cardinal front half-close vowel without a glide /e / as is illustrated in:

(69a) 'wait' rendered as / wet / for
(69b) /weIt /
(70a) 'engage' produced as / ɛngedʒ / for
(70b) / IngeIdʒ /
(71a) 'case' produced as / kes / for
(71b) / keIs /
72a) 'shame' produced as / ʃem / for
72b) / ʃeIm /
73a) 'fail' produced as / fel / for
73b) / feIl /

Similarly, the back closing diphthong / əʊ / tends to be substituted with the cardinal back half-close vowel / O / as in the following:
(74a) 'donor' pronounced as / donɔ / for
(74b) / dəʊnə /
(75a) 'exposure' produced as / ɛkspoʒɔ / for
(75b) / ɪkspəʊʒə /
(76a) 'boat' produced as / bot / for
(76b) / bəʊt /
(77a) 'spoke' pronounced as / spok / for
(77b) / spəʊk /
(78a) 'programme' pronounced as / program / for
(78b) / prəʊgræm /

The Consonant-Related Peculiarity

The peculiarities examined in this section comprise the substitution of consonants, spelling-induced peculiarities, those that relate to the omission of the intrusive and the linking 'r' and the syllabic consonants, and consonant deletion.

The Substitution of Consonants

Sierra Leoneans tend to replace some consonants. For example, they replace the voiceless dental fricative /θ/ with the voiceless alveolar plosive /t/ (as shown in 79a-82a) and the voiced dental fricative /ð/ with the voiced alveolar plosive /d/ (as illustrated in 83a – 86a). This accounts for the development of homophones that are unfamiliar in native English as seen in:
(79a) 'with' produced as / wit / for
(79b) / wɪθ /
('with' is made homophonous with 'wit')
(80a) 'through' pronounced as / tru / for
(80b) / θru /
('through' is made homophonous with 'true')
81a) 'death' rendered as / dɛt / for
81b) / dɛθ /
('death' is made homophonous with 'debt')
(82a) 'both' pronounced as / bot / for

82b) / bəʊθ /
       ('both' is made homophonous with 'boat')
83a) 'brother' rendered as / brɔda / for
83b) / brʌðə /
       ('brother' is made homophonous with 'broader')
84a) 'mother' produced as / mɔda / for
84b) / mʌðə /
       ('mother' is made homophonous with 'murder')
85a) 'then' pronounced as /d ɛ n / for
85b) / ðɛn /
       ('then' is made homophonous with 'den')
86a) 'those' produced as / doz / for
86b) / ðəʊz /
       ('those' is made homophonous with 'doze')

Moreover, the velar nasal / ŋ / which in native English is used to phonemically represent inter alia the '– ing' in word final position tends to be substituted with the alveolar nasal. This is evident in:

(87a) 'interesting' pronounced as / intrɛstin / for
(87b) /Intrɛstɪŋ/
(88a) 'funding' rendered as / fɔndin / for
(88b) / fʌndɪŋ /
(89a) 'marching' produced as / matʃin / for
(89b) / mɑtʃɪŋ /
(90a) 'waiting' rendered as / wetin / for
(90b) / weɪtɪŋ /
(91a) 'wrong' pronounced as / rɔng / for
(91b) / rDŋ /
(92a) 'along' rendered as / alɔng / for
(92b) / əlDŋ /
(93a) 'among' pronounced as /amɔng / for
(93b) / əmʌŋ /

Spelling-Induced Peculiarity

As shown in the vowel-related peculiarities that involve spellings (see pp 9-10), the subjects also have the tendency of pronouncing some English consonants as they are spelt. This is evident in the

voiced and voiceless alveolar fricatives as is seen in the following examples:
94a) 'because' produced as / bikɔs / for
94b) / bIkDz /
95a) 'islamic' pronounced as / islamik / for
95b) / IzlæmIk /
96a) 'preside' pronounced as / prisaid / for
96b) / prIzaId /
97a) 'is' rendered as / is / for
97b) / Iz /
98a) 'resource' produced as / risɔs / for
98b) / rIzɔs /

The other spelling-related peculiarities which are related to other consonants are evident in the following examples:
99a) 'regime' produced as / rɛdʒim / for
99b) / reIʒim /
100a) 'situation' rendered as / sitwɛʃɔn / for
100b) / sItʃueiʃən /
101a) 'could' pronounced as / kuld / for
101b) / kʊd /
102a) 'building' rendered as / bjuld ĩ / for
102b) / bIldIŋ /
103a) 'limbs' produced as / limbs / for
103b) / lImz /

The Omission of the Linking and the Intrusive 'R'

In native English, it is common in connected speech for the linking / r / forms of words to be used before a vowel. This phenomenon which is referred to as the linking – r is lacking in Sierra Leonean English as is shown below in 104a – 106a. Similarly, in native English the r – which is referred to as the 'intrusive r'– is inserted between two vowels (with the exception of close vowels or diphthongs that end with a close element) at word boundaries where there is none in the spelling. As the examples in 107a – 109a show, there is the tendency among Sierra Leoneans not to use this feature.

104a) 'He promised to see us after a while' rendered as
/ hi prɔmist to si ɔs afta e wail / for
104b) / hI prDmIst tə si əs aftər ə37waIl /
105a) 'We don't care about their party' produced as
/ wi dont kia abaut dia pati / for
105b) wI dəʊnt kɛər əbaʊt ðɛə pɑti
106a) 'She is the mother of the rebel leader' produced as
/ ʃI is di mɔda ɔf di rebɛl lida / for
106b) / ʃI Iz ðə mʌðər əv ðə rɛbəl lidə /
107a) 'The mayor and his thugs are responsible for the crisis' produced as
/ di mejɔ an his tɔgs a rɛspɔnsibul fɔ di kraisis / for
107b) / ðə mɛər ən hIz θʌgz ə rɛspDnsəbəl fə ðə kraIsIs /
108a) 'There is no law and order in the country' is produced as
/ dia is no lɔ an ɔda in di kɔntri / for
108b) / ðɛə Iz nəʊ lɔr ənd ɔdə In ðə kʌntri /
109a) 'We saw an entire structure being demolished' rendered as
/ wi sɔ an ɛntaia strɔ ktʃɔ bin dimɔliʃt / for
109b) / wi sɔr ən IntaIə strʌktʃə biIŋ dImDIIʃt /

The Omission of the Syllabic Consonants

In native English, there are some consonants that constitute syllables. These consonants are the bilabial nasal /m/, the alveolar nasal /n/ and the alveolar lateral /l/. On the other hand, Sierra Leoneans tend to insert a vowel phoneme before any of these consonants in order to form a syllabic peak. For example,

110a) 'hospital' rendered as / hɔspitul / for
110b) / hDspItəl /
111a) 'honourable' produced as / hɔnɔrebul / for
111b) / Dnərəbəl /
112a) 'bottom' pronounced as / bɔtɔm / for
112b) / bDtəm /
113a) 'Britain' pronounced as / britin / for
113b) /brItən /
114a) 'cotton' produced as / kɔtin / for
114b) /kDtən /

Consonant Deletion

In native English, there can be as many as three consonants in the onset and as many as four consonants in the coda of a syllable (Roach:2000). On the contrary, the Sierra Leonean speaker tends to reduce the final consonant clusters by deletion. This can be observed in:

115a) 'kind' in 'kind man' produced as / kaın / for
115b) / kaInd /
116a) 'just' in 'just below' produced as / dʒɔs / for
116b) / dʒʌst /
117a) 'missed' in 'missed the door' pronounced as / mis / for
117b) / mIst /
118a) 'called' in 'called my name' pronounced as / kɔl / for
118b) / kɔld /

The Suprasegmental Features

The peculiarities in this section include features like syllable-timing, down-drift, tonality, lack of attitudinal intonation and of contrastive stress.

Syllable Timing

In native English, every word of more than one syllable has at least one of its syllables stressed. This contributes to the rhythm of English as the stressed syllables occur at regular intervals of time irrespective of how many unstressed syllables there may be. This is why English is referred to as a stress-timed language. For their part, Sierra Leoneans tend to give every syllable equal prominence making all of them to be pronounced with the same duration. This is what is referred to as syllable-timing. This difference accounts for the almost regular intervals with which English syllables tend to be pronounced. This is particularly evident in Sierra Leoneans' use of the strong forms of words where native speakers use the weak forms. Examples include:

119a) 'It was not so full of challenges' produced as:
/ it | wɔz | nɔt | so | ful | ɔf | tʃa | 'len | dʒis /
(9 foot beats)
for

119b) It wəz' | "nDt 'səʊ | 'fʊl əv| 'tʃællIndʒIʌ|
(4 foot beats)

120a) 'There are some advantages and disadvantages in this aspect' rendered as:
/ di | a | a | sɔm | ad | van | te | dʒis | and | dis | ad | van | te | dʒis | in | dis | a |spɛkt |
(18 foot beats)
for

120b) ðɛə ə səm 'əd | 'vəntIdʒIʌən dIsəd | 'vəntIdʒIz In ðIs | 'æspɛkt |
(4 foot beats)

121a) 'I also participated in the planning' produced as:
ai | ɔl | so | pa | ti | si | pe | tɛd | in | di | plæ | nin
(12 foot beats)
for

121b) αI | 'ɔlsəʊ pα | 'tIsIpeItId In ðə |plænIŋ|
(4 foot beats)

122a) 'One has to do a study of the city' produced as:
'wɔn | 'has | 'to | 'du | e | 'stɔ | di | ɔf | di | 'si |ti
(11 foot beats)
for

122b) 'wʌn | 'həz tə | 'du | ə 'stʌdI əv ðə | 'siti|
(5 foot – beats)

It can be observed from the above that owing to the equal prominence given to all syllables, the speech pattern of the educated Sierra Leonean is rather slow, disjointed and monotonous.

Downdrift

Closely related to the feature of syllable timing, downdrift is concerned with making every syllable slightly lower in pitch than the one preceding it. In native English, every stressed syllable may be said at a slightly lower pitch than the one preceding it, while an unstressed syllable may be said at the same pitch as a stressed syllable or even at a higher pitch than a stressed syllable. This tendency seems to be absent among educated Sierra Leoneans who seem to produce syllables that become increasingly low in pitch as they move from one syllable to the other. This is shown in the following examples:

123a) 'Other countries don't have the same culture that we have' produced as

'ɔdā 'kɔ̄ntriz 'dŌnt 'hav 'di 'sem 'kɔltʃɔ 'dāt 'wi 'hāv̄ for

123b) ʌðə kʌntriz dəʊnt hæv ðə seIm kʌltʃə ðət Wl həev

124a) 'It was not so full of challenges' rendered

'Īt 'wɔz 'nɔt so 'ful 'ɔf 'tʃalendʒis For

124b) It wəz 'nDt səʊ 'fʊl əv 'tʃ ælIndʒIz

125a) 'There are some advantages and disadvantages in this aspect' produced as

'dia 'a 'sɔm 'advantedʒis 'and 'disadvantedʒis 'in 'dis 'aspɛkt for

125b) ðɛə ə 'səm əd'vɑntIdʒIz ən dIsəd 'vɑntIdʒIz In ðIs 'æspɛkt

126a) 'One has to do a study of the city' produced as

40

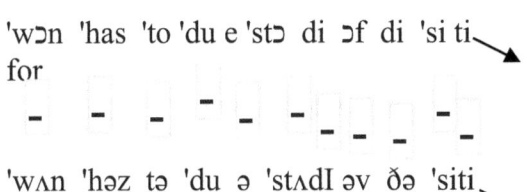

'wɔn 'has 'to 'du e 'stɔ di ɔf di 'si ti
for

126b) 'wʌn 'həz tə 'du ə 'stʌdI əv ðə 'siti

Significantly, in native English, 'wh' questions tend to end with a rising pitch. However, Sierra Leonean speakers have the inclination towards downdrift in 'wh' questions. This is shown in the following examples:

127a) 'Where is it in its completed form now?' rendered as

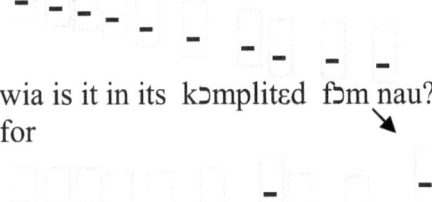

wia is it in its kɔmplitɛd fɔm nau?
for

127b) wə Iz It In Its kəmplitId fɔm naʊ?

128a) 'Where were you when you were at school? produced as

wia wia ju wɛn ju wia at skul?
for

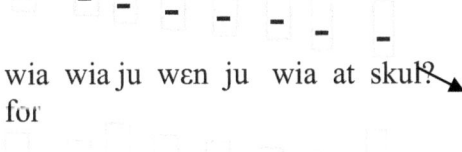

128b) wə wə jʊ wɛn jʊ wə ət skul?

129a) 'How long have you been away from your wife? produced as

au lɔng hav ju bin awe frɔm jɔ waif?
for

129b) aʊ lDŋ həv jʊ bIn əweI frəm jə waif?

Tonality

Sierra Leoneans also have the tendency to shift the stress in some English disyllabic and polysyllabic words. For example,

130a) 'support' (as a noun) pronounced as | 'sɔpɔt | for
130b) / sə'pɔt /
131a) 'advice' pronounced as / 'advais'/ for
131b) / əd'vaIs /
132a) 'address' pronounced as | 'adrɛs | for
132b) / ə'drɛs /
133a) 'affront' rendered as | 'afrɔnt | for
133b) / ə'frʌnt /
134a) 'educate' pronounced as / ɛdju'ket / for
134b) / 'ɛdʒʊk₁eIt /
135a) 'demonstrate' produced as |dɛmɔn'stret | for
135b) / 'dɛmən₁streIt /
136a) 'emphasize' produced as | ẽfa'saiz | for
136b) / 'ɛmfə₁saiz /

It can be observed from the above polysyllabic words (see 134a – 136a) that the syllables with the secondary stress in native English tend to be given the primary stress by the subjects.

The Lack of Attitudinal Intonation

According to native English usage, intonation does not only show whether an utterance is a statement or a question, but it also conveys attitudinal information about the speaker. In other words, through his speech, we are able to know whether a speaker is, for example, polite or impolite, certain or uncertain. This means that if a speaker's voice goes from high to low, which is referred to as falling pitch, that gives finality to what he says. If, on the other hand, his voice moves from low to high, that is, he makes an utterance with a rising pitch, he is inviting the listener to continue with the conversation. Moreover, if his voice moves from fall to rise on the same word (that is, he uses a fall-rise pitch), this means that he agrees with a statement with some doubt. Finally, if his voice moves from rise to fall (that is, if he uses a rise-fall pitch), he is expressing strong feelings of approval, disapproval or surprise. Roach (2000: 155-158) demonstrates this phenomenon in native English by using the monosyllabic words 'yes' and 'no'. Sierra Leonean speakers, however, tend not to use intonation to convey this kind of attitudinal information; instead, additional words are employed to convey it. For example,

137a) Question: Are they not the ones that should pave the way for the others?

Response: Certainly, certainly, Mr. Moderator those people that have been elected to Parliament should be the role models by now.
rendered as:
Question: a de nɔt di wɔns dat ʃuld pev di we fɔ di ɔdaz

Response: satenli satenli mista mɔdretɔ doz pipul dat have bin ilɛktɛd to palimɛnt ʃuld bi di rol modɛls bai nau
for

137b) sɜtnlI mIstə mDdrəreItə ðəʊz pipəl ðət

həv bIn IlɛktId tə pɑləmənt ʃəd bI ðə rəʊl mədəlz baI naʊ

138a) Question: 'So in actual fact meningitis affects every age?

Response: Yes, yes meningitis affects me, affects every
age but is more common in childhood
produced as:
Question: so in actʃual fakt mɛnindʒaitis afɛkts ɛvri edʒ?

Response: jɛs, jɛs mɛnindʒaitis afɛkts mi,
afɛkts ɛvri edʒ bɔt is mɔ kɔmɔn in tʃaildhud

for
138b) jɛs mɛnIndʒaItIs əfkɛts ɛvrI eIdʒ bət It IZ
mɔ kDmən In tʃaIldhƱd ↑

It can be observed from the above that whereas the native English speaker tends to use the rise-fall pitch to show certainty and the fall-rise pitch to show uncertainty, the Sierra Leonean speaker is inclined to employ additional words to show his attitudes as is respectively shown in (137a) and (138a) above.

The Lack of the Contrastive Stress

Native English uses contrastive stress for the purpose of emphasis, contrast or emotion. For example, the sentence, 'Smith works here' can be normally produced as / smIΘ w3ks hIə / where each word is stressed. The situation will, however, be different if one of the items is given extra stress at the expense of the others. In other words, if there is an extra stress on 'Smith,' it means it is Smith I am talking about and nobody else. Furthermore, if the stress is on 'teaches', it may mean he does not live here, he teaches here. Finally, if the extra stress is on 'here', it means it is here that he works and nowhere else. Significantly, however, it would appear that Sierra Leoneans tend to use clefted sentences in these circumstances. For example,

139a) 'What I am saying here is that Bo and Kenema need to be
properly restructured'
rendered as:

/ wat ai am sein 'hia is dat bo an kɛnɛma nid to bi prɔpali ristrɔktʃɔd' / for:
139b) / 'bəʊ ən 'kɛnɛmə nid tə bI prɒpəli rIstrIʌktʃəd /

140a) 'I have no doubt that she would do likewise or even better in her new appointment'
rendered as:
/ai hav no daut dat ʃi wuld du laikwaiz ɔ ivin bɛ ta in ha nju apɔintmɛnt/ for:
140b) /ʃi wʊd də laIkwaIz ɔ IvIn bɛtə In ə nju əpɔInmənt/

141a) 'Then we can say in no uncertain terms people here have benefitted from income distribution'
rendered as:
/dɛn wi kan se in no ɔnsaten tams pipul have bɛnifitɛd frɔm ĩkɔm distribjuʃɔn/ for:
141b) / ðən wI kən seI pipəl həv bɛnIfIted frəm Iŋkʌm dIstrIbjʊʃən /

142a) 'It was we who actually advocated right through this country'
produced as:
/it wɔz wi hu aktʃuali advokɛtɛd rait tru dis kɔntri/ for:

142b) / 'wI ædvəʊkeItId raIt θru ðIs kʌntri /

143a) 'It is a very very major social problem in our societies today'
produced as
/it is e vɛri vɛri medʒɔ soʃial prɔblɛm in aua sosaitiz tode/ for:
143b) /It Iz ə 'meIdʒə səʊʃəl prɒbləm In aʊə səʊsaItiz tədeI/

The Lexical Peculiarities in the English of Educated Sierra Leoneans

The peculiarities that are discussed in this section are categorised into collocation, word modification, idiom, innovation and aboriginal peculiarities.

Collocation

The use of certain words in collocation with others is very much unlike native English usage. This phenomenon is evident from the inability to grasp the complex ways in which words are paired up in native English, the use of L_1 words borrowed from the English lexicon and the use of English words that reflect the subjects' cultural setting.

Collocation in Native English

In native English, there is the predictable connection of words which Sierra Leoneans seem to be unfamiliar with. Their apparent unfamiliarity with such collocational pairs in native English can be observed as follows:

1a) ... three judges will have to preside <u>on</u> the matter and eventually deliver a ruling on that matter.
1b) ... three judges will have to preside <u>over</u> the matter and eventually deliver a ruling on that matter.

2a) President Koroma must <u>make</u> consultations and objectively try to...
2b) President Koroma must <u>have</u> consultations and objectively try to...

3a) ... to <u>undertake</u> a coup against the APC government then under the leadership of late Joseph Saidu Momoh.
3b) ... to <u>stage</u> a coup against the APC government then under the leadership of late Joseph Saidu Momoh.

4a) One only hopes the scathing attack is not associated <u>to</u> rumours of witch hunt

4b) One only hopes the scathing attack is not associated <u>with</u> rumours of witch hunt

5a) Sahr Issa Mansaray of the Ahmadiyya Secondary School in Freetown said the Scholarship given to them by the People's Choice Awards <u>created</u> big impacts on the...

5b) Sahr Issa Mansaray of the Ahmadiyya Secondary School in Freetown said the Scholarship given to them by the People's Choice Awards <u>had</u> big impacts on the...

First Language Induced Collocation

This sub-section deals with peculiarities that are related to the use of English words (which now exist in Krio) with different meanings in native English. Examples of these peculiarities include:

6a) I will <u>hang heads</u> with the elders before...
6b) I will <u>confer</u> with the elders before...
7a) The secrets began to unfold when one of them could not hide his <u>mind</u> but...
7b) The secrets began to unfold when one of them could not hide his <u>feelings</u> but...
8a) Sahr first impressed me when he took the bold <u>mind</u> to...
8b) Sahr first impressed me when he took the bold <u>step</u> to...
9a) He explained that the speed at which the vehicle was moving was 70 kilometres per hour when the <u>back</u> tyre suddenly exploded.
9b) He explained that the speed at which the vehicle was moving was 70 kilometres per hour when the <u>rear</u> tyre suddenly exploded.
10a) ... when Siaka Stevens' secret police officers made the eyes of Sierra Leoneans <u>ran water</u>
10b) ... when Siaka Stevens' secret police officers made the eyes of Sierra Leoneans <u>flow with tears</u>
11a) Pa Santigie took permission from the Town Chief for the <u>Medicine Man</u> to perform the ceremony.
11b) Pa Santigie took permission from the Town Chief for the <u>Sorcerer</u> to perform the ceremony.

12a) Also, Bailor Sow who is a <u>butcher man</u> at the market said the need to ...
12b) Also, Bailor Sow who is a <u>butcher</u> at the market said the need to...
13a) NPA <u>Man</u> Refute Story
13b) NPA <u>Official</u> Refute Story

Culturally Induced Collocation

There is also the tendency to use English words in a way that reflects the Sierra Leonean cultural milieu. In other words, some English words tend to collocate to refer to people (or things) which do not exist in native English settings. This can be observed in:

14a) The <u>witch doctor</u> said it would cost me if I object his advice
14b) The <u>occult healer</u> said it would cost me if I object his advice

15a) ... in an alleged plot to shoot and kill the complainant <u>with a witch gun</u>
15b) ... in an alleged plot to shoot and kill the complainant <u>with a gun that has mystical powers</u>
16a) ... and the things to be included would be a goat, a red cock, two five-gallon palm oil, <u>black soap</u> etc.
16b) ... and the things to be included would be a goat, a red cock, two five-gallon palm oil, <u>soap used for medicinal purposes</u> etc.
17a) I did not want to hear any more about <u>woman damage</u>.
17b) I did not want to hear any more about <u>the fine for having an affair with a married woman</u>.
18a) I hear your husband paid five pounds as <u>bride price</u> for you.
18b) I hear your husband paid five pounds as <u>trousseau</u> for you.

Word Modification

It would appear in Sierra Leonean usage that some words are used in senses which are quite different from their use by native speakers of English. In other words, the meanings of some native English words are extended, some have their meanings reduced and others have their meanings changed.

The Extension of Word Meaning

This sub-section deals with the extension of the meanings of native English words. For example,

19a) ... the parents then rushed to the school and <u>met</u> their daughter in a bad state.
19b) ... the parents then rushed to the school and <u>found</u> their daughter in a bad state.
20a) APC <u>Youth</u> exposes NEC Commissioner
20b) APC <u>Activist</u> exposes NEC Commissioner
21a) He further maintained that the educational system in Sella Limba Chiefdom is very poor; noting that if one wants to have <u>better</u> education the individual should have to...
21b) He further maintained that the educational system in Sella Limba Chiefdom is very poor; noting that if one wants to have <u>good</u> education the individual should have to...
22a) ... where the patient was being <u>escorted</u> by a volunteer.
22b) ... where the patient was being <u>accompanied</u> by a volunteer.

23a) Not less than five wards have been <u>shut</u> down at the painful expense of...
23b) Not less than five wards have been <u>closed</u> down at the painful expense of...
24a) The <u>marriage</u> between Marima and Moseray Bai Koroma was an occasion of great celebration.
24b) The <u>wedding</u> between Marima and Moseray Bai Koroma was an occasion of great celebration.
25a) ... I got an accident and my heap was severely <u>damaged</u>.
25b) ... I got an accident and my heap was severely <u>injured</u>.
26a) The news spread that Sergeant Musuba's home was in shambles as his wife cared for no <u>strangers</u>...
26b) The news spread that Sergeant Musuba's home was in shambles as his wife cared for no <u>guests</u>...
27a) A poda poda <u>apprentice</u>, Sahr John, was yesterday sent to...

27b) A poda poda <u>conductor</u>, Sahr John, was yesterday sent to...
28a) We have been parading behind the men for a long time now let's parade behind our <u>colleagues</u>.
28b) We have been parading behind the men for a long time now let's parade behind our <u>female mates</u>.
29a) ... he will take the full responsibility of taking care of the baby after Kadi would have safely <u>delivered</u>.
29b) ... he will take the full responsibility of taking care of the baby after Kadi would have safely <u>given birth</u>.
30a) I would call my friend Olu Gordon of Peep Newspaper to <u>provoke</u> him after we would have swept the votes in Freetown.
30b) I would call my friend Olu Gordon of Peep Newspaper to <u>tease</u> him after we would have swept the votes in Freetown.

The Restriction of Word Meaning

There is also the tendency to reduce the referential meanings of words. This is what the following examples indicate:

31a) According to our report, Mohamed Sheriff and the deceased Baindu Ali had been <u>seeing each other</u> for four years and were preparing to get married.
31b) According to our report, Mohamed Sheriff and the deceased Baindu Ali had been <u>in courtship</u> for four years and were preparing to get married.
32a) In those days it was the <u>educated</u> and skilled that were employed with all the best jobs going to...
32b) In those days it was the <u>learned</u> and skilled that were employed with all the best jobs going to...
33a) Yet, we are proud to say that an illiterate man has been a greater asset to the upliftment of mankind than all the <u>bookmen</u> of this world put together.
33b) Yet, we are proud to say that an illiterate man has been a greater asset to the upliftment of mankind than all the <u>learned</u> of this world put together.
34a) ... I got up and reassured her that Tony had never <u>touched</u> me or told me that he was interested in me.

34b) ... I got up and reassured her that Tony had never <u>had an affair with</u> me or told me that he was interested in me.

The Change of Word Meaning

Sometimes the referential meanings of lexemes are completely changed. For example,

35a) My husband is bedridden, so I have to feed him, change his diapers when he <u>toilets</u>...

35b) My husband is bedridden, so I have to feed him, change his diapers when he <u>defecates</u>...

36a) In the last five years or more the Government, individual politicians, internal agencies, <u>academicians</u> and...

36b) In the last five years or more the Government, individual politicians, internal agencies, <u>academics</u> and...

37a) ... to reverse those negative traits that have brought upon us the negative consequence of the <u>bad heart</u>, pull-him down syndrome.

37b) ... to reverse those negative traits that have brought upon us the negative consequence of the <u>jealousy</u>, pull-him down syndrome.

Idiomaticity

This section involves the tendency to use native English idioms differently and to use idioms borrowed from the local languages of Sierra Leone.

Native English Idiom

Some elements of native English idioms are sometimes modified. This is illustrated in the following sentences:

38a) Obviously, the police is not helping with <u>regards</u> to...

38b) Obviously, the police is not helping with <u>regard</u> to...

39a) Hawa Mansaray of no. 12 Bai Bureh in the eastern part of Freetown is alleged to have burnt the private <u>part</u> of her daughter.

39b) Hawa Mansaray of no. 12 Bai Bureh in the eastern part of Freetown is alleged to have burnt the private <u>parts</u> of her daughter.

40a) ... how <u>comes</u> you are here?

40b) … how <u>come</u> you are here?
41a) The ball is now <u>on</u> Ernest Koroma's court.
41b) The ball is now <u>in</u> Ernest Koroma's court.
42a) You cannot eat your cake and have it.
42b) You cannot have your cake and eat it.
43a) The English have a saying that a stitch in <u>times</u> saves nine
43b) The English have a saying that a stitch in <u>time</u> saves nine

44a) As counting continues…SLPP, APC <u>neck neck</u>.
44b) As counting continues…SLPP, APC <u>neck and neck.</u>
45a) A man can work <u>donkey years</u> in the country and not have anything to show for all those years
45b) A man can work <u>donkey's years</u> in the country and not have anything to show for all those years

Local Idiom

There is also the tendency to use idioms that are borrowed from the local languages. For example,

46a) Knowing fully well what had been <u>cooked</u> for him, the Leone Stars Captain hired a taxi driver who hastily escaped with him to the airport.
46b) Knowing fully well what had been <u>plotted</u> for him, the Leone Stars Captain hired a taxi driver who hastily escaped with him to the airport.
47a) Mr. Alie Jafaar gave me a <u>raw</u> Benjamin Franklin 100 dollar note…
47b) Mr. Alie Jafaar gave me a <u>brand new</u> Benjamin Franklin 100 dollar note…
48a) Cidi wanted to attack Hakeem and snatch me away but I never <u>showed him the face</u>.
48b) Cidi wanted to attack Hakeem and snatch me away but I never <u>entertained the idea</u>.
49a) Hindolo, I can't <u>keep you</u> any longer. I'm in love with someone else.
49b) Hindolo, I can't <u>date</u> you any longer. I'm in love with someone else.

50a) Even when Bee used to advise Sirian that she cannot grow more than her hair she never listened, thinking that her <u>bottom connection</u> will protect her.
50b) Even when Bee used to advise Sirian that she cannot grow more than her hair she never listened, thinking that her <u>sexual favours</u> will protect her.
51a) ... some of the <u>area boys</u> went ahead and burnt down the jeep belonging to the junta.
51b) ... some of the <u>locales</u> went ahead and burnt down the jeep belonging to the junta.
52a) ... not when those <u>sweet 16s</u> were around
52b) ... not when those <u>young attractive ladies</u> were around

Innovation

There is the tendency to use certain words which may look like English words but do not occur in the lexicon of native users. This is what is observed in:

53a) As far as I am concerned, Khali who has raised an army exceeding one thousand men and who has overruled the whole of Robut must be seen as the <u>undisputable</u> strong man of...
53b) As far as I am concerned, Khali who has raised an army exceeding one thousand men and who has overruled the whole of Robut must be seen as the <u>indisputable</u> strong man of...
54a) ... was known throughout Rokantha as a very firm man who <u>seldomly</u> speaks.
54b) ... was known throughout Rokantha as a very firm man who <u>seldom</u> speaks.
55a) ... not to be seen tearing people apart causing <u>hatredness</u> and chaos in institutions
55b) ... not to be seen tearing people apart causing <u>hatred</u> and chaos in institutions
56a) ... that will only show an <u>over-ambitiousness</u> on your part.
56b) ... that will only show an <u>over-ambition</u> on your part.
57a) ... where she discovered that all the doors were <u>widely</u> opened.

57b)   ... where she discovered that all the doors were <u>wide</u> opened.

58a)   ... to prevent its <u>reoccurrence</u> during the second <u>rounds</u>.
58b)   ... to prevent its <u>recurrence</u> during the second <u>round</u>.

Aboriginal Words

There is also the use of untranslated non-English words in English. This tendency is demonstrated in:

59a)   N'fa Ali Cessay a Gambian national was arrested at the Freetown International Airport three weeks ago while attempting to smuggle <u>diamba</u>.
59b)   N'fa Ali Cessay a Gambian national was arrested at the Freetown International Airport three weeks ago while attempting to smuggle <u>cannabis</u>.
60a)   ... they buried <u>juju</u> in various parts of the country to attract huge membership and wrest power from the ruling party.
60b)   ... they buried <u>charms</u> in various parts of the country to attract huge membership and wrest power from the ruling party.
61a)   Passengers observe that almost all <u>poda poda</u> drivers are fond of playing loud music.
61b)   Passengers observe that almost all <u>mini bus</u> drivers are fond of playing loud music.
62a)   <u>Bondo</u> is a common practice in the country and it usually happens when schools are in session...
62b)   <u>Female circumcision</u> is a common practice in the country and it usually happens when schools are in session...

The Grammatical Peculiarities in the English of Educated Sierra Leoneans

This section deals with the noun, pronoun, determiner, verb, preposition, adjective, word class and syntax-related peculiarities.

Noun

The deviations in this category are related to pluralisation. That is, the distinction between countable and uncountable nouns with respect to pluralisation is hardly made in certain cases. For example,

1a) ... causing major <u>damages</u> on the administrative building.
1b) ... causing major <u>damage</u> on the administrative building.
2a) Already, there are strong <u>evidences</u> via NEC officials pilfering the...
2b) Already, there are strong <u>pieces of evidence</u> via NEC officials pilfering the...
3a) I have been following your <u>advices</u>
3b) I have been following your <u>pieces of advice</u>
4a) And what was the grandfather's reaction to these strange <u>behaviours</u> of his grandson, Foday?
4b) And what was the grandfather's reaction to this strange <u>behaviour</u> of his grandson, Foday?
5a) This reason should not be underestimated as there are proofs to show that NEC <u>staffs</u> are...
5b) This reason should not be underestimated as there are proofs to show that NEC <u>staff members</u> are...
6a) This, in her opinion, justified the appropriation of <u>properties</u> belonging to the writer.
6b) This, in her opinion, justified the appropriation of <u>property</u> belonging to the writer.
7a) It is the inciting <u>languages</u> from the media that is causing the violence
7b) It is the inciting <u>language</u> from the media that is causing the violence
8a) ... no matter how high a man is he is going to account for his <u>works</u>
8b) ... no matter how high a man is he is going to account for his <u>work</u>
9a) We have arrested several culprits and their <u>equipments</u>
9b) We have arrested several culprits and their <u>equipment</u>
10a) ... needed arms and <u>ammunitions</u> to dislodge the illegal regime by force of arms.

10b) ... needed arms and <u>ammunition</u> to dislodge the illegal regime by force of arms.

Pronoun

This is concerned with pronoun usage. For example, there is the use of the 'subject' form of the relative personal pronoun where the native English speaker would preferably use the 'object' form and vice versa. This is evident in:

11a) ... and this can be done through <u>we</u> the parents.
11b) ... and this can be done through <u>us</u> the parents.
12a) The other day somebody who knows your family more than <u>me</u> was telling me that...
12b) The other day somebody who knows your family more than <u>I</u> was telling me that...

There is also the tendency to use different forms of the demonstrative pronoun. For example,

13a) ... the completed nomination forms and objectives for parliamentary candidates would have been submitted to the Commission while <u>that</u> of the presidential candidates are to be submitted by July 7th.
13b) ... the completed nomination forms and objectives for parliamentary candidates would have been submitted to the Commission while <u>those</u> of the presidential candidates are to be submitted by July 7th.
14b) Now Clifford's fear is not the money he lost or the pain he suffered but the safety of his life and <u>that</u> of Nigerians.
14b) Now Clifford's fear is not the money he lost or the pain he suffered but the safety of his life and <u>those</u> of Nigerians.

Also, there is the tendency to use the reflexive pronoun where the native English speaker would prefer the reciprocal pronoun as seen in:

15a) You can still transform the love you have for <u>yourselves</u> to a brotherly one.
15b) You can still transform the love you have for <u>each other (one another)</u> to a brotherly one.
16a) ... and as years went by, the two men saw <u>themselves</u>.
16b) ... and as years went by, the two men saw <u>each other</u>.

Verb

This section is concerned with concordial usage, the use of infinitive/participle and tense/aspect.

Concord

Concordial rules are observed differently from native English. For instance,

17a)   ... the training of the youths <u>constitute</u> a security threat and therefore a cause for concern.

17b)   ... the training of the youths <u>constitutes</u> a security threat and therefore a cause for concern.

18a)   A team of medical doctors and dentists from the United States of Africa, upon the encouragement of the Hon. Minister of Lands Alfred Bobson Sesay, <u>are</u> currently offering...

18b)   A team of medical doctors and dentists from the United States of Africa, upon the encouragement of the Hon. Minister of Lands Alfred Bobson Sesay, <u>is</u> currently offering...

19a)   Those who thought the APC's twenty four years implacable notoriety of vandalism and kleptomaniac activities <u>are</u> now history, should think again.

19b)   Those who thought the APC's twenty four years implacable notoriety of vandalism and kleptomaniac activities <u>is</u> now history, should think again.

20a)   Among the Commission's most prominent achievements <u>was</u> the facilitation of a dialogue among political parties and the subsequent agreement and signing of a Code of Conduct that...

20b)   Among the Commission's most prominent achievements <u>were</u> the facilitation of a dialogue among political parties and the subsequent agreement and signing of a Code of Conduct that...

21a)   She was one of those young, beautiful, professional, well poised women who <u>was</u> coming up, trying to...

21b) She was one of those young, beautiful, professional, well poised women who <u>were</u> coming up, trying to...
22a) Secretary General of RUFP Jonathan Kposowa said that Fatou Sankoh together with other members <u>have</u> visited the...
22b) Secretary General of RUFP Jonathan Kposowa said that Fatou Sankoh together with other members <u>has</u> visited the...
23a) It is neither the APC nor the SLPP that <u>pay</u> our salaries at the end of the month.
23b) It is neither the APC nor the SLPP that <u>pays</u> our salaries at the end of the month.
24a) ... the leones <u>are</u> not flowing
24b) ... the leones <u>is</u> not flowing
25a) All the people wanted <u>were</u> for Sankoh and his boys to...
25b) All the people wanted <u>was</u> for Sankoh and his boys to...
26a) "It is you who <u>is</u> frustrated," he said.
26b) "It is you who <u>are</u> frustrated," he said.

Infinitive/Participle

Infinitives tend to be used where participles would be preferable by the native speaker. For example,
27a) ... who are committed <u>to see</u> his dream of taking Sierra Leoneans to the promise land achievable at all cost.
27b) ... who are committed <u>to seeing</u> his dream of taking Sierra Leoneans to the promise land achievable at all cost.
28a) I am looking forward <u>to have</u> a united and prosperous Sierra Leone.
28b) I am looking forward <u>to having</u> a united and prosperous Sierra Leone.
29a) The reason why I am keen <u>to see</u> the Koindu trade revived is because...
29b) The reason why I am keen <u>to seeing</u> the Koindu trade revived is because...
30a) P.C. Sinnah Yovoni who together with the Resident Minister South ...symbolically presented fifty-six she goats to President Koroma as a means to <u>develop</u> and <u>multiply</u> the resources of Sierra Leone.

30b) P.C. Sinnah Yovoni who together with the Resident Minister South ...symbolically presented fifty-six she goats to President Koroma as a means to <u>developing</u> and <u>multiplying</u> the resources of Sierra Leone.

Conversely, the choice of a participle rather than an infinitive, is also observed. This can be seen in:
31a) ... he went abroad <u>choosing</u> another disgruntle politician from the same party.
31b) ...he went abroad <u>to choose</u> another disgruntle politician from the same party.
32a) So, you see why it makes no sense <u>talking</u> about the looting of...
32b) So, you see why it makes no sense <u>to talk</u> about the looting of... 33a) Speaking on the day, the women urged the newly elected government to give space to women to continue to <u>proving</u> their mettle.
33b) Speaking on the day, the women urged the newly elected government to give space to women to continue <u>to prove</u> their mettle.
34a) ... and if I hear you call that illegitimate child your daughter again, you will cease <u>to be</u> my son.
34b) ... and if I hear you call that illegitimate child your daughter again, you will cease <u>being</u> my son.

Tense and Aspect

This sub-section involves inflection and aspectual usage. For example, a verb is not inflected where the context would require it to be inflected. This is what is shown in:
35a) If perpetrators of violence <u>have</u> your interest at heart, then violence would not be a priority for them at this crucial time of transition.
35b) If perpetrators of violence <u>had</u> your interest at heart, then violence would not be a priority for them at this crucial time of transition.
36a) Berewa added that if the APC and the SLPP were honest, they <u>will</u> not go around...

36b) Berewa added that if the APC and the SLPP were honest, they <u>would</u> not go around...
37b) I think it is high time we <u>define</u> the preventive measures.
37a) I think it is high time we <u>defined</u> the preventive measures.

Conversely, a verb tends to be inflected where in the context it would not be inflected in native English as seen in:

38a) ... when suddenly he saw large crowd of boys <u>entered</u> his shop shouting that they were supporting the former ruling SLPP government.
38b) ... when suddenly he saw large crowd of boys <u>enter</u> his shop shouting that they were supporting the former ruling SLPP government.
39a) This man made him <u>lost</u> his sense of thought.
39b) This man made him <u>lose</u> his sense of thought.
40a) Manso Bangura was on a taxi heading for Sorie Magbele at Queens port where he heard people <u>talked</u> about...
40b) Manso Bangura was on a taxi heading for Sorie Magbele at Queens port where he heard people <u>talk</u> about...

The 'to' also tends to be part of the infinitive in an environment where it is not used in native English. For example,
41a) The horrifying news made me <u>to collapse</u> in my office.
41b) The horrifying news made me <u>collapse</u> in my office.
42a) ... which made the country <u>to look</u> to the East for assistance.
42b) ... which made the country <u>look</u> to the East for assistance.

There seems to be a difference in aspectual usage sometimes resulting in inflecting stative verbs for the progressive aspect. For example,
43a) I know that they <u>are hearing</u> my inquiries but they've simply decided to...
43b) I know that they <u>hear</u> my inquiries but they've simply decided to...
44a) The fact that he does not want anyone to know he <u>is having</u> an affair with you shows...

44b)　The fact that he does not want anyone to know he <u>has</u> an affair with you shows...
45a)　The DPP told the court that he <u>is seeing</u> four different types of parcel which are not...
45b)　The DPP told the court that he <u>sees</u> four different types of parcel which are not...

The perfective aspect is also used where the native speaker would prefer the past tense. The following sentences illustrate this tendency,

46a)　The Sierra Leone Red Cross Society of the western area branch <u>have</u> on Saturday 24th March 2007, <u>opened</u> a Child Advocacy and Rehabilitation (CAR) project centre at...
46b)　The Sierra Leone Red Cross Society of the western area branch on Saturday 24th March 2007, <u>opened</u> a Child Advocacy and Rehabilitation (CAR) project centre at...
47a)　Fourah Bay College, the University of Sierra Leone's Faculty of Social Sciences and Law, <u>has celebrated</u> its annual faculty week on Monday 11th June.
47b)　Fourah Bay College, the University of Sierra Leone's Faculty of Social Sciences and Law, <u>celebrated</u> its annual faculty week on Monday 11th June.
48a)　The Chief Electoral Commissioner Miss Christiana Thorpe <u>has disclosed</u> on Friday to journalists that...
48b)　The Chief Electoral Commissioner Miss Christiana Thorpe <u>disclosed</u> on Friday to journalists that...

Determiner

This section deals with differences in the use of the determiner, the inclusion and the omission of the article.

Different Determiner

The differences in usage in this respect can be viewed from the use of articles and indefinite determiners. For example, there appears to be a difference in the use of articles as seen in:
49a)　... disenfranchised from <u>a</u> SLPP candidate of their choice.
49b)　... disenfranchised from <u>an</u> SLPP candidate of their choice.

50a) ... after he was also docked for stealing <u>a</u> L6 Motorola mobile phone valued at Le300,000.
50b) ... after he was also docked for stealing <u>an</u> L6 Motorola mobile phone valued at Le300,000.
51a) ... and was taken to the hotel that was managed by <u>an</u> European.
51b) ... and was taken to the hotel that was managed by <u>a</u> European.

Also, some indefinite determiners tend to be used in ways which native speakers would not:

52a) ... to the extent that it sometimes took <u>one</u> whole week without running an errand for the former administrative clerk.
52b) ... to the extent that it sometimes took <u>a</u> whole week without running an errand for the former administrative clerk.
53a) ... he needed to rest for <u>one</u> whole week and should eat rice with chicken soup.
53b) ... he needed to rest for <u>a</u> whole week and should eat rice with chicken soup.
54a) ... had been <u>less</u> complaints of pilfering of passengers' luggage.
54b) ... had been <u>few</u> complaints of pilfering of passengers' luggage.
55a) I kept on praying fervently and after <u>few</u> months, another young man approached me.
55b) I kept on praying fervently and after <u>a few</u> months, another young man approached me.
56a) Youthful side George FC must be commended for resisting the might of their counterpart, and making <u>few</u> attacks...
56b) Youthful side George FC must be commended for resisting the might of their counterpart, and making <u>a few</u> attacks...

57a) I read through the pages of our local tabloids <u>some few</u> days ago...

57b) I read through the pages of our local tabloids <u>a few</u> days ago...

Article Inclusion

There is the tendency to include the article where the native speaker would consider it undesirable:

58a) Yet she brought herself up struggling politically and got to the limelight and eventually became <u>a</u> Minister.
58b) Yet she brought herself up struggling politically and got to the limelight and eventually became Minister.
59a) ... that will show <u>an</u> over-ambitiousness on your part.
59b) ... that will show over-ambitiousness on your part.
60a) ... but equally promoted his son Osman Conteh to the rank of <u>a</u> captain without merit.
60b) ... but equally promoted his son Osman Conteh to the rank of captain without merit.
61a) He has threatened on several occasions to disrupt my work as <u>a</u> Member of Parliament...
61b) He has threatened on several occasions to disrupt my work as Member of Parliament...
62a) Three years later, his friend returned to Sierra Leone with <u>a</u> sad news that...
62b) Three years later, his friend returned to Sierra Leone with sad news that...
63a) Speaking at the graduation ceremony of Njala Universiy students on the Coronation Field in Bo, Kabba said that he was not talking as <u>a</u> President but as a Lawyer
63b) Speaking at the graduation ceremony of Njala Universiy students on the Coronation Field in Bo, Kabba said that he was not talking as President but as a Lawyer.

Article Omission

There is also an apparent tendency to omit the article where the native speaker would consider it desirable. This is illustrated in:

64a) ... to state that they have never received anything from ø government.

64b) ... to state that they have never received anything from the government.
65a) ... and he took it at the last minute when it mattered ø most.
65b) ... and he took it at the last minute when it mattered the most.
66a) If readers could recall a year or two, Motuba had written ø series of articles demonstrating...
66b) If readers could recall a year or two, Motuba had written a series of articles demonstrating...
67a) Tina frankly told Kholifa that she had ø long time relationship with...
67b) Tina frankly told Kholifa that she had a long time relationship with...
68a) What will it profit us if as leaders we are to gain the whole world ... only to ultimately loose our souls ... by continuously being rated ø least in the world?
68b) What will it profit us if as leaders we are to gain the whole world ... only to ultimately loose our souls ... by continuously being rated the least in the world?
69a) 10 Youths Leave For ø UK
69b) 10 Youths Leave For the UK

Adjective

The deviations in this category are based on usage. Sierra Leoneans tend to use the superlative form of the adjective where native English would prefer the comparative form and vice versa. For example,

70a) What makes the matter worst for the SLPP is...
70b) What makes the matter worse for the SLPP is...
71a) ... on the question of whether the nation is better or worst off now than before.
71b) ... on the question of whether the nation is better or worse off now than before.
72a) Big cities like Bo, Kenema and Freetown are the worse in terms of...
72b) Big cities like Bo, Kenema and Freetown are the worst in terms of...

Preposition

This section deals with differences in prepositional usage, prepositional inclusion and prepositional omission.

Prepositional Usage

In the majority of cases, prepositional peculiarities are concerned with the choice of prepositions. For example,

- 73a)   ... for wanting to use and misuse them in the guise of change <u>at</u> the detriment of their future.
- 73b)   ... for wanting to use and misuse them in the guise of change <u>to</u> the detriment of their future.
- 74a)   Bee is waiting <u>on</u> this day as the creature no longer depends on the Kabba Tiger
- 74b)   Bee is waiting <u>for</u> this day as the creature no longer depends on the Kabba Tiger
- 75a)   Mr. Blair made the apology <u>over</u> UN Radio after...
- 75b)   Mr. Blair made the apology <u>on</u> UN Radio after...
- 76a)   He told me that he has a wife and a seven year old girl child and they live <u>at</u> Conakry.
- 76b)   He told me that he has a wife and a seven year old girl child and they live <u>in</u> Conakry.
- 77a)   ... a lot of my friends congratulated me <u>for</u> my presence in the show.
- 77b)   ... a lot of my friends congratulated me <u>on</u> my presence in the show.
- 78a)   Whoever does not ask from Allah, He becomes angry <u>at</u> him.
- 78b)   Whoever does not ask from Allah, He becomes angry <u>with</u> him.
- 79a)   ... daily market activities are moving smoothly <u>under</u> the hot burning sun.
- 79b)   ... daily market activities are moving smoothly <u>in</u> the hot burning sun.
- 80a)   ... three judges will have to preside <u>on</u> the matter and eventually deliver a ruling on that matter.

80b) ... three judges will have to preside <u>over</u> the matter and eventually deliver a ruling on that matter.
81a) We were so closed that we sometimes sleep together <u>on</u> the same bed
81b) We were so closed that we sometimes sleep together <u>in</u> the same bed

Prepositional Inclusion

Prepositions are sometimes included where native speakers would not make use of them:

82a) The basketball competition will comprise <u>of</u> 20 teams competing for...
82b) The basketball competition will comprise 20 teams competing for...
83a) When Hawa sat <u>to</u> the G.C.E. O'Level exams...
83b) When Hawa sat the G.C.E. O'Level exams...
84a) ... to discuss <u>about</u> the ugly situation in the constituency
84b) ... to discuss the ugly situation in the constituency
85a) Mr. Sesay's defence was that he requested <u>for</u> sex from...
85b) Mr. Sesay's defence was that he requested sex from...
86a) And the time they reach <u>at</u> school they are already late.
86b) And the time they reach school they are already late.
87a) ... this was because the government failed to give them what they demanded <u>for</u>.
87b) ... this was because the government failed to give them what they demanded.

Prepositional Omission

In some instances, prepositions are omitted where they would be used by native English speakers:

88a) I didn't want to wake them ø.
88b) I didn't want to wake them <u>up</u>.
89a) He who earlier said he believe ø nothing else other than his parents, had changed his mind drastically.
89b) He who earlier said he believe <u>in</u> nothing else other than his parents, had changed his mind drastically.

90a) The witch doctor said it would cost me if I object ø his advice.
90b) The witch doctor said it would cost me if I object <u>to</u> his advice.

Word Class

The native English use of similar morphological forms which can function in different syntactic slots (for example, nominal, adjectival, adverbial, and so on) may account for the use of items in the following examples where other items would be preferable in native English:

91a) The blood of a five <u>months</u> old baby was reported...
91b) The blood of a five <u>month</u> old baby was reported...

92a) ... while Margai was invited for a two <u>hours</u> lecture by the students of Njala (Bo campus).
92b) ... while Margai was invited for a two <u>hour</u> lecture by the students of Njala (Bo campus).
93a) ...who announced that the Consular Section of the embassy was now <u>opened</u> to the public.
93b) ...who announced that the Consular Section of the embassy was now <u>open</u> to the public.
94a) Speaking to the Exclusive early this week in Makeni, Mr. John said the people in the north are <u>matured</u> politically...
94b) Speaking to the Exclusive early this week in Makeni, Mr. John said the people in the north are <u>mature</u> politically...
95a) ... where she discovered that all the doors were <u>widely opened</u>.
95b) ... where she discovered that all the doors were <u>wide</u> <u>open</u>.
96a) The Kabba/Berewa SLPP Government is fully aware that most places in the interior, and even parts of the city, are either impassable or inaccessible during the <u>raining</u> season.
96b) The Kabba/Berewa SLPP Government is fully aware that most places in the interior, and even parts of the city, are either impassable or inaccessible during the <u>rainy</u> season.

Syntax

This section deals with the relationship between words in sentence structure, which may not have been dealt with in other aspects of grammar. It includes imbalance, repetition, structural omission, structural differences, the use of the universal tag, the placement of modifier, reduplication and responses to yes/no questions.

Imbalance

There appears to be a logical imbalance in structuring certain words or expressions:

97a) ... will become a source of motivation and inspiration for our development agenda rather than <u>source</u> of neglect or complacency.

97b) ... will become a source of motivation and inspiration for our development agenda rather than <u>a source</u> of neglect or complacency.

98a) They prefer to cope with this ignominious position for the rest of their lives rather than <u>risk</u> coming back home.

98b) They prefer to cope with this ignominious position for the rest of their lives rather than <u>to risk</u> coming back home.

99a) ... my party is capable of fighting corruption, <u>provide</u> better education, proper health system and justice for all.

99b) ... my party is capable of fighting corruption, <u>providing</u> better education, proper health system and justice for all.

100a) ... which is generally considered to be free, fair and <u>not characterised by violence</u> which used to be the hallmark of pre-war elections.

100b) ... which is generally considered to be free, fair and <u>violence-free</u> which used to be the hallmark of pre-war elections.

101a) They have the mandate of protecting lives and properties and <u>to keep the peace</u>.

101b) They have the mandate of protecting lives and properties and <u>of peace keeping</u>.

102a) ... a good number of PMDC executive members and supporters both <u>in the Western Area</u> and <u>the provinces</u> have defected to the SLPP.

102b) ... a good number of PMDC executive members and supporters both <u>in the Western Area</u> and <u>in the provinces</u> have defected to the SLPP.
103a) ... people who came into the game either for temporary recognition or <u>to make money</u>.
103b) ... people who came into the game either for temporary recognition or <u>for money making</u>.
104a) <u>Pa Santigie took permission from the Town Chief</u> for the Medicine Man to perform the ceremony and <u>a date was fixed for the next day in the evening</u>.
104b) Pa Santigie took permission from the Town Chief for the Medicine Man to perform the ceremony and <u>they fixed a date for the next day in the evening</u>.
105a) After three hours, <u>Mrs. Catherine Donanldon regained consciousness</u> and <u>was advised by Dr. Sam Macdonald</u> to have some rest.
105b) After three hours, <u>Mrs. Catherine Donanldon regained consciousness</u> and <u>Dr. Sam Macdonald advised her</u> to have some rest.

Repetition

There is also the tendency to repeat words or ideas which do not seem to contribute anything to the total meanings of structures:

106a) As Aminata's father was uttering these words, he was <u>retreating backwards</u> cautiously.
106b) As Aminata's father was uttering these words, he was <u>retreating</u> cautiously.
107a) The Assistant Secretary General <u>attributed</u> the gains made by the party <u>due</u> to hard work...
107b) The Assistant Secretary General <u>attributed</u> the gains made by the party to hard work...
108a) Bear in mind that the election is going to be a <u>secret ballot</u> wherein...
108b) Bear in mind that the election is going to be a <u>ballot</u> wherein...

109a) Government should <u>suspend</u> payment of funds earned from mining operations to chiefdoms and sections <u>temporarily</u> and…

109b) Government should <u>suspend</u> payment of funds earned from mining operations to chiefdoms and sections and…

110a) They also said they were all arrested in the <u>afternoon hours</u> at <u>2 pm</u>.

110b) They also said they were all arrested at 2 <u>pm</u>.

111a) He died in the battle to <u>return</u> the APC <u>back</u> to power.

111b) He died in the battle to <u>return</u> the APC to power.

112a) <u>Among</u> the weapons discovered <u>include</u> is a point 22 revolver and a point 39 special 100 live rounds, four cartoons of 54.2 live rounds ammunition.

112b) <u>Among</u> the weapons discovered is a point 22 revolver and a point 39 special 100 live rounds, four cartoons of 54.2 live rounds ammunition.

113a) … <u>let</u> us <u>don't</u> allow them to leave us in pieces but in peace.

113b) … <u>let</u> us not allow them to leave us in pieces but in peace.

114a) During the court proceedings, the accuse who is a <u>tailor by profession</u> was reportedly worried because…

114b) During the court proceedings, the accuse who is a <u>tailor</u> was reportedly worried…

115a) The starting point will be to identify the <u>most major</u> of these amateur leagues…

115b) The starting point will be to identify the <u>major</u> of these amateur leagues…

116a) … making it the <u>most unique</u> city in the world.

116b) … making it the <u>unique</u> city in the world.

117a) Similarly, University Lecturers always have to be dynamic as the community <u>in</u> which they live <u>in</u>.

117b) Similarly, University Lecturers always have to be dynamic as the community <u>in</u> which they live.

118a) The many Lawyers and Legal minded Parliamentarians including the Osho Williamses, the Serry-kamals, the Edie Turays, the Mabinty Mansarays, the Chernor Maju Bahs and

many others with similar capabilities are the ingredients <u>of</u> which a strong parliament is made up <u>of</u>.
118b) The many Lawyers and Legal minded Parliamentarians including the Osho Williamses, the Serry-kamals, the Edie Turays, the Mabinty Mansarays, the Chernor Maju Bahs and many others with similar capabilities are the ingredients which a strong parliament is made up <u>of</u>.

Structural Omission

This sub-section involves the tendency to omit the comparative, content and function words.

Comparison

Comparisons tend to be made without the use of a comparative word:
119a) Motuba wants SLFA to pay attention to other sports discipline ø than only concentrating on football.
119b) Motuba wants SLFA to pay attention to other sports discipline <u>rather than</u> only concentrating on football.
120a) …came from the realisation that women are ø devoted, competent and capable than men in promoting politics and maintaining good governance in any nation.
120b) …came from the realisation that women are <u>more</u> devoted, competent and capable than men in promoting politics and maintaining good governance in any nation.
121a) Nothing makes you ø happy than to know your family supports you in life.
121b) Nothing makes you <u>happier</u> than to know your family supports you in life.
122a) … and I have a ø fierce challenger than Margai.
122b) … and I have a <u>fiercer</u> challenger than Margai.

Content and Function Words

Content and function words also tend to be omitted where native speakers would consider them preferable:

123a) … but this year they feel that the less privileged are not enjoying Ø as they should enjoy Ø in the society.

123b) ... but this year they feel that the less privileged are not enjoying <u>themselves</u> as they should enjoy <u>themselves</u> in the society.
124a) ... but he had never Ø and will not succeed.
124b) ... but he had never <u>succeeded</u> and will not succeed.
125a) <u>While ø waiting for the election results</u>, a report reached the African Champion ...
125b) <u>While we were waiting for the election results</u>, a report reached the African Champion ...
126a) <u>For their loyalty ø and support for</u> the newly installed All Peoples Congress (APC) government, some members of the party were seen...
126b) <u>For their loyalty to and support for</u> the newly installed All Peoples Congress (APC) government, some members of the party were seen...
127a) This, he noted, was as a result of the fact that <u>access ø and uptake of</u> services for children and...
127b) This, he noted, was as a result of the fact that <u>access to and uptake of</u> services for children and...
128a) No sooner he assumed the mantle of leadership of Africa's most populous nation ø the price of oil jumped in the international market. (see p VI)
128b) No sooner he assumed the mantle of leadership of Africa's most populous nation <u>than</u> the price of oil jumped in the international market.

Structural Differences

This section deals with the position of pronouns and modifiers.

Pronoun

This sub-section involves pronouns in compound subjects/objects and pronoun copying.

Pronoun in Compound Subject/Object

In compound subjects/objects, as opposed to what obtains in native English, the first person pronoun (the personal pronoun I/me) tends to come first as observed in:

129a) The diary starts when <u>I and a close colleague</u>...
129b) The diary starts when <u>a close colleague and I</u>...
130a) It is a sad memory for <u>me and my sisters</u>

130b) It is a sad memory for <u>my sisters and me</u>
131a) Will you go to school, then, and leave <u>me and my wife</u> in peace?
131b) Will you go to school, then, and leave <u>my wife and me</u> in peace?

Pronoun Copying

Pronouns tend to be used in situations where they are not desirable in native English:

132a) Saturday's election, though the turn out in the initial stage was low, <u>it</u> turned out to be a big success.
132b) Saturday's election, though the turn out in the initial stage was low, turned out to be a big success.
133a) Mr. Donald Oluwole James I think <u>he</u> should begin to share some of the responsibilities of running the office.
133b) Mr. Donald Oluwole James I think should begin to share some of the responsibilities of running the office.
134a) According to the victims, Mohamed Kamara, a class III pupil of the Kulafai Islamic School <u>he</u> and a number of his neighbourhood friends were playing in an empty space…
134b) According to the victims, Mohamed Kamara, a class III pupil of the Kulafai Islamic School and a number of his neighbourhood friends were playing in an empty space…

The Placement of the Modifier

Modifiers are sometimes placed where the native speaker would not:

135a) The Freetown based legal luminary Chernor M. Bah is aspiring for a parliamentary seat under the All People's Congress (APC) party for Constituency 110, which comprises the two communities <u>in the forthcoming presidential and parliamentary elections</u> scheduled for August 11.
135b) The Freetown based legal luminary Chernor M. Bah is aspiring for a parliamentary seat <u>in the forthcoming presidential and parliamentary elections scheduled for</u>

August 11 for Constituency 110, which comprised the two communities under the All People's Congress (APC) party

136a) According to members of the PMDC resident in the UK and USA who are Pujehun descendants they had paid for air time (2 hours) which started at 8:00 p.m. on Friday <u>to the Management of the Station</u> to "sensitise" the people of Pujehun on the August elections.

136b) According to members of the PMDC resident in the UK and USA who are also Pujehun descendants they had paid <u>to the Management of the Station</u> for air time which started at 8:00 p.m. on Friday to "sensitise" the people of Pujehun on the August elections.

137a) ... a young guy called Cidi whom I knew his girl friend some years back <u>boldly</u> met me and proposed love to me.

137b) ... a young guy called Cidi whom I knew his girl friend some years back met me and <u>boldly</u> proposed love to me.

138a) The people of Mabarr Chiefdom attempted to walk up to the Provincial Commissioners and District Commissioner to seek redress but they could <u>only</u> see the Pronivial Commissioner, Peter Duncan.

138b) The people of Mabarr Chiefdom attempted to walk up to the Provincial Commissioners and District Commissioner to seek redress but they could see <u>only</u> the Pronivial Commissioner, Peter Duncan.

139a) ... the total for the academic year is Le135,000 not considering whether the parent of the child <u>only</u> earns Le 200,000 per month as salary.

139b) ... the total for the academic year is Le135,000 not considering whether the parent of the child earns <u>only</u> Le 200,000 per month as salary.

140a) Massaquoi was allegedly accused of disclosing the location of ballot boxes to SLPP party stalwarts <u>at their Kissy warehouse</u>.

140b) Massaquoi was allegedly accused of disclosing the location of ballot boxes <u>at their Kissy warehouse</u> to SLPP party stalwarts.

Universal Tag

There is a tendency to consistently use one question tag where native speakers would prefer other forms:

141a) You are happy for his death, <u>not so</u>?
141b) You are happy for his death, <u>aren't you</u>?
142a) If the SLPP had won we will be out in the cold licking our wounds, <u>not so</u>?
142b) If the SLPP had won we will be out in the cold licking our wounds, <u>won't we</u>?
143a) In other words, if one fails to adhere to the law, that person also is corrupt <u>not so</u>?
143b) In other words, if one fails to adhere to the law, that person also is corrupt <u>isn't he</u>?

Reduplication

There appears to be a tendency to use reduplicated morphemes as opposed to what obtains in native English:

144a) George Oluwole Cole <u>pondered and pondered</u> before...
144b) George Oluwole Cole pondered hard before...
145a) Section Chief Alpha Sulaiman <u>stammered and stammered</u> for sometime, but could not come with a reply.
145b) Section Chief Alpha Sulaiman stammered for sometime, but could not come with a reply.
146a) The court messengers <u>searched and searched</u> but found no blanket or cement.
146b) The court messengers searched hard but found no blanket or cement.

Responses to Negative Yes/No Questions/Statements

There appears to be a tendency to respond differently to yes/no questions/statements from native English:

147a) **Question:**
Komba Mondeh: Don't you want to retain your position as Inspector General of Police?
Response:

Acha Kamara: Of course yes. But I think you are missing the point
For:
147b) Acha Kamara: Of course no. But I think you are missing the point.
148a) Statement:
Pupil J: Yesterday we did not discuss anything about how our pending topic simply because you were not present.
Response:
Teacher: Yes, I know but this was not my fault as I went to another college for a part time lecture yesterday but forgot to inform the class.
For:
148b)
Teacher: No, I know but this was not my fault as I went to another college for a part time lecture yesterday but forgot to inform the class.

The Discoursal Peculiarities in the English of Educated Sierra Leoneans

The peculiarities in this section include form of address, proverb and riddle, phatic communion and style.

Form of Address

There is the tendency to use specific titles before the names of people. For example,

1. Addressing participants, the Resident Minister East <u>Hon</u>. Sahr Randoff Fillie Faboe informed his audience that…
2. <u>Hon</u>. Benjamine Davies said he served in the British Navy for…

3. The president of Sierra Leone, <u>Hon</u>. Ernest Bai Koroma of the ruling All People's Congress (APC) yesterday Wednesday...
4. <u>Hon</u>. Sam Sumana apologised on behalf of the APC
5. The decision according to the presidential spokesperson, <u>Hon</u>. Alpha Kanu came in the wake of...
6. Statement by <u>Alhaji Dr</u>. Ahmad Tejan Kabba
7. Meanwhile, up to now <u>principal</u> Karim Sesay who had openly shown his support and sponsorship of...
8. The Chairman of the Political Parties Registration Commission <u>justice</u> Sydney Warne praised NEC for...
9. The first he said would be held the day the party's leader, <u>Prof</u>. Abdul Khady Koroma arrives from America...
10. A vehicle owned by <u>Ambassador</u> Joe Blell, outgoing Minister of Defence was looted.

Proverb and Riddle

Proverbs which are unfamiliar in native English are sometimes used.
11. As <u>the fingers are not the same</u>, so we too are not the same in terms of financial capability.
12. No matter how big, a tree cannot make a forest.
13. Can we therefore say a sheep head and a goat head are the same?

Similarly, expressions which are foreign to the native speaker because of their cultural implications are sometimes used:
14. Fatmata narrated that upon performing their ceremony, <u>a black locked padlock</u> was discovered together with <u>human hair, five hundred Leones coin and tied beads</u> under the steps leading to the compound.
15. She explained further that additional <u>blood was also drained from the walls of the victim's house</u>.
16. The Director of Works Mathew Allen <u>scratched his head</u> feeling embarrassed that the Chief Clerk could raise a point that was not relevant to the meeting.
17. Provincial Commissioner Mark Prince <u>bit the end of his pencil</u> and said...

18. When questioned by District Commissioner William Parker, he fell flat on the ground and held the white man's feet weeping, "please sir forgive me...

19. ... where the nine month pregnant Fatmata was expected to either accept that she stole the gold or would be subjected to the dangerous oath-taking that could lead to her death in less than twenty four hours.

20. You will stay here with me for it will be a great loss to me if you go back, considering that I bought you from your parents for ten pounds ten shillings (a husband speaking to his wife).

21. ... he never border to come and look at his baby.

22. The problem now is that I am pregnant but doesn't know the actual person who impregnated me. Both of them have expressed ownership and desire to take care of the pregnancy.

23. ...Kaday, I am not married, ... I am here to look out for a wife. I have decided to marry you (a man conversing with a woman).

24. Mammy Sallay almost shed tears when she said, "Ina, at the age of nineteen, I was married to your father...

25. The search for children had taken Biareh far and wide, first in his search for the right woman who would deliver his sons primarily and daughters secondarily.

Phatic Communion

This section is concerned with the tendency to respond to greetings differently from native English.

26) Alimamy: Hello Tamba and Yabome! How are you doing?
    Tamba and Yabome:
        We're doing fine.

27) Saffa: Welcome guys, how is the day?
    Kpana: It's fine with me.
    Vamboi: It's fine with me too.

Style

There are certain words and constructions in native English which tend to belong mainly to a formal written language or to a very formal spoken style. However, Sierra Leoneans have the tendency to use such words and constructions in their casual conversation or writing. For example,

28) Clifford: As far as I <u>am</u> concerned nothing seems to be working. If at all <u>they are</u> working, <u>they are</u> going at a snail pace.
    Memunatu: I agree things are going at a snail pace like you said, but I <u>do not</u> subscribe to the fact that nothing seems to be working.
    Clifford: You people are misunderstanding me. When I say things <u>are not</u> working, I simply meant that...
29) Lawrence: Ha! Ha! Ha! <u>What is</u> your qualification?
    Clifford: Keep quiet! <u>I am</u> not talking to you.
    Lawrence: To be frank enough, <u>I am</u> not worried about having a job... as long as <u>I am</u> able to make ends meet. What <u>I am</u> worried about is whether this Government will deliver. I say so because the way <u>I am</u> looking at things, the people around him will continue to confuse him so much that <u>he will</u> find himself preoccupied.
30) Lawrence: May be the man <u>does not</u> want to be messed up by these our old APC thirsty politicians.
    Clifford: Forget it, the man made a blunder, by not accepting a ministerial job. Becoming a Minister in the current government <u>does not</u> mean the end of his career as leader of the PMDC (Friends conversing at an entertainment centre).
31) Marah: Sir Albert to be honest with you, the government of Tejan <u>did not</u> give much help to members of the Young Generation.
    Sir Albert: You mean with all the sacrifices the youths made for the restoration of the SLPP that nearly caused their lives, you <u>did not</u> compensate them?..

How do you expect these young men to take over the leadership of the party when they <u>are not</u> empowered, or do you think the party belongs to you and your children? Actually <u>you have</u> caused the whole conversation to become unpleasant to me… I helped Tejan to complete his university education in England but you people <u>did not</u> suffer for the party as these young men did… <u>I am</u> really in sympathy with these youths.

Conclusion

From the above, it can be observed that the features highlighted across the four language levels (that is phonology, lexis, grammar and discourse) take specific patterns. This systematicity in their use contributes to making the users sound like Sierra Leoneans and not like Englishmen.

CHAPTER THREE

THE EXISTENCE OF THE HIGHLIGHTED FEATURES IN OTHER ENGLISH VARIETIES

Introduction
This chapter seeks to investigate whether the above-mentioned features of the Sierra Leonean English variety can be found in other English varieties with a view to confirming whether or not they are peculiar to that variety.

The Phonological Features in other English Varieties
This section deals with the segmental and suprasegmental features in other English varieties.

The Segmental Features in other English Varieties
In this sub-section, some English varieties are examined in relation to features such as vowel merging, vowel substitution, spelling-induced peculiarities, nasalisation, the merging of diphthongs, the substitution of consonants, the omission of the linking and the intrusive 'r', the omission of syllabic consonants and the deletion of consonants.

Vowel Merging
It can be observed that the tendency of merging RP vowels is not peculiar to the Sierra Leonean English variety. Huber (2006:850), for example, highlights this tendency in Ghanaian English involving RP minimal pairs such as | i – I|, |U: – ʊ | and |ɔ : - D | ; | 3 : | - | ɛ | and / ɑ: / - | æ | - / ʌ /. This fusion of RP vowels, Huber contends, has led to the emergence of homophones. Bobda (2006: 885 -889) also identifies this tendency in Cameroon English citing instances such as the merging of the front close | i | and the front half close | I | vowels, the back open | D | and the back half open | ɔ | vowels; the neutralisation of the front open / æ / and the central back open / ɑ / vowels by the central / a / vowel. Furthermore, in his discussion of

the neutralisation of RP vowels in Singapore English, Wee (2006: 1025) cites Hung (1995: 29) who observes that even though Singaporeans can identify and even ridicule vowel length differences in other English varieties, 'in their own spontaneous, natural speech, no distinction is normally made..." Wee (2006: 1025-1026) observes that this tendency accounts for the development of homophones in Singapore English involving words like pool/pull and beat/bit.

It can also be observed that this tendency is evident in native English varieties. For example, Hughes and Trudgill (1987: 31-32) cite words such as 'city', 'money' and 'coffee' as well as the weak forms of 'me', 'he' and 'we' where the front close | i | vowel tends to be produced. Similarly, Trudgill and Hannah (1985:84) state that the distinction between the back open / ɒ / and the back half-open | ɔ | vowels tends not to be evident in Scottish English. In most Scottish varieties, also, they contend, the distinction between the front open / æ / and the central back open / ɑ / vowels appears non-existent. Hughes and Trudgill (1987:30) also highlight this tendency in Scottish and Irish accents. Finally, the distinction between the centralised back half-close / ʊ / and the back close / u / vowels tend to be neutralised in most types of Scottish English (Trudgill and Hannah 1985:83).

One can deduce from the above that the tendency of merging RP vowels is not peculiar to the Sierra Leonean English variety.

Vowel Substitution

The tendency of substituting some RP vowels can also be observed in other English varieties. For example, Huber (2006: 851) cites Bobda (2000a:254) who states that 'the replacement of / æ / vowel by / a / is a feature found in all African Englishes, east, west, and south." Huber (2006:851) discusses the tendency of substituting RP vowels by citing among others the central half-open / ʌ / vowel which tends to be replaced by the back half-open / ɔ / and more frequently by the central open /a / and occasionally by the front half open / ɛ / vowels. Significantly, the tendency of replacing the central half open / ʌ / vowel by the back half open / ɔ / vowel is evident in almost all West African English varieties (see Todd (1982: 288) and Trudgill and Hannah (1985: 102). Moreover, Bobda (2006: 885-894) indicates how some RP vowels tend to be substituted in Cameroon English. For example, the back closing diphthong is inclined to be replaced by the cardinal vowel / O /, together with / ɔ / and / U /; the central half-open / ʌ / vowel tends to be produced as / ɔ / and the front closing diphthong is rendered as / e /, / a / and / ej /. In addition, Baskaran (2006:1040) investigates this tendency in Malaysian English where RP diphthongs appear to be produced in such a way that they seem to be monophthongs. He provides the following as examples of this tendency:

/ eI / realised as / e / example [mel] 'mail'
                                      [relwe] 'railway'
/ əʊ / realised as / o / example [fo: to] 'photo'
                                      [slo] 'slow'
/ ɛə / realised as / ɛ / example [ðɛ] 'there'
                                      [hɛ] 'hair'

The tendency to substitute RP vowels can also be discerned in some native English varieties. For example, Hughes and Trudgill (1987: 28-29) contend that the central half open / ʌ / vowel does not exist in the north and Midlands of England and that in most parts of the north, it tends to be replaced by the back open / D / vowel. They also observe that the central half-close / 3 / vowel is absent in Tyneside speech and appears to be replaced by the back half-open / ɔ / vowel in a broad Tyneside accent.

One can deduce from the above that the tendency of substituting RP vowels is not distinct to the variety under review.

Spelling-Induced Peculiarity
The tendency to pronounce words as they are spelt can be discerned in some English varieties. For example, Bobda, (2000a) contends that spelling serves as a guide to pronunciation in all African accents of English. He states among other things that 'All African speakers

of English are likely to pronounce the 'b' of bombing, plumber, the 'g' of 'hunger', 'singer', the 'i' of parliament, the 'c' of 'indict', 'victuals', the 'w' of 'Greenwhich' (Bobda 2000a: 253). Similarly, Ahmar (2006: 1012) highlights this tendency in Pakistani English where for example the bilabial and the alveolar plosives tend to be germinated respectively in 'happy' (rendered as / hæppI /) and 'letter' (produced as / lettʌr /). He further illustrates this tendency in the non-reduction of vowels citing as an example the word 'of ' which is rendered as / əv / in RP. He states that whereas the labio-dental fricative, tends to be voiced in RP, this tendency does not occur in Pakistani English because of the influence of spelling.

One can infer from the above that the above tendency is not peculiar to the Sierra Leonean variety.

Nasalisation

The nasalisation of English vowels is a feature that appears to characterise several English varieties. In investigating Nigerian English, for example, Gut (2006: 822) observes that the Yorubas tend to nasalise vowels that precede nasal consonants leading to the disappearance of the latter if they occur in word final position. He illustrates this tendency in the word 'win' which is rendered as / wĩ /.

Huber (2006: 857) describes this tendency to be strong among educated Ghanaians particularly when the vowels precede the alveolar nasal. In this circumstance, Huber contends, the nasal is either reduced or completely dropped. He cites the following as examples of this tendency in Ghanaian English:
twenty [twɛnti – tw☐ⁿti – twẽti]
nine [nain – naĩᵐ - na ĩ]
(Huber, 2006: 857)
Huber argues that this tendency among Ghanaians has led to the existence of near-to homophones evident in pairs of words such as can – car, been – bee, and coffin – coffee.

One can deduce from the above that this peculiarity-type is not exclusively evident in the Sierra Leonean variety.

The Substitution of Consonants

Some RP consonants tend to be substituted in several English varieties. For example, Platt et al. (1984: 38) refer to the tendency of replacing the voiced and the voiceless dental fricatives / ð / and / θ / by the voiced and voiceless alveolar plosives / t / and / d / respectively. In other words, citing Bansal (1978:2), they state this tendency can be observed in Indian English, where the voiced alveolar plosive / d / can be heard in words such as 'the', 'this' and 'that' while the voiceless alveolar plosive / t / can be heard in 'thick' and 'Thursday'. They also contend that this tendency obtains in Sri Lankan English, West Indian English and some African Englishes. Similarly, in Malaysian English, Baskaran (2006:1045) observes that the dental fricatives / θ / and /ð/ are inclined to be rendered as the corresponding alveolar plosives / t / and / d / respectively. He considers the following as examples of this tendency:

[tik] 'thick'   [tɔ:t] 'thought'
[tri] 'three'   [də] 'the'
[dis] 'this'   [fa:də] 'father'
[dəm]'them'   [e:də] 'either'
                       [ra:də] 'rather'

(Baskaran, 2006: 1045)

In addition, Huber (2006: 858) highlights the replacement of the velar nasal / ŋ / by the alveolar nasal / n / in progressives or deverbal nouns in Ghanaian English citing examples such as 'morning', 'leading' and 'the meeting', which are respectively pronounced as [mɔnin], [lidin] and [dɛ mitin]. He observes that whereas RP does not inter alia allow [ŋg] sequence in the coda, this is not the case in Ghanaian English where, for example, the expression 'sing a song' and the words 'among' and 'bring' are respectively produced as [siŋg ɛ sɔŋg], [amɔŋg] and [briŋg].

Significantly, Hughes and Trudgill (1987: 36) identify this tendency in native English varieties. In other words, citing words that take the – ing suffix such as 'singing' and 'walking' respectively pronounced as / sIŋIn / and / wɔ:kIn /, they observe that the velar nasal is mostly replaced by the non-RP speakers by the alveolar nasal. They also highlight the tendency in western central England for words that end with the velar nasal in other varieties and are spelt 'ng' to be pronounced as / ŋg /. They illustrate this tendency in words such as 'singer' and 'thing' which are respectively pronounced [sIŋgə] and [θIŋg].

From the above, one can state that this tendency is not distinctive of the variety under reference.

The Omission of the Linking and the Intrusive 'R'
The tendency of using the linking and the intrusive 'r' in native English seems absent in some English varieties. For instance, Baskaran (2006: 1045) observes that liaison is rare in Malaysian English and that even when it does occur, it is more pronounced in the use of linking 'r'. Mesthrie (2006:1108) also states that: 'Linking [r] is absent in Ghanaian English, Cameroon English and Liberian standard English and is rare to non-existent in varieties of South African English.' Bobda (2006:894) in his discussion of some differences between Cameroon English and RP cites one of his works (Bobda 1994:254-55). In this work, the absence of the linking 'r' in Cameroon English is one of the differences noted between the two varieties as shown in the following phrases 'their opponents', 'our ancestors', 'further amount' 'your advice' and 'for a period' which are respectively rendered as [diɛ 'ɔ pɔnɛnts], [awa an'sɛstɔs], [fɔda amaunt], [jua 'advais] and [fɔ e piriɔd]. Furthermore, Wee (2006:1029) cites Brown (1988: 119) who contends that since colloquial Singapore English words appear to be separated by glottal stops, this has hindered the possibility of using both the linking and the intrusive [r] in that variety. Mesthrie (2006:961) also makes a similar observation with regard to Indian South African English.

One can conclude from the above that the tendency of omitting both the linking and the intrusive 'r' is not peculiar to the Sierra Leonean English variety.

The Omission of the Syllabic Consonants
This peculiarity-type also exists in other English varieties. In his investigation of the forms of consonant cluster simplification strategies in Nigerian English for example, Gut (2006) highlights inter alia the tendency to insert the epithentic vowel [U] or [i] between word – final syllabic consonants and the preceding consonants. This tendency, which he observes is mainly evident among Hausa speakers of English, can lead to the omission of syllabic consonants. He cites the following as examples of this tendency:
bottle [bɔtul]
button [bɔtun]
cattle [katul]
silk [silik]
(Gut, 2006:824)

Wee (2006) also investigates this tendency in Singapore English. That is, instead of retaining the RP feature of making the lateral / l / and the nasals / m, n, ŋ / syllabic, Wee observes that a schwa tends to be inserted to take the nucleus position in Singapore English, thereby shifting the lateral and the nasal to the coda position. He provides the following as examples:

	RP	CollsgE
button	[bʌtn̩]	[batən]
bottle	[bɔtl̩]	[bɔtəl]
whistle	[wIsl̩]	[wIsəl]

(Wee, 2006: 1026)
From the above, one may venture to state that this peculiarity-type is not distinctive to the Sierra Leonean variety.

Consonant Deletion
This peculiarity-type is also evident in other English varieties. In examining Cameroon English, for instance, Bobda (1994:249-253) identifies variables that account for this tendency in relation to

cluster simplification in coda position. These variables include the following:

1) The final segment in a cluster is normally deleted and not the one that precedes it excluding words such as [fit] 'fifth', [hɛp] 'help', and [fIm] 'film'.
2) The plosives [t, d, p, k] are especially likely to be deleted as shown in 'past', 'missed', 'cold', 'end', 'grasp', 'jump', 'task', 'd
3) The phenomenon of deletion is more likely in the context of a following consonant than in that of a following vowel;
4) A final stop which agrees in terms of voicing with the preceding sound is more likely to be deleted than the one which does not. This can be seen in 'cold' and 'colt', 'hand' and 'grant', 'send' and 'sent', 'veld' and 'belt';
5) A final stop that agrees in place of articulation with the one that precedes it is more prone to be deleted than the one that does not. This is seen in 'planned' and 'programmed', 'sunk' and 'sulk';
6) A final stop that is not preceded by a morpheme boundary is more likely to resist the deletion than the one that is. The examples are 'find' and 'fined', 'mind' and 'mined', 'left' and 'laughed'.

Sey (1973) also observes this peculiarity-type in Ghanaian English citing examples such as the following:

/ pas / 'past' / mis / 'mist'
/ pos / 'post' /tɛ:n / 'tend'
Sey (1973: 15)

One can infer from the above that this peculiarity-type is not peculiar to the Sierra Leonean variety.

The Suprasegmental Features in other English Varieties

This section deals with the investigation of features such as syllable timing, downdrift, tonality, lack of attitudinal intonation and of contrastive stress.

Syllable Timing

This tendency exists in many English varieties. For example, Baskaran (2006) states that 'rhythm in Malaysian English is more often one of a syllable-timed nature – where all syllables (stressed as well as unstressed) recur at equal intervals of time' (Baskaran 2006: 1044). Similarly, Wee (2006) identifies this tendency in Singapore English where 'all syllables take up the same amount of time, regardless of whether the syllables are stressed or not (Wee, 2006:1030). Furthermore, Spencer (1971:26) observes that educated West Africans have the tendency to produce a syllable isochronous rhythm. Gut (2006: 827-829) reinforces this view when he states that there is the proclivity to 'syllable timing in Nigerian English, a tendency which, citing Udofot, (2003) is reflected by the fact that vowel reduction tends not to occur in this variety leading to "a more equal duration of syllables" (Gut, 2006:828). Gargesh (2006:1001) also illustrates this tendency in Indian English in the sentence 'I'm thinking of you' which is produced as:

['aːI 'am 'tʰIŋking 'ɔ f 'juː]

wherein the shortened forms of the first person singular pronoun (I), the auxiliary (am) and the preposition (of) are not reduced.

One can discern from the above that this peculiarity-type is not distinct to the Sierra Leonean variety.

Downdrift

Other English varieties tend to have this peculiarity-type. In describing Ghanaian English, for instance, Huber (2006) observes that there is 'a general lowering of absolute pitch as the utterance proceeds' (Huber, 2006:862). Also, it is noted that Black South African English tends to be characterised by 'a general lowering of pitch through the course of a sentence combined with a weakening of the intensity (Rooy, 2006:951).

It may therefore be accurate to infer from the above that this peculiarity-type is not peculiar to the Sierra Leonean variety.

Tonality

This tendency also exists in other English varieties. For instance, citing Tay (1993: 27-28), Wee (2006:1030-1031) identifies sources of differences between Singapore English and native English. These include the use of equal stress for native English primary and secondary stress, the equal placement of stress in Singapore English (as opposed to native English) in some words that have different grammatical classes, the non-distinction of Singapore English (in terms of stress placement) between a phrase and a compound and the different placement of stress in certain English words. Bobda (2006) also illustrates this tendency in Cameroon English where he observes that 'thousands of words are stressed differently from the patterns in native Englishes' (Bobda, 2006: 896). He identifies two sources through which Cameroon English differs from native English. These are the movement of stress from the syllable of a word to a subsequent one and the movement of stress from the syllable of a word to a previous one. The first tendency, Bobda observes, has 12 possible patterns of stress while the second tendency has 6 (Bobda, 2006: 896-898).

Significantly, Trudgill and Hannah (1985: 42-43) highlight the sources of differences in stress placement between North American English and RP. These sources are the use of French words in American English that have different stress patterns from RP, the placement of stress in the first syllable of some words, differences in stress placement in compound words, differences in stress placement in polysyllabic words ending in -ory, -ary, and differences in the placement of the stress on family names and names of places.

From the above, it could be observed that this peculiarity-type is not a distinctive feature of the variety in Sierra Leone.

The Lack of Attitudinal Intonation

The lack of attitudinal intonation in the variety under-review also tends to occur in other English varieties. Platt et al (1984) for instance contend that some of the New Englishes – as opposed to the established varieties - do not use content words to express attitude; rather, they tend to make adequate use of discourse particles for this purpose. They illustrate this tendency in Philippine and Singapore Englishes (1988: 141-143). Similarly, Malaysian English tends to use particles such as 'lah', 'man' and 'ah' to express emotions and attitudes (Baskaran, 2006: 1044). Mesthrie and Bhatt (2008:137-138) describe the particles "La" and "What" as the most common discourse-pragmatic particles in Singaporean English. They cite Wong (2004) who describes three forms of "La" which contain three different pitch heights, namely low, mid-risising and high-falling tones each with a different attitudinal function. In addition, Gut (2006: 818) describes the intonation pattern of Nigerian English as simple since it is mostly characterised by the falling tone. That is, citing Eka (1985) and Gut (2003), he contends that complex tones such as fall-rises and rise-falls (which illustrate the native speaker's attitude) are uncommon in the Nigerian variety.

It can thus be deduced from the above that the tendency not to use intonation to convey attitude is not distinctive to the Sierra Leonean variety.

The Lack of the Contrastive Stress

The tendency of not using the contrastive stress seems to exist in other English varieties. Platt et al. (1984), for instance, observe that instead of using a contrastive stress, Singapore English has the tendency to either place the lexical item to be emphasised at the beginning of the sentence or use a discourse particle. They illustrate the former phenomenon as follows:

> This kind cannot get already
> (You can't get this kind anymore)
> (Platt et al. 1984: 141)

Similarly, Baskaran (2006) opines that Malaysian English tends not to have contrastive stress. In other words, a statement is emphasised or contrasted by lengthening and stressing particular syllables. He refers to the following conversation to illustrate this tendency:

> Speaker 1: 'How many years are you going away for?'

Speaker 2:   'Three years!' / 'θrii 'ji: az /
(Baskaran, 2006: 1042)

Moreover, Trudgill and Hannah (1985) state that in West African English, there is the tendency to use a clefted version in order to express a contrast. They cite the following as an example of this tendency:
Did John go to the store?
No, Bill went.
No, it was Bill who went.
(Trudgill and Hannah, 1985: 103)

Similarly, Gut illustrates this tendency in Nigerian English where he observes that the sentence 'Mary did it' tends to be rendered as 'It was Mary who did it' (Gut, 2006:826).

One can deduce from the above that the tendency not to have sentence stress for emphasis or contrast is not peculiar to the Sierra Leonean variety.

The Existence of the Lexical Features in other English Varieties
This section seeks to investigate the lexical features relating to the Sierra Leonean variety with a view to ascertaining their existence or otherwise in other English varieties. This includes collocation, word modification, idiom, innovation and aboriginal-related features.

The Collocation-Related Peculiarity in other English Varieties
This section involves the collocations of native English, first language induced collocation and the use of English words that reflect the subjects' cultural milieu.

Native English Collocation Peculiarity
The tendency to use collocations differently from native English can also be observed in other English varieties. Sey (1973: 46-53), for example, observes this tendency in Ghanaian English. That is, he outlines five analogies which account for this peculiarity-type. First,

a preposition which collocates with a given word may also collocate with another word which has similar semantic associations. He contends that because for example 'for' collocates with 'reprimand' and 'from' collocates with 'withdraw', in native English, there is the tendency for these words to respectively collocate in Ghanaian English with 'warned' and 'vacate'. Secondly, through analogy, an inference can be drawn in relation to the kind of preposition which a given word is likely to collocate with. He cites examples such as 'deprive' and 'prevent' which respectively collocate with 'from' and 'against'. Also, a preposition that collocates with a given word class is likely to collocate with a similar word which belongs to another word class. That is, he contends that because, for example, the preposition 'of' collocates with the noun 'satisfaction' in native English, there is the likelihood for it (that is, the preposition) to collocate with the adjective 'satisfied' in Ghanaian English. Moreover, Sey observes that there is the tendency among Ghanaians to inter-change prepositions (particularly the prepositions 'by' and 'with') that are perceived as notionally related. Finally, he highlights the likelihood of inter-changing prepositional phrases that appear similar citing inter alia examples such as 'charge with' and 'charge for', and 'wait for' and 'wait on'.

Similarly, Coomber (1995: 16) investigates this tendency in Kenyan English providing the following examples:
> The papers will go a long way in making our members informed.(Nation 26th May, 1994; p. 14)
> ... to make lecturers... involved in the decision making process
> (Nation 2nd June, 1994; p. 7)

> Dr. Kituyi said the biggest mistake the Minister had done was
> to give new powers... (Nation 17th June, 1994; p. 4)

It can be deduced from the above that this peculiarity-type is not unique to the Sierra Leonean variety.

First Language-Induced Collocation

This tendency can also be observed in other English varieties. For example, Todd and Hancock (1986) identify this tendency in Nigerian and East African Englishes. In other words, they state that in Nigerian English, there are certain collocations such as 'smell pepper' (which means 'suffer'), 'spray money' (which means 'to attach money to musicians, dancers as a mark of appreciation) and 'to wash an event' (that is to celebrate an event by 'washing' it down with drinks) are inter alia examples of expressions borrowed from the local languages of Nigeria (Todd and Hancock, 1986: 306). They also state that in East African English, there are expressions from the local languages of East Africa such as 'clean heart' that is 'pure' and 'dry coffee' that is "coffee without milk or sugar' (Todd and Hancock, 1986: 171). Furthermore, Platt et al. (1984: 95-99) also highlight this tendency in inter alia West African, Indian, Singapore and Philippines Englishes. In other words, citing Gonzalez, 1983: 158-159), they identify expressions which tend to occur in Philippines English. Some of these expressions which come from the local languages of the Philippines include 'brown-out' (a short interruption to electricity supply) 'bed-spacer' (someone who rents a bed in a room or dormitory) and 'high hat' (someone who puts on airs, a snob) (Platt et al., 1984: 98).

From the above, one may infer that this peculiarity-type is a non-distinctive feature of the variety under review.

Culturally-Induced Collocation

There is the tendency in some English varieties to use English expressions which reflect their settings. For example, Spencer (1971:28-29) identifies English collocations which reflect the natural and cultural environment of West Africa. Examples of such collocations include 'silk cotton tree', 'cutting-grass', 'chewing stick', 'head-tie' and 'market mammy'. Similarly, Kachru (1985: 41), in examining collocations in South Asian English, argues that the most productive class are those that 'are culture-bound, context-bound, or register-bound' Kachru (1985:41). Examples of the culture-bound collocations include 'rice-eating ceremony,' 'nose-screw' which mean 'a decorative gold or silver ornament for the nose used by women' and 'brother-anointing ceremony.'

It can be drawn from the above that this peculiarity-type is not unique to the variety under discussion.

Word Modification Peculiarity in other English Varieties

This peculiarity-type investigates the modification of the meanings of words in other English varieties. This involves the extension, reduction and change of the meanings of words.

The Extension of the Meanings of Words

This tendency can be observed in many other English varieties. In his examination of East African English, for example, Schmied (2006: 942) argues that words that are regarded as 'confusables' are likely to lead to the extension of the meanings of such words or would relegate specific features associated with them. One of the examples he cites is the word 'escort' which implies 'a special guard or act of courtesy' but tends to expand its meaning among East Africans to mean 'to accompany.' This tendency is also evident in Nigerian English where 'battery charger' now means 'a person who repairs batteries' and 'essential commodities' refers to 'scarce consumer goods' (Todd and Hancock, 1986: 306) and in Ghanaian English where among others 'cloth' has the additional meaning 'any Ghanaian dress' and 'concert' which means 'any other stage performance' (Sey, 1973:71). In addition, Platt et al. (1984: 102-103) illustrate this tendency in Singapore, Sri Lankan and Philippines Englishes, among others.

From the above, one may infer that this peculiarity-type is a non-distinctive feature of the variety under reference.

The Restriction of the Meanings of Words

The tendency to semantically restrict lexical items can be identified in other English varieties. For instance, Sey (1973) investigates this tendency among educated Ghanaians citing inter alia the following words as examples: 'donation', 'fitter' and 'tribunal' whose meanings have been respectively restricted to 'gifts of money given to relations of a deceased person to help them to meet the high cost of funerals' (Sey, 1973: 92) 'a motor mechanic, or a person who does odd jobs on motor vehicles' (Sey, 1973: 93) and 'local courts for hearing minor cases according to native customary laws' (Sey, 1973: 95). Also, Schmied (2006: 943) identifies this tendency in East African English where the expression 'move with' has been taken to mean '[to] go out with friends or a boy/girl friend'. (Schmied 2006: 943)

One may use the above as a basis to assert that this peculiarity-type is not peculiar to the variety under discussion.

The Change of the Meanings of Words
The tendency to change the meanings of words can also be observed in other English varieties. What comes out clearly in these varieties is either the meaning of a word is completely changed or a central meaning is developed making other meanings marginal. This is evident in Ghanaian English in relation to words such as 'family', 'mat' and 'park'. 'Family' now has the central meaning 'a group of people descended from a common ancestor, a house, kindred or lineage' (Sey, 1973:119). 'Mat' is now used to refer to 'an object for sleeping on, and only marginally to mat in the context table mat, door mat etc' (Sey, 1973:120). Also, 'park' has the central meaning 'football field' relegating other meanings like 'a car park' and 'ornamental recreational grounds' to a marginal usage (Sey, 1973:121). Platt et al. (1984) are of the view that the tendency to change the meanings of words does exist in the new Englishes. They caution, however, that it is rare to have a complete change in the meaning of a word as the normal trend is that 'traces of the old meaning remain, even if they are only implied' (Platt et al., 1984: 101).

Idiom-Related Peculiarity in other English Varieties
This section is concerned with the modification of native English idioms and the use of local idioms in other English varieties.

The Modification of Native English Idioms

This tendency exists in other English varieties. Coomber (1995: 15) for example examines this tendency among educated Kenyans citing the following examples:

... must do everything possible to break the <u>vicious cycle</u> if we are to thrive.....
(<u>Standard</u>, 29th May, 1994; 13)

... that cases of cheating were <u>in increase</u> due to...
(<u>Times</u>, 3rd June, 1994; 3)

Matiba and Odinga ...have not been <u>on talking terms</u> since ...

(<u>Times</u>, 1st January, 1993; 1)

...Council workers had gone <u>on rampage</u> destroying windows...
(<u>Times</u>, 15th June, 1990; 2)

...because Kapten is <u>solid as rock</u> in Ford – K ...
(<u>Nation</u>, 22nd April, 1994; 4)

Sey, 1973; 56-61 also examines this tendency among educated Ghanaians pointing out examples such as:
He is <u>wide off</u> the mark (Sey, 1973: 58)
Since I sworn (i.e. swore) the great oath, things began <u>to have a new turn</u> (Sey, 1973: 58)

One thing for which the Kumasi Council deserves <u>a pat on the shoulders</u> is its efforts to construct roads and streets.
(Sey, 1973: 59)

I met the girl and found her to be on <u>the family way</u>.
(Sey, 1973: 59)

They insisted on '<u>collar</u>' '<u>jobs</u>' (Sey, 1973: 59)

Significantly, in this discussion of Ghanaian idiomatic usage, Sey (1973: 47) cites Hill (1965) who identifies a similar tendency in the Middle East, India and Indonesia as follows:
> I asked <u>from</u> him a question
> The farmers cut <u>off</u> their corn in August
> They kept the plan <u>in</u> secret
> I asked the question <u>for</u> four times
> Will you find <u>out</u> my dictionary, please
> He could not cope <u>up</u> with his work
> He wants to leave <u>up</u> his work.

This discussion shows that this peculiarity-type is not unique to the variety under reference.

The Use of Local Idioms

The tendency to use local idioms has also been observed in other English varieties. For instance, Todd and Hancock (1986: 496) recognise this tendency in West African English citing examples such as 'be in state' (which means to be pregnant), 'en-stool' (that is, instal a chief) and 'have long legs (that is, have influence). Platt et al. (1984: 108-110) also highlight this tendency in East African English, Nigerian English and Caribbean English, among others. That is, citing Hancock and Angogo (1982: 317), they illustrate this tendency in East African English in the expression 'to be on tarmac' which means 'to be in the process of finding a new job' (Platt et al. 1984:109). They also refer to Bashir (1981: 7-8), Bokamba (1982: 89), Bamgbose (1983: 106-7), Jibril (1982: 81-82) and Sey, 1973: 76-78) in associating this tendency with Nigerian English using the following example among others as a basis: 'to put sand in someone's gari' which means 'to threaten someone's livelihood or to interfere with someone's good fortune' (Platt et al. 1984: 109). Also, referring to Craig (1982: 202), they illustrate this tendency in Caribbean English as follows: 'hard ears' and 'cut your eye' which mean to be 'persistently disobedient or stubborn and 'make a contempt gesture with the eyes' respectively.

One can deduce from the above that this peculiarity-type is not unique to the variety under reference.

Innovation-Related Peculiarity in other English Varieties
The other English varieties have also been observed to tend to have in their lexicons words that can be mistakenly viewed as part of native English lexicon. Todd and Hancock (1986: 306) describe this tendency in Nigerian English citing words such as 'arranger' which means 'someone who arranges illegal money transactions', 'decampee' which means 'one who switches to a different political party' and 'jambite' which has the meaning 'a first-year undergraduate student'. Similarly, Platt et al. (1984) identify this tendency in Singapore English where the suffix 'o' is used to form a new adjective or noun such as 'stingko' which is used to mean 'smelly', 'cheeko' which means someone with 'a roving eye and likes to go after girls' and 'cracko' which means 'a crazy fellow' (Platt et al., 1984: 95). Citing Mehrotra (1982: 160), they also highlight this tendency in Indian English where the female suffix '-ess' is used to distinguish a male and a female that belong to the same profession – a tendency that has led to the emergence of the word 'teacheress' in that variety (Platt et al. 1984: 96) Moreover, they refer to Gonzalez who highlights the emergence of 'new' words in Philippine English such as 'jeepney', and 'bannanacue' or 'bananaque' which respectively mean 'a small bus' and 'a special type of banana on a stick and cooked like barbecued meat' (Platt et al., 1984:96).

The above examples lend credence to the view that the innovation-related peculiarity tends not to be peculiar to the variety under review.

Aboriginal-Related Peculiarity in other English Varieties
This tendency can also be discerned in other English varieties. For example, Hannah and Trudgill (1985: 111-112) contend it to be 'one distinctive characteristic of Indian English.' Some of the examples they cite to illustrate this tendency include:

      bandh   a total strike in an area
      crore   ten million

darzi tailor
dhobi washerman
lakh one hundred thousand
(Trudgill and Hannah, 1985: 111)

Moreover, Ajani (2007) in investigating Nigerian English observes this tendency by referring to Soyinka's collected plays 2, citing the following sentences:

"Towards the end of this speech the sound of 'gangan' drums is heard coming from the side opposite the house. A boy carrying a drum on each shoulder" (CP2: 152).

"A man in an elaborate 'agbada' outfit with long train and a cap is standing right downstage with a ... of notes in his hand" (CP2: 167).

The words 'gangan' and 'agbada' are borrowed from Yoruba and respectively mean 'a type of drum used to sing the praises of people', and 'suit'. Similarly, this tendency exists in South African English which has borrowed words from Zulu such as 'impi' (that is African warrior band) and 'indaba' (which means conference) and Afrikaans including words such as 'dorp' 'kraal', 'sjambok' and 'veld' which respectively mean 'village' 'African village', 'whip' and 'flat, open country' (Trudgill and Hannah, 1986: 27).

Significantly, in some native varieties, words tend to be borrowed from aboriginal languages. Trudgill and Hannah (1985: 21) for example, observe this tendency in Australian English citing as examples words such as 'boomerang', 'dingo' (a wild dog) and 'billabong' (a cut-off river channel).

It can be discerned from the above that this peculiarity-type is not exclusively distinctive to the Sierra Leonean variety.

The Existence of the Grammatical Features in other English Varieties

This section seeks to examine the grammatical features in other English varieties. The features that will be examined are noun, pronoun, verb, adjective, determiner, preposition, word class and syntax-related.

The Noun-Related Peculiarity in other English Varieties

The tendency not to distinguish between count and mass nouns in terms of pluralisation can also be discerned in other English varieties. Sey (1973), for example, identifies this tendency among educated Ghanaians as seen in some of his following examples:

The teachers will be given the respects they deserve. (Sey, 1973:26)
The headmaster of the school lighted the firewoods (Sey, 1973: 27)

Similarly, Todd and Hancock (1986: 307) demonstrate this tendency among educated Nigerians as follows:

Thank you for your advices
We have ordered these equipments

Trudgill and Hannah (1985: 107) also describe Indian English in relation to this tendency as inter alia seen in:

Many aircrafts have crashed there
We ate just fruits for lunch
Do not throw litters on the street
The meeting was surrounded by secrecies

It can be drawn from the above that the tendency to pluralise mass nouns is typical of but not peculiar to the variety under reference.

The Pronoun-Related Peculiarity in other English Varieties

There are English varieties that tend to use pronouns differently from
native English. This difference can be viewed in relation to the case form
of personal pronouns, the number of the demonstrative pronoun and

the use of the reflective pronoun instead of the reciprocal pronoun. In his examination of these tendencies in Kenyan English, Coomber (1995: 6) highlights the use of the 'subject' form instead of the 'object' form of the pronoun. He illustrates this tendency as follows:

> ... the government is abolishing the ginning monopoly held by ... most of <u>who</u> are insolvent...(Nation, 24th May, 1995: 12)
> ... the government should not provoke the area residents <u>who</u> he described as peace loving... (Standard, 29th May, 1995: 4)
> ... against some civil servants <u>who</u> he ordered out of the district.
> (Nation, 29th May, 1995: 13)

With regard to the different use of the demonstrative pronoun, McCormick (2006: 997) demonstrates this tendency in Cape Flats English where among other things, the demonstrative pronoun tends to be used in the singular form irrespective of the number of its referent:

> <u>That is</u> other people's constitutions
> <u>That's</u> sandwiches

For their part, Alo and Mesthrie (2006:822) point out the tendency to use the reflexive pronoun in Nigerian English where native English would prefer the reciprocal one:

> Adebanjo and Suliat love <u>themselves</u>
> After greeting <u>ourselves</u>, Tolu and I started to work
> James and Lanre like quarrelling with <u>themselves</u>

The above examples show that this peculiarity-type is not unique to the Sierra Leonean English variety.

The Verb-Related Peculiarity in other English Varieties

This section involves concordial use, the use of infinitive/participle and tense/aspect.

Concordial Use

As opposed to native English, the subject and the verb tend not to agree in some English varieties. Coomber (1995: 10-11) for example, highlights this tendency in Kenyan English citing the following examples among others:

…since no valid service of the principal election documents were affected…

(Times, 3rd June, 1994: 5)

Among the areas affected by low level of illiteracy were Oltepesia near Magadi

(Times, 1st January, 1993: 4)

Gyasi (1991: 30) also illustrates this tendency in Ghanaian English as follows:

The burial of dead bodies are becoming expensive.

Importantly, this tendency is evident in some native English varieties. Filppula (2006: 88-90) for example highlights this tendency in Irish English providing inter alia the following examples from southern Irish English:

"Oh, my mother and father was born and reared in Dublin. (Dublin, M.L.)

… and I think at the pace the people is going they are not going to stick it. (Wicklow: M.K.)

Oh well, only they gets pensions, you know and I get the old-age pension (Kerry J.F.)

Similarly, Anderwald (2006: 182-185) observes this tendency in the English of the southeast of England where she points out among other things the singular forms of BE follow the existential 'there' including situations in which the subject is plural:

There's no false ceiling, there's no columns. (FRED IND 007)

There was some papers wanted urgently. (FRED IND_006)

From the above examples, one could deduce that this peculiarity-type is not peculiar to the Sierra Leonean variety.

Infinitive/Participle
The tendency not to distinguish between infinitive and participle constructions is evident in other English varieties. Schmied (2006: 931-932) for example, illustrates this tendency among educated East Africans as follows:

> Would you mind <u>to tell</u> us uh a brief background about ICAC and uh what are you going to discuss in Arusha
> (ICE-EA: SIB 041 T)

> He has indicated to want to stop <u>to deliver</u> what he has.
> (ICE- EA: S/BO31T)

Similarly, Chisanga (1989:65) highlights this tendency in Zambian English citing the following examples:

> Workers suspected <u>to have</u> stolen funds or committed any other acts which led to the Northern Co-operative Union incurring Losses must be reported to the police for action
> (TZ 11/1/85, P. 5)

> The energy plan should be capable <u>to handle</u> problems on a long term basis, it should be able to find answers to problems of how to use our surplus hydro-electricity if our neignbours stop importing (ST 22/12/85 p. 1).

Sey (1973: 37) contends that this tendency is best evident in Ghanaian English in the verb 'to stop' as shown in the following sentence which, it would appear, gives credit where censure is intended:

> Our politicians have stopped <u>to think</u>

For his part, Baumgardner (1993: 259) observes this tendency in Pakistani English as opposed to native English:

They are not eligible <u>to enter</u> the contest (StBrE)
Students who are likely to be admitted by the end of January 1987 are also eligible <u>for appearing</u> in the qualifying examinations. (PaKE)
His is not prepared <u>to repay</u> the money. (StBrE)
It is believed that PLA is prepared <u>for filing</u> an insurance claim. (PaKE)

The discussion above shows that this peculiarity-type does exist in the Sierra Leonean variety but it is not unique to it.

Tense and Aspect

The deviations that fall within this category can also be discerned in other English varieties. For example, Sey (1973: 35) points out the tendency among educated Ghanaians not to inflect verbs where native English prefers it:

I <u>will</u> like to go right now
I won't even if I <u>can</u>

Jowitt (1991: 117) also illustrates a similar tendency in Nigerian English as follows:

Yesterday they go to your office

Furthermore, Rahman (1990: 54) investigates how the differences between native English and Pakistani English in aspectual usage are evident in the inflection of stative verbs to show progression:

I am <u>seeing</u> the sky from here
They were <u>having</u> a horse.

Baskaran (2006:1077-1078) also illustrates this tendency in Malaysian English as follows:

That bottle is <u>containing</u> sulphuric acid
I am <u>smelling</u> curry in this room
She is <u>owning</u> two luxury apartments.

In addition, Trudgill and Hannah (1985) observe this tendency in Scottish English as shown in: I'm <u>needing</u> a cup of tea (Trudgill and Hannah, 1985: 86) and in Southern Irish English as illustrated in:

> I'm <u>seeing</u> it very well
> This is <u>belonging</u> to me
> (Trudgill and Hannah, 1985: 94)

Also, the use of the perfective aspect instead of the past tense distinguishes native English from some English varieties. For example, Rahman (1990: 58) examines the tendency to neutralise these two grammatical categories in Pakistani English.

> I <u>have seen</u> him yesterday

Todd and Hancock (1986:497) also identify this tendency in West African English providing the following example:

> I <u>have gone</u> to Jos two years ago

Finally, Schmied (2006: 931) recognises the use of the 'to' infinitive in East African English. That is, he states that educated East Africans tend to regularise seeming irregularities by applying analogy. This accounts for the use of the expression '<u>made him to do</u>' which is semantically analogous to 'force him to do'.

It can be inferred from the above that this peculiarity-type is typical of but not unique to the Sierra Leonean variety.

The Determiner-Related Peculiarity in other English Varieties

This section involves the use of determiners differently from native English, the inclusion and omission of determiners.

Determiner Usage Related Peculiarity

The tendency to use determiners differently from native English can be observed in some English varieties. Huber and Dako (2006: 860) for example observe how, through analogy, the definiteness distinctions that obtain in native English are neutralised in Ghanaian English:

> He started at <u>an</u> early age of 15
> (analogous to StBrE He started work at an early age)
>
> I had <u>a</u> shock of my life yesterday
> (analogous to StBrE I had a shock yesterday)

They also point out the tendency to interchange the indefinite determiner as shown in the following sentence which is concerned with a discussion about some variations on the weather forecast every evening:

>There will be Ø few scattered showers over the country
>(Huber and Dako, 2006: 861)

It can also be noted from Sey (1973: 30) that Ghanaians use the indefinite determiner differently from native English. That is, he contends that the use of the singular indefinite article 'a' in conjunction with the determiner 'few' which suggests plurality is considered illogical by educated Ghanaians. Therefore, they tend to either omit the singular article 'a' in a plural expression as in (This money is given to the girl to buy few articles) or substitute the singular article with 'some' which suggests plurality as in ("Some few minutes past nine I leave the office").

Chisanga (1989: 66) observes that educated Zambians seem to prefer the collocation of 'some' with the indefinite determiner to express plurality:

>The night was just O.K. except that I had <u>some few</u> friends visiting me. (JM. p. 282)

>… after <u>some few</u> minutes…, one of them raised a Chitenge material… He wanted to know who the owner was. This was when the owner realised that a Chitenge material was missing in his basket. (MBL 6)

One can infer from the above that this peculiarity-type is not unique to the variety under reference.

Determiner Inclusion-Related Peculiarity
The inclusion of the determiner (that is, both the definite and the indefinite articles) where native English will not consider it desirable is a tendency that can be discerned in some English varieties. Mesthrie (2006: 970), for example, indicates this tendency

in Black South African English citing inter alia the following examples:

> I was on a maternity leave
> You're going to have a trouble
> You might create a chaos

Chisanga (1989: 66) also observes this tendency in Zambian English as follows:

> Mr. Liso was not available for a comment
> (TZ 4/3/85, P. 5)

There was a great scope for the area covered in the article (TC)
Similarly, Coomber (1995: 5) illustrates this tendency in Kenyan English as seen in the following examples among others:

> ... changed the picture of the university education in the country
> (Nation, 2nd June, 1994; 7)
> ... there is no such a thing as a pure and/or perfect university ...
> (Nation, 16th August, 1994; 6)

Significantly, this tendency is also observed in some native English varieties. For example, Filppula observes this tendency in Irish English citing among others the use of the article before names of diseases and ailments and before names of social institutions:

> And that cured the whooping cough...some children does be terrible bad with it, whopping cough (Wicklow: T.F.)

> But he's the measles, and he, he's off school for a while (NITCS: NK43)

> I left the school in early age, nearly fourteen, you know. (Dublin: W.H.)

> ...mm, best singer now, he's away in, in the present time in the hospital (NITCS: CM129)

One can use the above instances to infer that this peculiarity-type is not unique to the Sierra Leonean variety.

Determiner Omission-Related Peculiarity
The tendency to omit the determiner (that is, both the definite and the indefinite articles) appears to be common in some English varieties. For instance, Schmied (1989: 92-93) demonstrates this tendency in Indian and East African Englishes respectively as follows:
> I really want to spend sometime in ... a village, definitely if I get ... chance.
> (Platt/Weber/ Ho, 55)

> Ironically, a technician of Zanzibar television was discouraging installation of a TV station for ... Mainland on the argument of...cost of booster stations.
> (SUNDAY NEWS 10/4/83 Tanzania)

Huber and Dako (2006: 859-860) also identify this tendency among educated Ghanaians. That is, they attribute some of the examples of this tendency to analogy as seen in:
> My sister became Ø teacher in Achimota
> (analogous to StBrE she became chairperson)

> She was on her way to Ø bank
> (analogous to StBrE she was on her way to church)

> When we talk of the freedom of Ø press.
> (analogous to StBrE when we talk of the freedom of speech)

Furthermore, the determiner 'one' tends to substitute the article in some cases. Todd and Hancock, 1986: 497) illustrate this tendency in West African English as in: 'I bought one fine car' and in Southern African English as in, 'I stay in one lovely hostel' and 'One lady told me.' (Todd and Hancock, 1986: 431)

This tendency can also be observed in some native English varieties. Beal (2006: 120-121) highlights the omission of the indefinite article in some Northern dialects namely Yorkshire and Lancashire:

> It were ... lovely summer (Shorrocks, 1999: 47)
> Ay, but he were ... ironmonger (Shorrocks, 1999: 47)
> I'd buy ...house there if I'd got t' money (CSU)

One may deduce from the above that this peculiarity-type is typical of but not unique to the variety under review.

The Adjective-Related Peculiarity in other English Varieties

The tendency not to distinguish between the comparative and superlative forms of the adjective can be seen in other English varieties. Mesthrie (2006: 821) highlights this tendency in Nigerian English:

> His condition is now getting worst.

One cannot therefore limit this peculiarity to the Sierra Leonean English variety.

Preposition-Related Peculiarity in other English Varieties

This section is concerned with the use of prepositions differently from native English, prepositional inclusion and prepositional omission. These tendencies tend to exist in other English varieties.

Prepositional Usage-Related Peculiarity

The tendency to use prepositions differently from native English is evident in some English varieties. For example, Chisanga (1989: 65-66) observes this tendency in Zambian English using as examples the prepositions in and at as follows:

> Mr. Zulu named the officer as Constable Daka who was shot in the shoulder when police were chasing the men. Mr. Dako has been admitted in Ndola Central Hospital
> (TZ 4TH March, 1985: 5)
>
> ... I was traveling from Lusaka ... while waiting for a bus, a man came at the station...
> (RM ii)

Todd and Hancock (1986: 307) also illustrate this tendency in Nigerian English as seen in:
The victim, died <u>by</u> twelve O'clock
Mr. Olu is the Principal <u>for</u> our school
<u>On</u> the long run, this won't work

Similarly, Coomber (1995: 8-9) highlights this tendency in Kenya as shown in the following examples among others:
… because of increased demand <u>of</u> fish both for local consumption and export. (Nation, 28th May, 1994: 1)

The Minister of Education… raised a total of … to assist in funeral expenses <u>of</u> the 18 students who… (Times, 3rd June, 1994: 2)

The Kenya National Chamber of Commerce and Industry yesterday complained <u>over</u> the low trade practices… (Times, 15th June, 1990: 10)

… Freedom of movement is restricted <u>to</u> opposition leaders while KANU leaders moved from corner to corner without hindrance.
(Standard, 29th May, 1994: 5)
Significantly, this tendency is also shown to exist in some native English varieties. For example Filppula (2006: 97-99) identifies it in Irish English as inter alia illustrated in:
One year then he took the half of them <u>on</u> me. (Wicklow: Mrs. Γ.)

But eh, there was some island, like, where there was a man living.
And he was marooned, like, and there was no one in it but himself like and this day the fire went out <u>on</u> him, like (Clare: F. K.).

One may thus assert that this peculiarity-type is typical of but not unique to the Sierra Leonean variety.

Prepositional Inclusion-Related Peculiarity

The tendency to include the preposition where native English considers it undesirable can be seen in other English varieties. Huber and Dako (2006: 854-55) for instance demonstrate this tendency in Ghanaian English as follows:

>They requested <u>for</u> higher pay
>We were encouraged to voice <u>out</u> opinion

Also, Todd and Hancock (1986: 425) observe this tendency in Philippine English citing the following as one of their examples:

>He emphasised <u>on</u> the importance of hard work.

Similarly, citing Crewe (1977: 56; 58-9), Platt et al. (1984: 84) refer to this tendency in Singapore English as seen in:

>They discussed <u>about</u> the mistakes and emphasised <u>on</u> the need for greater care.

They also point out this tendency in West African English as illustrated in inter alia:

>(WR) The High Commissioner also stressed <u>on</u> the importance of Ghanaian students registering their names and their addresses with this office.
>(Platt et al., 1984: 84)

One may therefore state that this peculiarity-type is typical of but not unique to the variety under reference.

Prepositional Omission-Related Peculiarity

The tendency to omit the preposition where native English would consider it mandatory is also evident in other English varieties. Coomber (1995: 9-10) for instance highlights this tendency in Kenyan English as illustrated in among others:

>…after learning that it was to be presided …by the Ford-Ken boss…
>(Standard, 29th May, 1994: 3)

... the Okero Commission which was set ...by the president...
(Nation, 4th June, 1994: 4)

...that the opposition supporters were being discriminated
...
(Times, 30th May, 1994: 4)

Similarly, Platt et al. (1984: 83) illustrate this tendency in Indian English:

'I applied ...couple of places in Australia' and by citing (Tay and Gupta, 1981: 29) do likewise in respect of Singapore English:

(WR) Our mutual benefit schemes provide you and your family ...financial relief in emergencies.
Moreover, Mahboob (2006: 1052) observes this tendency in Pakistani English using the expression 'to dispense' as an example.

The above examples show that though this tendency is typical of the variety under review yet it is not unique to it.

Word Class-Related Peculiarity in other English Varieties
The tendency to use certain items differently from native English can be observed in other English varieties. Mesthrie (2006: 821) highlights this tendency in Nigerian English where adjectives can function as verbs:
> He naked himself
> She jealoused her elder sister

Similarly, Mugler and Tent (2006: 777) identify this tendency in Fiji English where both nouns and verbs can function as adjectives. This is respectively demonstrated in the following examples among others:
> Urgently wanted experience digger operators

[....] (Position Vacant, Fiji Times, 15/2/2003)

Two bedrooms furnished flat 2 minutes walk to city/CWM, all amenities, quiet, <u>secured</u>
(To Let, Fiji Times, 15/2/2003)

Also, Coomber (1995: 6-7) demonstrates this tendency in Kenyan English as illustrated in among others the following:
... because he had made <u>elaborated</u> consultations with his people...
(Nation, 21st May, 1994: 2)

... who died on Friday in a <u>horror</u> traffic accident.
(Standard, 29th May, 1994: 2)

Furthermore, Shorrocks (1999:199) cited in Beal (2006: 121) examines this tendency in English dialects in the North of England where "a great many adverbs in the dialect have the same form as the adjective:"
I told thee <u>confidential</u>
Do it <u>good</u>
A <u>high</u> technical job

It could be observed from the above that this tendency is evident in other English varieties and is therefore not unique to the variety under reference.

Syntax-Related Peculiarity in other English Varieties
This section involves imbalance, repetition, structural omission, structural difference, the use of the universal tag, the placement of the modifier, reduplication and responses to yes/no questions.

Imbalance-Related Peculiarity
In some English varieties, some words or expressions that are joined by the coordinating conjunction tend to be grammatically different. Nimako (2004) for example, observes this tendency in educated Ghananian English as shown in:

It said that not only <u>is the exhibition meant to create a platform for Ghanaians living in the US</u> but it also <u>serves as a source of foreign exchange in the country</u>.
Nimako (2004: 60)

The politician was both <u>against the Government</u> and <u>the Opposition</u>
Nimako (2004: 61)

Coomber (1995: 13) also illustrates this tendency in Kenyan English as follows:
A doctor does not only <u>do his profession credit</u> but also <u>serves the cause of human rights</u>. (Nation, 28th May, 1994: 3)

Perhaps it would make sense <u>to detain Galete</u> rather than <u>releasing him into the freedom</u>... (Nation, 28th May, 1994: 9)

... the statement was aimed at <u>tarnishing the name</u> ...and <u>to mislead members of the public</u>. (Nation, 3rd June, 1994: 3)

This tendency is therefore typical of but not unique to the Sierra Leonean variety.

Repetition-Related Peculiarity

The repetition of words or ideas that do not contribute to the general meaning of a structure is a tendency that cuts across some English varieties. Schmied (2006:941), for instance, highlights the sources of this tendency in East African English. In the first place, he states that the process of word formation may account for the repetition of semantic elements. He refers to the possibility of merging the suffix '-able' and the modal auxiliary 'can' which makes for example the use of 'can' and 'traceable' in an expression redundant. He also discusses the case of the modifying elements which may intrinsically have the features of what they modify. He cites as examples the use of the adjective 'secret' in relation to 'ballot' and 'perhaps' in the context of the modal 'may'. He further mentions the possibility of blending in a structure a Latin prefix and a Germanic participle both of which have the same meaning as seen in the use of 're' and 'back' in '<u>return</u> <u>back</u> home.' Furthermore, Schmied contends that in an event in which the meaning of an expression is thought to have been reduced as seen for example in the substitution of the preposition 'in' with 'during' to express the feature [+ DURATION], this may lead to redundancy when the latter is followed by 'the course of'. Finally, Schmied observes subtle cases of redundancy in situations such as 'include and so on' which both convey the idea of incompletion and 'reason and because' which both convey the idea of 'cause'.

Also, in his description of Cape Flats English, McCormick (2006: 1002) identifies the following redundant expressions as typical of that variety: 'my utmost best', 'I'd rather prefer', 'more happier' and 'more superior'.

Finally, this tendency can also be seen in native English usage. For example,
> That's the way it was that sunny day in the rich,
> red-carpeted, high white-ceilinged dining-room
> of the Half Moon Hotel at 2:15 <u>P.M. in the afternoon</u>.
> (Dundy, 2005:50) (emphasis mine)

One could deduce from the above that this peculiarity-type is not unique to the variety under review.

Structural Omission-Related Peculiarity in other English Varieties

This section examines the omission of the comparative word and content and function words.

The Omission of the Comparative Word

The non-use of the comparative word in comparative statements is a tendency that can be discerned in other English varieties. For example, Mesthrie (2006: 969) demonstrates this tendency in Black South African English as follows:

> ... if you are not in a hurry, you can take it today – now – than Thursday.
> ... my school was one of the radical schools that you can ever find.

Chinebuah (1976), cited by Bokamba (1992:134) and by Alo and Mesthrie (2006: 819) also illustrates this tendency in Nigerian English:

> It is the youths who are Ø skilful in performing tasks than the adults.

> He has Ø money than his brother.

Also, Coomber (1995: 14) identifies this tendency in Kenyan English citing the following examples among others:

> On that particular day Wabo had been at the site since 6 a.m. a bit late...than his usual time... (Standard, 29th May, 1994: 41)

> He said spoken words had the power of persuasion ...than written ones... (Nation, 2nd August, 1994: 3)

One could discern from the above that this peculiarity-type is not unique to the variety under discussion.

The Omission of Function and Content Words

Content and function words tend to be omitted in other English varieties. Mesthrie (2006: 824) for instance contends that in Nigerian English, there is the tendency to use the verbs 'enjoy' and 'disappoint' elliptically. He cites Jowitt (1991: 115) who illustrates this tendency:

> She promised to come, but I did not expect to see her – she always likes to disappoint Ø.

Baskaran (2006: 1080) also illustrates this tendency in Malaysian English as seen in:

> She wrote the letter but forgot to post Ø.

Coomber (1995:14) also demonstrates a similar tendency in Kenyan English:
> ... this is why I am telling you to build good schools ... so that your children can pass... and become doctors...
> (Nation, 8th July, 1994; 2)

Finally, Mahboob (2006: 1051-52) cites Rahman (1990: 57) who examines the tendency to omit inter alia the auxiliary 'do' in Pakistani speakers' casual speech.
> How you got there?

Therefore, the omission of content and function words is a tendency that is not unique to the Sierra Leonean variety.

Structural Difference-Related Peculiarity

This section involves the use of pronouns in compound subjects/objects, and pronoun copying in some English varieties.

Pronoun in Compound Subject/Object

The tendency to make the first person pronoun always preceding in compound subjects can also be discerned in other English varieties. McCormick (2006: 999), for example, illustrates this tendency in his discussion of the accusative form of a pronoun in subject position in Cape Flats English:
> Now me and Elizabeth speaks English
> Me and my first baby were here.

Also, Beal (2006:117) illustrates this tendency in his discussion of the case form of pronouns in the Northern English dialects. The examples he cites which demonstrate this tendency in the Northern English dialects include:
> They used to lock me and my mum in the top bedrooms (NECTE)
> Me and my mum and dad are going for a meal (NECTE)

It could be observed thus from the above that this tendency cannot be found in the Sierra Leonean English variety alone.

Pronoun Copying-Related Peculiarity

The tendency to include pronouns where native English would consider it undesirable is evident in other English varieties. Mbangwana (2006: 906) for example observes this tendency in Cameroon English. He gives the following examples of this tendency among others:

There are some students whom I am teaching them to write

The other teacher that we were teaching English with her went away.

Similarly, Chisanga (1989:69) indicates this tendency in Zambian English using inter alia the following examples:

> Mr. Chongwe, he has left the bank. He now works on the (TC).
> The Form Vs, they have to sit for the examinations before Christmas (TC)

Furthermore, this tendency is evident in Malaysian English as seen in:

> My brother, he is an engineer
> (Baskaran, 2006: 1080)

The above discussion reveals that this tendency exists in other English varieties besides the variety under reference.

The Modifier Placement-Related Peculiarity

In some English varieties, the modifier tends to be placed differently from what obtains in native English. Bhatt (2006: 1023-25) for example, highlights this tendency in Indian English. He mentions inter alia the tendency for presentationally-focused subject noun phrases to be placed in the canonical subject position and not at the right-edge of the clause. He illustrates this by giving the following examples among others:

> Her mother only is doing this to her
> (Response to: What did her mother do?)

She <u>only</u> told me to write Ø like this
(Response to: why didn't you ask your teacher to show you how to write an essay? [Ø] = 'essay'

Baskaran (2006: 1081) also demonstrates this tendency in Malaysian English as seen in:
They must admit <u>immediately</u> to the offence.

From the above discussion, one could state that the tendency to position the modifier differently from native English is not evidenced only in the Sierra Leonean variety.

Universal Tag-Related Peculiarity

The tendency to use universal tags such as 'is it?' 'isn't it?' and 'not so?' regardless of person, tense and the auxiliary of the main verb can be observed in some English varieties. Sey (1973: 43) for instance contends that the tag questions 'isn't it' | 'not so?' are used by educated Ghanaians of varying academic levels and that these tags are in free variation with the native English ones. He gives the following as examples of this tendency:

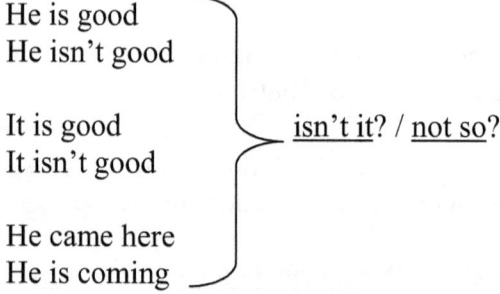

```
He is good
He isn't good

It is good              isn't it? / not so?
It isn't good

He came here
He is coming
```

Also, Schmied (1989: 93) cites Arya (1979:74) who illustrates this tendency in Indian English:
You are coming this evening, <u>isn't it</u>?
Furthermore, Rahman (1990:55) demonstrates this tendency in Pakistani English:
You are ill, <u>isn't it</u>?

Significantly, Penhallurick (2006: 103) observes that the use of 'isn't it' as an interrogative tag is common in Welsh English. He cites his previous work (Penhallurick, 1991: 204-205) in which he gives 'fourteen examples of this tendency in Welsh English some of which include:

>You have to rig him up in his clothes, <u>isn't it</u>?
>We saw some the other day, <u>isn't it</u>?
>They had them in their hair, <u>isn't it</u>?

One may infer from the above that this peculiarity-type is not unique to the Sierra Leonean variety.

Reduplication-Related Peculiarity

The tendency to reduplicate certain elements can be observed in some English varieties. Mesthrie (2006: 825) for instance illustrates this tendency in Nigerian English as shown among others in the following:

>He likes to talk about <u>small-small</u> things
>'... insignificant things'
>
>Tell Mr. Bello to come <u>now-now</u>
>'... at once.'

In addition, Kachru (1983: 78-79) cited by Bhatt (2006: 1028) illustrates this tendency in Indian English as seen in 'different different things'. Finally, Wee (2006: 1065-67) observes the types of reduplication in Singapore English. They are nominal reduplication (as seen in for example, 'Where is your boy-boy (boyfriend/son)? (2006: 1066); adjectival reduplication (as seen in for instance 'Don't always eat sweet-sweet (very sweet things)'and verb reduplications shown in for example, 'Don't always stay in the house. Go outside walk-walk (stroll)' (2006: 1067).

One may thus observe that this peculiarity-type is not unique to the variety under reference.

Responses to Negative Yes/No Question/ Statement-Related Peculiarity

The tendency to respond to negative questions/statements differently from native English is evident in some English varieties. Huber and Dako (2006:857) for example, state that Ghanaians (like other West Africans) tend to respond to the form instead of to the content of yes/no questions. They give the following examples:

    Q: Isn't your mother at home?
    A: <u>Yes</u>
    (What you say is true) she is not at home'; or 'she is there' 'she is at home.'

Chissanga (1989:67) also makes a similar observation in relation to the educated African who is prone to respond to the question;
    Didn't the college send you an application form? (TC)
as follows:

i)   <u>Yes</u>, meaning 'yes, the college did not send me an application form' or

ii)   <u>No</u>, meaning 'no, the college did send me an application form.

Kachru (1986: 51) cites his previous work (Kachru, 1969: 652-53) where he considers 'the response of 'no' where a native speaker would expect 'yes' as a feature that is distinct to both African and South Asian Englishes.

One could observe from the above that this peculiarity-type is not exclusively distinct to the variety under reference.

The Discoursal Features in other English Varieties

This section is concerned with features such as forms of address, proverbs and riddles, style and phatic communion.

Form of Address-Related Peculiarity in other English Varieties

The tendency to use titles before the names of people can be observed in some English varieties. For example, Akere (1982: 96)

cited by Platt et al. (1984: 154) illustrates this tendency in Nigerian English as follows:
Alhaji Chief Doctor + last name (for a person who is a medical doctor or Ph.D holder who has taken a chieftaincy title and has also made a Muslim pilgrimage to Mecca and Madina).

In the same way, Wa Thiong'o demonstrates this tendency in Kenyan English where titles such as 'Mualimu' (Teacher), Petals of Blood (1977: 35) 'Bwana' (sir) Weep Not, Child (1964: 12) and 'Afande' ('sir' among soldiers) Weep Not, Child (1964: 116) are in use.

Also, Schmied (2006:942) highlights the tendency to use word forms in the form of kinship terms in African English. He contends that in Africa, as opposed to British societies, kinship terms are reduced to the social features of seniority (age), solidarity, affection and role-relations. The examples he uses to show this tendency include the terms 'mother' (used to point to the co-wives or sister of someone else's mother); 'father' (used to refer to all elderly men); and 'brother' and 'sister' (used to point to people without blood ties but from the same village or town).

One could deduce from the above that this peculiarity-type is common to other English varieties and is therefore not unique to the one under discussion.

Proverb And Riddle-Related Peculiarity in other English Varieties

The tendency to use proverbs and riddles can also be observed in some English varieties.

Achebe – a Nigerian – for example, uses proverbs as a way of expressing the thought and culture of the Ibos in Nigeria. His often quoted definition of a proverb as "the palm-wine with which words are eaten" Things Fall Apart (1958: 5) is proved by his effective use of them. In No Longer At Ease, for example, before Obi leaves for England through a scholarship granted him by the Umuofia

Progressive Union, one of the elders of the union advises him against rushing into the pleasures of the world too soon "like the young antelope who danced herself lame when the main dance was yet to come." <u>No Longer At Ease</u> (1966: 11). In another development, Obi's apparent indifference to his mother's death is attributed by an elderly member of the Umuofia Progressive Union (Lagos Branch) to '[this] thing called blood,' suggesting that Obi's reckless behaviour reflects that of his late father. This prompts the president of the union to make the following proverbial statement:

> 'You see that,' said the president. 'A man may go to England, become a Lawyer or a Doctor, but it does not change his blood. <u>It is like a bird that flies off the earth and lands on an ant-hill. It is still on the ground</u>' <u>No Longer At Ease</u> (1966:160) (emphasis mine).

Similarly, in <u>Arrow of God</u> (1966: 55) Achebe brings to light the case of the Chief Priest who sends one of his sons to join the Christian church, a move that is not expected of the custodian of the traditional religion. This is what he says to his son:

> I want one of my sons to join these people and be my eyes there. If there is nothing in it you will come back. But if there is something there you will bring home my share. <u>The world is like a mask dancing</u>. <u>If you want to see it well you do not stand in one place Arrow of God</u> (1966: 55) (emphasis mine).

The proverb of dancing mask (which has its roots in the Igbo culture) shows the Chief Priest's willingness to come to terms with the harsh reality that is steadily dawning on their society.

Generally, in West African English, proverbs can be translated from local languages or co-mixed with English utterances:

> 'A single finger cannot catch a louse.'
> 'He who attempts to shake a stump only shakes himself.'
> 'However much a parrot speaks, it is still a bird.'

Achebe also demonstrates the Igbo cultural belief in <u>A Man of the People</u> as follows:

> The Minister stepped out ... acknowledging cheers with his ever-present fan of animal skin which they said <u>fanned away all evil designs and shafts of malevolence thrown at him by the wicked.</u> <u>A Man of the People</u>, (1966: 7) (emphasis mine)

Achebe similarly demonstrates the Umuofians' belief in their gods and ancestors as illustrated in the oracle's response to Unoka's enquiry about the cause of his unyielding harvests after offering sacrifices to the gods:

> You have offended neither the gods nor your fathers. And <u>when a man is at peace with his gods and ancestors</u>, his harvest will be good or bad according to the strength of his arm. (<u>Things Fall Apart</u>, 1958: 14) (emphasis mine)

It would appear therefore that the proverb and riddle-related peculiarity is not limited to the Sierra Leonean variety.

Phatic Communion-Related Peculiarity in other English Varieties

The tendency to respond to greetings differently from native English is also evident in other English varieties. Sekyi-Baidoo and Koranteng (2008:119) illustrate this tendency in inter alia
Ghanaian spoken English
as follows:

How are you?	-	<u>Fine</u>
How are you doing?	-	<u>Fine/I'm doing fine</u>
How's life?	-	<u>Fine/ Okay</u>
How is life?	-	<u>So – so</u>

This tendency is also evident in Kenyan English as Wa Thiong'o (1977:35) demonstrates in the following conversation:

'How are you, Mwalimu'?	-	Abdulla asked
'<u>I am fine</u>…'	-	Munira said

Mugler and Tent (2006:787) also mention common greeting forms in Fiji English which include 'how's it? And 'how's the life?'

From the above examples, one could state that this tendency is typical of but not unique to the Sierra Leonean English variety.

Style-Related Peculiarity in other English Varieties

The tendency to use formal words and constructions in casual conversational English can be discerned in other English varieties. For example, Adichie demonstrates this tendency in <u>Purple Hibiscus,</u> as shown in the following dialogues between familiars:

'Do you want me to adjust your seat, to make more room for you?'

'No, <u>I am</u> fine. <u>I am</u> an old man now and my height is gone. I <u>would not</u> have fit in this car in my prime. In those days, I plucked icheku from the trees by just reaching out high; I <u>did not</u> need to climb.' <u>(Purple Hibiscus)</u> (2006: 84)

'We cannot sit back and let it happen, mba. Where else have you heard of such a thing as a sole administrator in a university.'

'A governing council votes for a vice chancellor. <u>That is</u> the way it has worked since this university was built, <u>that is</u> the way <u>it is</u> supposed to work, Oburia.'

'They said <u>there is</u> a list circulating Ifeoma, of lecturers who are disloyal to the university. They said they might be fired. They said your name is on it.'
'<u>I am</u> not paid to be loyal. When I speak the truth, it becomes disloyalty.'

'Ifeoma, do you think you are the only one who knows the truth? Do you think we <u>do not</u> all know the truth, eh? <u>Purple Hibiscus</u> (2006: 217)

Similarly, Wa Thiong'o (a Kenyan) illustrates this tendency in Petals of Blood as shown in the following dialogues, among others:

> 'Do you know, it is so funny that when you go to a new place the men treat you as if you were a virgin... so you will find us barmaids, wherever there is a bar in Kenya. Even in Ilmorog.'
>
> It is difficult to sleep early in such a vast wilderness,' Karega said.
> 'Wanja is telling you about her life in the bar wilderness?' he asked as he sat down so that Wanja was between them.
>
> It is not a very beautiful wilderness,' Wanja said. 'but it is not all bad. for a woman, anyway, it is a good feeling when a thousand eyes turn toward you and you feel that it is your body that is giving orders to all those hearts. Petals of Blood: (1977: 129)

It can be observed that the absence of contractions from the above dialogues accounts for their formality when they are supposed to be casual conversations between (among) familiars. This peculiarity-type is therefore not unique to the Sierra Leonean English variety.

Conclusion

The discussion so far has highlighted that the tendencies identified in the chapter are common to the Sierra Leonean English variety. However, since they can also be noticed in other English varieties, these tendencies cannot be said to be unique to that variety. It is the recognition of this developing trend that prompts us to contend that the features are typical of but not exclusive to the variety under reference.

CHAPTER FOUR

THE CAUSES OF THE FEATURES OF THE SIERRA LEONEAN ENGLISH VARIETY

Introduction
This chapter is concerned with the possible causes of the phonological, lexical, grammatical and discoursal features of the variety under reference.

The Causes of the Phonological Features
This section involves the possible causes of the subjects' segmental and suprasegmental peculiarities.

The Causes of the Segmental Features

In this section, the possible causes of the vowel and consonant-related peculiarities are examined.

The Causes of the Vowel-Related Peculiarity
The peculiarities that will be examined here are vowel merging, vowel substitution, spelling-induced, nasalisation, diphthong merging and diphthong substitution.

The Vowel Merging-Related Peculiarity
A possible factor for this peculiarity-type is native language transfer. In other words, native English has 12 pure vowels. On the other hand, apart from Temne which has nine vowels which are: / a, ʌ, ə, e, i, ɛ, o, ɔ, u /, most of the local languages of Sierra Leone have only seven. For example, Krio, Limba and Mende have the following vowels: / a, e, i, o, u, ɔ, ɛ /. In this circumstance, most Sierra Leoneans tend to merge distinctive vowels in RP English. For example, the distinction made by native English between the front close / i / and the centralised front half-close / I / vowels, (see 1a-

5a); the back open / ɒ / and the back half open / ɔ / vowels (see 6a – 10a); the front open /æ/ and the central back open / α / vowels (see 11a-20a) and the centralised back half close / ʊ / and the back close / u / vowels (see 21a -25a) seems not to be observed by most educated Sierra Leoneans. Instead, they tend to use the vowels that exist in their local languages with which they are familiar.

However, the tendency to merge the native English vowels may not completely be caused by the influence of Sierra Leonean languages. That is, the distinctive vowels in RP English tend not to be realised in all established native Englishes. For example, as has been highlighted before, (see p 82) the RP distinction between the front open / æ / and the central back open / α / vowels tends not to be observed in Scottish and most Irish accents (Hughes and Trudgill, 1987:30). The same is true of the front-close / i / and the centralised front half-close / I / vowels where the distinction tends not to hold with certain words. (Hughes and Trudgill, 1987: 31-32).

Additionally, in Scottish English, the RP back open / ɒ / and the back half-open / ɔ / vowels together with the centralised back half-close / ʊ / and the back close / u / vowels tend not to be viewed as distinct. Another possibility therefore is that the tendency to merge RP English vowels may have been caused by the influence of some native Englishes.

The Vowel Substitution-Related Peculiarity

This tendency involves the central half-open / ʌ /, (see 26a-31a), the central half-close / ɜ / (see 32a-40a) and the mid central / ə / vowels (see 41a-44a). As has been noted above, the absence of these [substitution in English. It has however, been also discerned that both the central half-open / ʌ / and the central half-close / ɜ / vowels tend to be substituted in some native Englishes (as shown in p 83). It is possible therefore for this tendency to influence the speech patterns of Sierra Leoneans. This peculiarity-type may therefore be both first language and native English-induced.

The Spelling-Induced Peculiarity

This peculiarity-type may be due to the inconsistences between the spellings of native English words and their pronunciations. It is observed that letters that are considered silent in RP are normally produced. This is probably as a result of the educational system in the country which puts premium on spelling and reading at the elementary level. Therefore, the 'a' in 'malaria','basically' and 'extraordinary' is produced distinctly. The same is also true of the 'o' in 'police', the 'i' 'medicine' and the 'e' in 'funeral'. Another possible cause of this peculiarity-type is analogy. In other words, the 'im' for instance in 'impasse, the 'south' in 'southern', the 'or' in 'doctor' the 'a' in the second syllable of 'transparent' and the 'day' in 'Monday' are rendered as such in analogy to 'impossible', 'south', 'or', 'parent' and 'day' respectively. The subjects' educational system and analogy are therefore possible causes of this peculiarity-type.

The Nasalisation-Related Peculiarity

The tendency to nasalise vowels is a distinct African feature. That is, there could be either an anticipatory or prolonged lowering of the velum in the environment of (a) nasal consonant(s). This is illustrated in the following Limba words:

bãnka	-	house
hãnda	-	your father
hũntũma	-	darkness

Krio also demonstrates this feature as seen in:

fãỹn	-	lovely
ũman	-	woman
trãnga	-	difficult
tr☐nk	-	energy, strength
mõni	-	money
nɔ̃ỹs	-	noise

The possibility therefore is that this peculiarity-type is first-language induced.

The Diphthong Merging-Related Peculiarity

This peculiarity-type may also be first language induced. That is, RP English has 8 diphthongs most of which do not exist in Sierra Leonean languages. Krio, for example, has only three diphthongs which are / ɔi, au, and ai /, Temne has 6 /ai, ʌi, ɔi, ui, ei, oi / and Limba has 6 / ɛi, ɔi, oi, ei, ui, ai /. It can be observed that the local languages do not have both the front half-open to mid central / ɛə / and the front half-close to mid central / Iə / diphthongs. Since the latter diphthong is more familiar, the subjects tend to merge it with the former diphthong. A possible cause of this peculiarity-type is therefore first language transfer.

The Diphthong Substitution-Related Peculiarity

This peculiarity-type involves the front closing / eI / and the back closing / əʊ / diphthongs which are respectively replaced by the cardinal front half-close / e / and the cardinal back half-close / o / vowels. Since the substituting vowels are present in the local languages of Sierra Leone, a possibility is that this peculiarity-type is first language induced.

But the influence may not be wholly that of Sierra Leonean languages. Trudgill and Hannah (1985) for instance identify many regional varieties of English spoken in Britain and elsewhere, that do not have the front closing diphthong / eI / but rather have the monophthong / e : /. Similarly, the back closing diphthong / əʊ / is not present in many regional varieties of English which have instead a pure long vowel varying between cardinal back half-close / o / and cardinal back half-open / ɔ/. One may therefore attribute this peculiarity-type to first language and native English influence.

The Causes of the Consonant-Related Peculiarity

This section involves consonant substitution, spelling-induced, the omission of the linking and the intrusive 'r', the omission of the syllabic consonants and the omission of consonants.

The Consonant Substitution-Related Peculiarity

This section involves the replacement of the voiced / ð / and the voiceless / θ / dental fricatives and the velar nasal / ŋ /. Both the voiced dental fricative / ð / and its voiceless counterpart / θ / do not exist in the local languages of Sierra Leone. Temne and Shebro have a sound which comes close to the voiceless apico-dental fricative, but in their case, the sound is a dental plosive rather than a fricative / t /. This can be seen for example in the Temne word / əntən / 'a dog'. Most of the Sierra Leonean languages including Krio, Limba and Mende replace the voiceless dental fricative /θ / with the voiceless alveolar plosive / t / while the voiced dental fricative / ð / is substituted with the voiced alveolar plosive / d /. This peculiarity-type may therefore be first language-induced.

As regards the velar nasal / ŋ /, it can be used in word final position. Temne for example has the words 'ŋaŋ' (bite) and 'haŋ' (until); Krio has 'tɔŋ' (town) and Limba 'feŋ' (fish), 'sandeŋ' (head tie), and 'manaŋ' (cow). However, the tendency to render the velar nasal as an alveolar nasal and to use the velar plosive to represent the 'ng' form has been shown to characterise some native Englishes (see pp 62 - 63). One cannot therefore rule out the influence of native English in relation to this peculiarity-type.

The Spelling-Induced Peculiarity

This section involves voicing voiceless sounds and producing silent letters. In relation to voicing, it is observed that the letter 's' is pronounced as it is spelt thus making it a voiceless fricative as opposed to RP where it is voiced. This can be observed in 94a-98a. Also, in 99a the letter 'g' in regime is produced as / dʒ / (in analogy to 'gin' and 'gesture') and in 100a the letter 't' is produced as / t / in analogy 'to 'sit' , 'wit' and 'bit'. With regard to the RP silent letters, it can be observed that in analogy to the phonemes / l + d / in 'killed' and / j + u / in 'buick', the 'l' in 'could' and the 'u' in 'building' are respectively pronounced distinctly. On the whole, owing probably to their educational background in which there is a correlation between the spelling of a word and its pronunciation, Sierra Leoneans tend to pronounce words differently from native English which has a highly inconsistent spelling system.

The Linking and the Intrusive 'R'-Related Peculiarity

The tendency to omit the linking '–r' may be attributed to our local languages. That is, in our local languages, when the frictionless continuant / r / comes at the end of a word, it is pronounced distinctly whether it is in isolation or in a structure. This can be seen in Krio words like 'kɛr' (to carry) 'wɛr' (to wear) and 'bɛr' (to bury). Similarly, Temne demonstrates this feature in words like 'thor' (to descend), 'mer' (to swallow) and 'mar' (to help).

As for the intrusive '–r' it has been stated earlier that words tend to be pronounced according to how they are spelt (see pp 31-32 and pp 35-36). It is therefore not surprising that the intrusive –r does not have a place in this variety. One may therefore consider the linking '–r' tendency to be first language induced and the intrusive tendency to be learning – induced.

The Omission of the Syllabic Consonants

Sierra Leonean languages have a simple CV syllable structure. That is, as opposed to RP native English, Sierra Leonean languages have a small number of clusters in the coda. Complex RP structures therefore tend to be simplified. In fact, the only local language that seems to have consonant clusters at word final position is Krio. But in this case, all the words that illustrate this feature in the language are borrowed from English (Coomber, 1969:64). Bobda (2007:417) also observes that when an alveolar follows another alveolar in word final position in African languages, this can lead to the insertion of a vowel between the consonants. This can be seen in 112a, 113a and 114a above. One may therefore conclude that this peculiarity-type is first language-induced

The Omission of Consonants

Bobda (2007: 417) contends that in African languages generally, when an alveolar follows another alveolar in word final position, there is the tendency to either drop the final consonant or insert a vowel between the cluster. The former tendency appears to exist in Sierra Leonean languages. In Krio, for example, the words 'want' (want)' 'lɛnt'(lend) and 'mɔs' (must) have their final alveolar sounds deleted when they are used in connected speech. It is this tendency that appears to account for the omission of the final alveolar consonant sounds in 115a-118a above. First language transfer is therefore a possible factor for this peculiarity-type.

The Causes of the Suprasegmental Features

This section involves syllable timing, downdrift, tonality, lack of attitudinal intonation and of contrastive stress.

The Syllable Timing Related Peculiarity

Sierra Leonean languages are characterised by the feature of syllable timing. That is, these languages tend 'to produce unstressed syllables with a quantity and an intensity which is stonger than in RP' (Maryns, 2000: 197). In Krio, for example, the sentence:

'The storm that takes away a mortar cannot leave a winnower' is rendered as: da/ briz / we / kɛr/ ma / ta / o/ do/ go/ nɔ/ to/ fa/ na/ i / go/ lɛf / (16 syllables)

One may conclude from the above that it is this tendency in the local languages that has been transferred to English.

The Downdrift-Related Peculiarity

The tendency to lower the voice pitch as we progressively move from one word to another in a sentence also appears evident in the Sierra Leonean languages. In Temne, for example, the sentence: 'the teacher spanks the child' is produced as:

```
- .
    - .
        -
          - -
```

ɔchicha ɔgbantha ɔwanth

Also, in Limba, the sentence 'Betty is cooking the rice' is produced

```
- -
    . -
       . -
          -
```

bɛti wototi si sa

Every syllable above is slightly lower than the one that precedes it. A possible cause of this type of peculiarity, therefore, is first language transfer.

The Tonal-Related Peculiarity

All Sierra Leonean languages (except Fullah) appear to be tonal, that is they use the relative differentiation of pitch on successive syllables to distinguish lexical items and also, in some cases to make morphological or syntactical distinctions. For example,

Krio:	/ `ko`ko /	=	root crop
	/ ´ko´ko /	=	node on the body
	/ `bɔ`bɔ /	=	little boy
	/ ´bɔ ´bɔ /	=	a kind of bean
Mende	/ `ndʒei /	=	water
	/ ´ndʒei /	=	goat
	/ `ka`li /	=	snake
	/ ´ka´li /	=	hoe
Temne	/ ´bi /	=	black
	/ `bi /	=	hole
	/ ´ba /	=	to have
	/ `ba /	=	to lay eggs

It can be observed that this tonal influence contributes to the shifting of the stress in some English polysyllabic words as shown in 134a-136a. In addition, Sierra Leoneans appear to be influenced by American word stress patterns where the first syllable tends to be stressed. (see 133a). Moreover, on the analogy of some English words with primary stress on the first syllable when used as nouns and on the second syllable when used as verbs, they tend to place the stress on the first syllable of two syllable nouns even when this is not the case in native English. (see 130a-132a of p 42). This peculiarity-type can therefore be first language, analogically and native English induced.

The Lack of Attitudinal Intonation-Related Peculiarity

In the local languages of Sierra Leone, additional words are mostly used to show a speaker's attitude. In other words, the languages do

not have the RP complex intonational feature such as the rise-fall and the fall-rise to show whether a speaker is certain or doubtful for instance of what he is saying. In Limba, for example, the sentence 'that was what he said' can literally be translated as:
/ Mɛnu domɛŋ ndɛ /

This sentence cannot for example, show a speaker's disbelief in what he has heard. In order to do so, additional words are to be used as in:

Mɛna domeŋ ndɛ kɛrɛ yaŋ niye la niŋ hula niya
Literal translation: That was said he but I
                    I do not him believe
Meaning: That was what he said but I don't believe/trust him

However, some local languages use tonal variation to express attitude. For example, in Temne, the word 'minɛŋ' can show two different meanings based on the tonal variations. That is 'mínɛŋ' with a Low High tone melody means 'it is me' while 'mìnɛŋ' with a Low Low tone melody means 'not me', 'I won't do it'. Similarly, in Mende, in response to the question 'Ngi pie, hi?' which means 'Can I do it this way?' one could say 'imm' which can have two meanings. That is 'ímm̀' with a High Low Low tone melody which suggests 'yes' with certainty while 'ímḿ' with a High High High tone melody which suggests 'yes' with doubt. One could therefore attribute this peculiarity to first language transfer and/or the ignorance of how attitudinal intonation is expressed in native English.

The Lack of the Contrastive Stress-Related Peculiarity
Emphasis seems to be made in the local languages of Sierra Leone by the addition of words. Whereas the sentence 'Abu drank the water' for example can carry an emphasis with the stress on Abu, this is not the case in the Sierra Leonean languages where additional words are to be used. This is illustrated in:
Krio: na Abu drink di wata

Literal Translation:	(It was Abu drank the water)
instead of:	Abu drink di wata
	(with the stress on 'Abu')
Meaning:	It was Abu who drank the water.

Temne:	Abɔ kɔnɔ mun ə mənt
Literal Translation:	Abu it was drank the water
instead of:	Abɔ ɔ mun ə mənt
	(with the stress on 'Abu')

Limba:	Na nde Abu wo thiyende maŋ mandi
Literal Translation:	It Abu who drank the water.
instead of:	Abu na thiyende mandi maŋ
	(with the stress on 'Abu')
Meaning:	It was Abu who drank the water

It is therefore likely that the tendency in the local languages to use words for emphasis accounts for the lack of contrastive stress in this variety.

Conclusion

The causes of the phonological peculiarities appear to be multi-faceted. That is, the possibilities appear to range from mother-tongue transfer, analogy and native variety influence. With regard to the influence of native English varieties, it is clear that our contact with native speakers of English is not limited to only RP speakers. This is becoming more and more evident with the influx into Sierra Leone of English speakers from America, Australia and other parts of Britain, and also with our exposure to a variety of radio and television programmes from different parts of the English-speaking world. In addition, Sumner (1965) observes that colonial education in Sierra Leone was partly influenced by English speakers with non RP accents who were exported to Sierra Leone via England. It would appear that these factors are to be considered for a comprehensive account of these peculiarity-types.

The Causes of the Lexical Peculiarities
This section is concerned with the collocation, word modification, idiom, innovation and aboriginal-related peculiarities.

The Causes Of The Collocation-Related Peculiarity
This section involves native English collocation, first language induced collocation and culturally induced collocation.

The Native English Collocation-Related Peculiarity
The peculiarities in this section show that Sierra Leoneans tend to view lexemes that are notionally equivalent as absolute synonyms. Such lexemes are therefore used inter-changeably in all contexts. However, in native English, lexemes do not have the same collocational range. Therefore, the verbs 'make' and 'undertake' do not respectively collocate with the nouns 'consultations' and 'coup'. On the other hand, Sierra Leoneans may know that the verbs 'sit' (analogous to 'preside') and 'associate' (analogous to 'attribute') pair up with 'on' and 'to' respectively, and therefore tend to collocate their synonymous pairs with the prepositions 'on' and 'to' (see 1a and 4a of p 46). Similarly, Sierra Leoneans' apparent incomplete knowledge of the pairing up of the verb 'have' with the noun 'impact' may cause them to collocate this noun with the verb 'create' (see 5a of p 47). One can therefore attribute this peculiarity-type to analogy and inadequate knowledge of native English rules.

The First Language-Induced Collocation Peculiarity
This peculiarity-type involves the use of cognate words that exist in both Krio and English and are formally and semantically isomorphous. Significantly, the two languages are related as Krio borrows several words from English. Usually, there is the tendency to use the cognates as if they applied in contexts of use in both languages and as if they were the same. Hence it is that 'hang' and 'heads', 'his' and 'mind', 'bold' and 'mind', 'back' and 'tyre' and 'run' and 'water' are translations of Krio expressions into English. (see 6a-10a of p 47). Furthermore, Krio morphology is illustrated in the use of the word 'man' which can collocate with other nouns to show special meanings. For example, it can collocate with a noun to

denote profession. It can also pair up with the name of a given political party to mean a member of that party (see 11a-13a of pp 47-48). This peculiarity-type is therefore first language-induced.

The Culturally-Induced Collocation Peculiarity

The tendency to use English words for referents that do not exist in the English lexicon can be as a result of the fact that English has now found itself in a cultural milieu that is different from that of the native speakers who are aboriginal users. In other words, in Sierra Leone, there are beliefs that there are people with certain mystical powers which the ordinary man does not have and there is a locally made soap which can be used to cure certain illnesses. Similarly, there is a traditional object which one could use to shoot and kill someone. Also, there is the practice of fining a man who has an affair with someone else's wife and in a wedding, the bridegroom is expected to give some amount of money or property before the ceremony is considered complete (see 14a-18a of p 48). These cultural beliefs and practices do not exist in the native setting and the tendency to express them in the language accounts for this peculiarity-type.

The Causes of the Word Modification-Related Peculiarity

This section involves the extension, reduction and change in the meanings of lexemes.

The Extension of the Word Meaning-Related Peculiarity

This peculiarity-type is first language-induced involving Krio which is the unofficial national lingua franca. That is, as opposed to native English lexemes, those of Krio function as if they were superordinate terms, while their English counterparts were subordinates. Therefore, for one Krio lexeme, the English language tends to have different lexemes which can be used in its place, each expressing a slightly different experience. This means that the different lexemes have slightly varied senses, while all these senses are expressed by a single lexeme in Krio. This is shown in lexemes such as 'meet', 'youth', 'escort', 'better', 'marriage', 'damage', 'apprentice', 'stranger', 'deliver' and 'colleague'. 'Meet' is now used to mean 'an accidental or deliberate encounter'; 'youth' can now be used to refer to someone who is not only 'young' but also 'politically active'; 'escort' now has the additional meaning of 'going with someone with or without the intention to protect him;' 'better' can now be used when no sense of comparison is implied; 'apprentice' now has the additional meaning of 'someone who works to get a pay' and not only 'to learn a trade'; 'marriage' is now used to cover both the 'occasion of uniting a couple and the union itself;' 'colleague' can now be used to mean 'one's work-mate' as well as 'one's friend'; 'damage' can be 'an experience that involves both living and non-living things'; 'deliver' can now mean 'to give birth with or without the aid of a midwife or a doctor' and 'provoke' can now mean 'to cause something to happen' and 'to tease.'

Another possible cause of this peculiarity-type is that Sierra Leoneans might not be aware of some specific contexts in which they are used in native English. This means that the all synonyms are perceived as absolute and therefore inter-changeable in all contexts. This peculiarity can also therefore be learning-induced.

The Restriction of the Word Meaning Related Peculiarity

It would appear that the peculiarities in this sub-section are influenced by Krio. In other words, since many words and expressions in English also exist in Krio, the subjects seem inclined to use some of these words and expressions even though they have a restricted meaning in Krio. Hence it is that 'education' is no longer related to moral values but to book learning, 'to see each other' now has the restricted meaning of 'courting' and to 'touch a woman' now means to have an affair with her (see 31a, 32a, and 34a of p 50). This peculiarity-type can therefore be first language-induced.

The Meaning Change-Related Peculiarity

This peculiarity-type comprises lexemes that appear to convey senses that are evident in Krio and which are different from native English. This means that the senses of the lexemes 'toilets' and 'bad heart' in Krio for example are different from those in native English. On the other hand, the suffix '-ian is used in native English to show profession as illustrated in lexemes such as 'physician', 'politician' and 'musician' (see p 51). It is probable that this accounts for the use of the suffix in 'academician' to denote someone who is in the academic field (see 36a of this same section). This usage can therefore be attributed to analogy. On the whole, this peculiarity-type can be explained in terms of first language transfer and analogy.

The Causes of the Idiom-Related Peculiarity
This section is concerned with the modification of native English idioms and the use of local idioms.

The Modification of the Native English Idiom-Related Peculiarity
This peculiarity-type can be traced to the apparent ignorance of the exact structures or forms of some native English idioms. It is observed that the number of an idiom, its verb, preposition or form can be changed. This can be respectively shown in 39a, 43a, 40a, 41a, and 45a of pp 51 - 52. Also, the modification can be as a result of giving a particular form to a given word in analogy to a similar one. This is evident in 'with regards to' in analogy to 'as regards' (see 38a of p 51). Sometimes, the whole structure of an idiom is changed as observed in 42a and 44a of p 52. On the whole, the idiomatic expressions are used in a slightly different morphological or structural form without consideration to the fact that such expressions normally have a fixed form. One can thus describe this peculiarity-type as learning-induced.

The First Language-Induced Idiom
The peculiarities in this section can be traced to the Sierra Leonean languages. This means that Sierra Leoneans tend to transfer idioms in their local languages – particularly Krio – to English. This peculiarity-type is therefore first language-induced.

The Causes of the Innovation-Related Peculiarity
This peculiarity-type can be traced to analogy. That is, owing to the flexibility of the English language, the subjects are inclined to employ affixation to make 'new' words in the language. For example, the suffix '-ly' is used to coin words such as 'seldomly'

and 'widely' (see 54a and 57a of p 53). Also, the suffix '-ness' is used to produce words like 'hatredness' and 'over-ambitiousness' (see 55a and 56a of p 31). In addition, the suffix '-s' is used to have the new word 'rounds' (see 58a of p 54). On the other hand, in recognition of the use of the prefix 'un' to show oppositeness of meaning and the prefix 're' before lexemes to connote repetition, the words 'undisputable' and 'reoccurrence' are coined (53a and 58a). This peculiarity-type can therefore be said to be learning-induced.

The Causes of the Aboriginal-Related Peculiarity

In this section, the peculiarities involve the use of lexemes from Sierra Leonean languages to cover areas like clothing, indigenous foods, traditional religious beliefs and local institutions. The lexemes used here are left unaltered in their substrate forms since they can better express meaning in the given contexts. In making a case for this peculiarity-type in South Asian English, Kachru (1982:333) contends that being a transplanted language this is the only way in which English can attain the level of functional appropriateness. By this, he means that the language has to transform its status as a mere guest or friend in the region to that of citing Raja: "one of our own, of our own caste, our creed, our sect and of our tradition" (Raja, 1978:421). One can therefore attribute these peculiarities to first language transfer.

Conclusion

One can observe from the above that the indigenous languages play an important role in the lexical peculiarities highlighted above. However, because English operates in Sierra Leone as a second language, one should not also lose sight of other factors which are common in a second language environment. These are the learning induced factors which appear to influence some collocational, idiomatic, word modification, phonological and innovation-related categories.

The Causes of the Grammatical Related Peculiarity

This section involves the causes of peculiarities such as noun, pronoun, verb, determiner, adjective, preposition, word class and syntax-related peculiarities.

The Causes of the Noun-Related Peculiarity

The peculiarities in this section can be caused either by the complexities involved in distinguisting nouns when they function as countable and uncountable nouns or by the insertion of the '–s' plural marker to an uncountable noun due to its semantic relationship with its countable counterpart.

As regards the delicacy in distinguishing nouns that can function as countable and uncountable, it can be observed that in native English, certain nouns can take the '–s' plural marker but not in all contexts. This depends on the subtle different meanings which a given noun may have. For example, the noun 'advice' takes the '–s' plural marker when it means 'notice' but it does not take it when it means 'suggestion.' The same is also true of 'language' which takes the plural marker if it means 'a system of communication' but does not take it if it means 'a particular style of speaking or writing;' 'property' which takes the marker if it means 'characteristic' or 'feature' but does not take it if it denotes 'a thing or things that is (are) owned by someone;' 'work' which takes the plural marker if it means a 'literary piece of writing' but does not take it if it has the meaning 'the use of physical strength or mental power in order to do or make something' and 'damage' which has the marker if it means 'an amount of money that a court decides should be paid to somebody by the person, company, etc. that has caused them harm or injury' but does not have it with the meaning 'physical harm caused to something which makes it less attractive, useful or valuable.' Jesperson (1970: 206-207) cited by Sey (1973: 27) observes this tendency when he states that: '... a great many words may in one connexion stand for something countable and in another for something uncountable.'

On the other hand, this tendency may also stem from the semantic relationship that exists between some countable nouns and their uncountable counterparts. In other words, an uncountable noun tends to become countable if it is similar in meaning with a countable one. For example, the nouns 'evidence' 'ammunition', 'staff', 'behaviour' and 'equipment' are clearly uncountable in native English usage. The synonyms or near-synonyms of these nouns are respectively the following countables: 'proof', 'weapon', 'worker', 'action' and 'tool'. The possible explanation here is that Sierra Leoneans are inclined to insert the '–s' plural marker to uncountable nouns since these nouns share a semantic relationship with other nouns that are labelled as countable nouns in native English (see 2a, 4a, 5a, 9a, and 10a of p 55). This peculiarity-type is therefore learning-induced.

The Causes of the Pronoun-Related Peculiarity

Pronouns tend to be used differently from native English in relation to case, the use of the reflexive/reciprocal pronoun and the demonstrative pronoun.

As regards the use of different cases, it can be observed that case distinction is not strictly evident in the local languages of Sierra Leone. In other words, in most of these languages, the same form of the first person plural is in subject and object positions. Krio, for example, uses the case form of the first person plural in the subjective and objective forms:

    wi go tɔŋ yɛstade
Meaning: we went to town yesterday

    i gi wi mɔni
Meaning: He gave us money

This type of peculiarity can therefore be first language-induced.

In Krio, also, the reflexive pronoun takes the place of the reciprocal pronoun as shown in:

    di bɔbɔ ɛn di titi lɛk dɛnsɛf
Literal translation: The boy and the girl love <u>themselves</u>
Meaning: The boy and the girl love each other.

One can therefore attribute this peculiarity to first language transfer.

As for the use of the demonstrative pronoun, it would appear that the speakers are aware of the relationship between 'these' and 'those' but may not know that the plural form of 'that' in native English is 'those'. One can therefore attribute this peculiarity to the partial knowledge of native English rules.

Generally, therefore, the peculiarities under reference can be attributed to first language transfer and incomplete knowledge of native English rules.

The Causes of the Verb-Related Peculiarity

This section comprises peculiarities relating to concord, infinitives/participles and tense and aspect.

The Concordial-Related Peculiarity

It is difficult to assume that Sierra Leoneans are not familiar with the concordial rules of native English. What may be certain is that in the first place, as opposed to native English rules, they tend to view an intervening phrase as a subject. Therefore, if there is a difference between what native English views as the subject and the noun in an intervening phrase, the number of the noun in the phrase will tend to influence the form of the verb. This is what is shown in 17a, 18a and 19a of p. 57 above. Secondly, when there is sentence inversion, they tend to regard as subject what the native speaker would not consider as such. This can lead to a difference in the number of the verb as shown in 20a above. Furthermore, in native English, the verb in an adjective clause introduced by 'who', 'which' or 'that' agrees with the antecedent of the relative pronoun. Where the antecedent is viewed differently from native English usage, they are likely to use a verb that is different in number from native English. This is so if the antecedent is different in terms of number. This is what 21a of the same section illustrates. The other peculiarities in this section are based on different perceptions. For example, a compound subject can be perceived as singular in native English but considered plural by educated Sierra Leoneans. This is what is shown when a singular subject is followed by the preposition 'together with' (as seen in 22a of the section), the use of the correlative conjunction to bring together singular subjects (as illustrated in 23a in the section). Similarly, a country's currency is viewed as a unit and is therefore considered singular. This is different from the perception in Sierra Leone which is plural when it is more than one (see 24a of the same section). This point of perception probably explains Lardo's (an American writer) use of the plural verb in the following sentence: They do have a good man qualified to practice in Florida, and he, with a team, are on their way here as we speak; McNally's Dilemma: (2000:57) (emphasis mine). In native English also, in sentences with linking verbs, the verb agrees with the subject not with the predicate nominative. This rule seems not to be observed because the predicate nominative is considered as the subject (see 25a). Finally, since the verb 'is' is used to point to one person or thing, the second person singular 'you' tends to pair up with 'is' in analogy to what obtains with the third person singular (see 26a). To conclude, these peculiarities can be accounted for as incomplete application of native English rules and different perceptions of certain grammatical forms.

The Infinitive/Participle-Related Peculiarity

In native English, the participle is used for general statements while the infinitive is preferred for specific and more immediate instances. This means that there are verbs that can use either of these elements based on the meaning the writer intends to express. In this vein, Sierra Leoneans' tendency of interchanging the two grammatical categories can be attributed to ignorance of the restrictions in native English rules.

One can rule out the influence of the Sierra Leonean languages since they also make a distinction between the two categories. In Krio, for example, one can state that:
Participle
i)   i lɛk rid
Meaning: He likes reading

Infinitive
ii) i lɛk fɔ rid
Meaning: He likes to read.

The distinction is also made in Mende as shown in:

i) Participle: ndopoi gahughuagɔ kɔgaalama
Meaning: The child likes reading

Infinitive:
ii) ndpoi gahuguagɔ kɔ i kɔlɔgaa
Meaning: the child likes to read.

One can therefore attribute this peculiarity-type to ignorance of native English rule restrictions.

The Tense/Aspect-Related Peculiarity
This section involves inflection, aspectual usage and the inclusion of the '–to' infinitive.

In terms of inflection, there are instances of uninflecting verbs that can be inflected in native English. One can trace this tendency to the existence in native English of a limited group of words that function both as verbs and as adjectives. Examples of such verbs include 'close', 'open', 'secure', 'free', 'advance' and 'develop'. In native English, these words have at least two adjectival forms which are the simple adjective and the past participle form. This is illustrated in:
i) It is an open secret.
ii) The library is opened to the public.

It would appear that the adjectival forms are indiscriminately interchanged here. One can thus attribute this peculiarity-type to Sierra Leoneans' partial knowledge of native English rules.

Sierra Leoneans also tend to inflect verbs that are uninflected in native English. A possible factor for this type of peculiarity is different perception from that of native English. That is, since Sierra Leoneans perceive the actions as occurring in the past, they consider it normal to inflect the verbs where native English would not. This is illustrated in 38a-40a of p. 60. Furthermore, in native English, the infinitive does not take 'to' when it comes after the verb 'make'. Sierra Leoneans seem unaware of this rule as is shown in 41a-42a of the same reference. This peculiarity may therefore be attributed to ignorance of native English rules.

With regard to aspectual usage, it can be observed that verbs that describe involuntary perception, those that describe inert cognition and have passive meaning, (that is, verbs of cognition) and relational verbs are regarded as stative in native English. This means that unlike dynamic verbs, these verbs do not take the '–ing' to express the progressive aspect. This distinction seems not to be made here (see 43a-45a of pp. 60 - 61). The peculiarity under reference can thus be traced to ignorance of the rules of native English. It should be noted that the influence of the Sierra Leonean languages with regard to this peculiarity-type may not be considered because while these languages can show the progressive aspect, this is not done by inflection.

The past tense is substituted for the perfective aspect. In native English, the various forms and usages relating to tense and aspect carry differences in meaning. This means that changing from one tense or aspect to another may be important in native English, but the meanings implied in the different forms and usages are even more important. For example, the perfective aspect is used to refer to an action that began in the past and is still going on and is finished by the time of speaking or writing with the emphasis on completion and continuity within a timeframe. On the other hand, the past tense is almost always used to refer to the past. It can for example, be used to refer to an action that has taken place over a period of time relating only to the past and completed. The peculiarities in 46a-48a portray the lack of awareness of the English rule that the notions of completion and continuity within a timeframe are essentially different. The peculiarity under reference can therefore be attributed to ignorance of native English rules.

One cannot, however, rule out the possible influence of the local languages for this peculiarity-type. This is because in these languages, the notions of completion and continuity can be viewed as one. This can be seen in the following Krio structures:

        di bɔbɔ dai yɛstade
Meaning: The boy died yesterday

        di bɔbɔ dɔn dai yɛstade
Meaning: The boy has died yesterday.

The same is also true of Temne which expresses this tendency as follows:

        ɔ wath ɔ fi dis
Meaning: The child died yesterday

        ɔ wath ɔ po fi dis
        The child has died yesterday.

This type of peculiarities can therefore be attributed to the subjects' ignorance of native English rules and the influence of local languages.

The Causes of the Determiner-Related Peculiarity

This section involves different determiner usage from native English, determiner inclusion and determiner omission.

The Determiner Usage Related Peculiarity

This peculiarity-usage deals with the use of articles and the indefinite determiner.

In native English, the choice between the indefinite articles ('a' and 'an') when they precede a singular noun depends on the sound of the first syllable of that word. In other words, the article 'a' is used if the first phoneme of the word is a consonant and 'an' is used if the first phoneme of the word is a vowel. The choice of the form of the indefinite article in 49a, 50a and 51a is determined by letters 's', 'l' and 'e' respectively. Thus this can be attributed to ignorance of native English rules.

It can also be observed that in Krio, the indefinite determiner 'one' tends to be used to replace the indefinite article where native English would prefer the use of the latter. It is possible that the Krio tendency has influenced this peculiarity-type as shown in 52a and 53a of p. 62.

In addition, native English makes a distinction between countable and uncountable nouns by using 'few' and 'less' before them respectively. This rule is not observed in 54a probably because of ignorance.

It is obvious that the omission of 'a' before 'few' is influenced by the plural form of the following noun (see 55a-56a). Alternatively, 'some' is used with 'few' to emphasize plurality (see 57a). Thus this peculiarity can be attributed to partial knowledge of native English rules.

The Determiner Inclusion-Related Peculiarity
In native English usage, some countable nouns do not take the indefinite article. Some of these nouns are those that relate to positions which people hold for a specific period. However, the knowledge that the indefinite article can be used before countable nouns may be responsible for its application in all cases. This is shown in 58a, 60a, 61a and 63a of p. 63. This type of peculiarity can thus be attributed to the over-generalisation of native English rules. Further, the use of the indefinite article with mass nouns, as in 59a and 62a may be due to ignorance of the native English rules.

The Determiner Omission-Related Peculiarity
In native English usage, the noun 'series' is perceived as singular and is therefore preceded by the indefinite article. Also, the abstract noun 'government' is preceded by the definite article when it is used in the generic sense. Moreover, the superlative can be preceded by

the definite article. This is also true of names of specific places. Sierra Leoneans' apparent ignorance of these rules seems to respectively account for the use in 66a, 64a, 65a, 68a and 69a of p. 64. This use can thus be attributed to the ignorance of native English rules.

The Cause(s) of the Adjective-Related Peculiarity

This peculiarity-type can be traced to partial knowledge of native English rules. The comparative and superlative forms of adjectives are changed as illustrated in 70a-72a.

The Cause(s) of the Prepositional-Related Peculiarity

The usage under consideration involves differences in prepositional usage, prepositional inclusion and prepositional omission.

The Prepositional Usage-Related Peculiarity

Native English considers prepositions to be different in significant ways. In other words, replacing a preposition in a given structure with another can lead to a difference in meaning. For example, the following structures are essentially different:

i) The scholarships are restricted <u>to</u> us the children of the less fortunate
ii) The scholarships are restricted <u>for</u> us the children of the less fortunate.

The sentences are different in that in the first sentence, the scholarships are said to be meant only for the children of the less fortunate. For its part, the second sentence means that the scholarships are not meant for the children of the less fortunate. However, in educated Sierra Leonean English usage, the meanings of prepositions tend to overlap. Therefore, 'wait' collocates with 'on' and 'for'; 'angry' pairs up with 'at' and 'with'; 'live' collocates with 'at' and 'in', 'sleep' matches with 'on bed' and 'in bed' (without any change of meaning) and 'under' and 'in' pair up with 'the sun' in each case. This is respectively shown in 74a, 78a, 76a, 81a, and 79a, of pp. 65 - 66. This tendency to overlap the meanings of prepositions is evident in the local languages. In Krio, for example, a single preposition would signal different relations. For example, the preposition 'na' has four different relations as illustrated in:

		meaning
i)	i de <u>na</u> os	He is <u>at</u> home
ii)	i kɔ mɔt <u>na</u> skul	He comes <u>from</u> school
iii)	put am <u>na</u> yu mɔt	Put it <u>in</u> your mouth
iv)	kɛr am <u>na</u> mi rum	Take it <u>to</u> my room

Similarly, in Temne, there are two main types of prepositions. They are 'ro' and 'ka' 'Ro' is used to denote places and things as is shown in:

    i tə kɔ <u>ro</u> məkeni   =   I will go to Makeni

'Ka' is designated to people as observed in:
    i kɔ ka ɔbay   =   I went to the chief

This peculiarity-type is therefore L_1 – induced

It can be noted also that some of the peculiarities that fall under this category can be traced to analogy. That is, synonymous lexemes in native English may have different prepositions. In educated Sierra Leonean English usage, however, there seems to be the assumption that because a given word collocates with a particular preposition, its synonymous pair can collocate with that same preposition. Hence it is that because the verb 'praise' can collocate with 'for', 'congratulate' also tends to be viewed as a collocational partner of this same preposition (see 77a of p. 65). The same is also true of 'detriment' and 'peril' in relation to their collocation with 'at', 'preside' and 'sit' in relation to the preposition 'on' and 'wire' and 'radio' in relation to the preposition 'over'. This is respectively illustrated in 73a, 80a and 75a. One can therefore assert that the peculiarity under consideration can be traced to analogy.

The Prepositional Inclusion-Related Peculiarity

The application of English rules in situations where they do not obtain in native English accounts for preposition-inclusion peculiarity, that is over-generalisation. In effect, in analogy with such verbs as 'consist', 'talk', 'ask', and 'arrive', there is the inclusion of the prepositions 'of', 'about', 'for' and 'at' respectively in 82a, 84a, 85a and 86a.

The Prepositional Omission-Related Peculiarity

There seems to be far more prepositions in English than in the local languages of Sierra Leone. And the relatively few prepositions in these languages are used to show grammatical relations. This is illustrated in p. 160 above where the Krio preposition 'na' indicates four grammatical relations. Therefore, structures are generated in English without prepositions because such structures do not require prepositions in the local languages. In the following Krio structures for example, prepositions are not used, but their use is considered mandatory in native English:

i) a biliv mi man
Literal translation: I believe my husband
Translation: I believe in my husband

ii) a wek am na mɔnin
Literal translation: I woke him in the morning
Translation: I woke him up in the morning

One can therefore adduce that this peculiarity-type is first language-induced.

The Cause(s) of the Word Class-Related Peculiarity

The conception of grammatical categories in Sierra Leonean English appears different from that of native English. For example, nouns that function as adjectivals in native English are treated as nominal with an '–s' plural marker acting as a suffix. This is what the peculiarities in 91a-92a of p. 67 illustrate. Verbs are also used in preference to adjectives as in 93a-96a. The most persistent of this peculiarity-type is the word 'mature'. This word hardly functions as a verb in Sierra Leone. When it is used as an adjective, however, it takes the participial adjective (like the '–ed' suffix in verbs) making it appear as a verb. This is probably due to its semantic relationship with verbs that have regular past participial forms. One can therefore attribute this peculiarity-type to partial knowledge of the different concepts of the grammatical categories in native English.

The Causes of the Syntax-Related Peculiarity

This section deals with imbalance, repetition, structural omission, structural differences, universal tag, reduplication and responses to yes/no questions.

The Imbalance-Related Peculiarity

The peculiarities under this category involve the use of parallel constructions in relation to the coordination of ideas. In native English, the coordinating conjunction is used to bring together grammatical structures that are parallel. This does not preclude the correlative conjunctions in which what follows the second half of the pair is the same as what follows the first half. On the other hand, in educated Sierra Leonean English usage, items that are brought together in a series could have different grammatical forms. Also, coordinating conjunctions (including correlative conjunctions) can bring together structures that are similar in content but different in grammatical form. One could attribute this set of peculiarities in 97a-105a to the incomplete application of native English rules.

The Repetition-Related Peculiarity

The peculiarities in this category are concerned with the use of words or expressions that are not desirable in native English. In other words, in native English, repetitions are allowed only for emphasis. However, it would appear here that the same idea is repeated even when emphasis is not intended. The general trend is to use words that repeat the sense of other words as in 'retreat' and 'backwards', 'attribute' (used as a verb) and 'due to', 'secret' and 'ballot', 'suspend' and 'temporal', 'afternoon' and 'pm,' 'return and back' and 'among' and 'include'. This is respectively illustrated in 106a-112a of pp. 69 - 70. There is also the case of using a modifier that repeats an idea already implied in the word modified as shown in 115a and 116a of the same section. Finally, function words can also be repeated in structures as indicated in 'let' and 'don't' (see 113a), 'in' (see 117a) and 'of' (see 118a). This feature can be attributed to ignorance of native English rules in relation to functions and meanings of words in a given structure.

The Causes of the Structural Omission-Related Peculiarity
This section involves the omission of the comparative word in a comparative structure and the omission of content and function words.

The Omission of the Comparative Word-Related Peculiarity
In native English, comparisons are made with the use of the comparative word. The omission of the comparative word here is due, perhaps, to the influence of the local languages which can express comparison without a comparative word. In Krio, for example, the sentence
'He is taller than I' is rendered as:
'i tɔl pas mi'

This sentence is also produced in Temne as follows:
ɔ bɔli ɔthaʃi mi

In both languages, no comparative word is used.

One can therefore state that this usage in 119a-122a is first language-induced.

The Omission of the Content and Function Word-Related Peculiarity
In this peculiarity-type, one can see the influence of the L_1 and that of the native variety at work. For example, in Krio, the word 'enjoy' does not require an object to make sense in a structure. It is this feature of Krio that might have been transferred to English (see 123a of p. 71). On the other hand, the subjects seem not to know that a verb has been omitted in 124a of the same section. This is also the

case with the omission of the subjects (see 125a), the particles in 126a-127a and the subordinator in 128a. In native English, when a similar idea is expressed by two different verb forms, both should be preserved. This also applies to prepositions that are different but express a similar idea. Moreover, sentences that have modifiers should also have what they have modified. The peculiarities under review show that the subjects appear to be unaware of these rules. One can therefore attribute these peculiarities to the subjects' ignorance of native English rules.

The Structural Difference-Related Peculiarity
This section comprises the order of pronouns and pronoun inclusion.

The Order of Pronoun-Related Peculiarity
In native English, the first person singular pronoun occupies the second position in compounds. But in Sierra Leone it can occupy the first position. One can trace this tendency to L_1-influence. That is, in Krio, for example, the first person singular pronoun always precedes in compounds as seen in:

i)   mi ɛn mi mama de go na di os
Literal Translation: I and my mother are going to the house
Meaning: My mother and I are going to the house

ii)   mi ɛn mi sista de kam
Literal Translation: I and my sister are coming
Meaning: My sister and I are coming

This peculiarity-type (see 129a-131a) is therefore L_1-induced

The Pronoun Inclusion-Related Peculiarity
Here, pronouns are used in situations where they are not used in native English. The influence of the local languages which use pronouns in such circumstances may account for this tendency. This can be seen in the sentence 'The children are coming' which is translated in the following languages as follows:
Limba

i)   mpati beŋ ti hiŋ bi si

Temne
ii)   ã ⁿ fɛth ã ⁿ tə der
Lit. Trans.   The children they are coming

This peculiarity-type (see 132a-134a of p. 73) can therefore be L_1-induced.

The Placement of the Modifier-Related Peculiarity
According to native English, the position of the modifier in a structure is important because it influences meaning. This can be illustrated in the position of the modifier 'only' in the following structures:
i)   He <u>only</u> died yesterday
ii)   He died <u>only</u> yesterday
iii)   <u>Only</u> he died yesterday

The meaning of the first sentence is that the only thing he did yesterday was to die. In sentence two, the meaning is that he died yesterday and no other day. The third sentence shows that he was the only one who died and no one else.

The random placement of modifiers as in 135a-140a (see pp.73 - 74) can be attributed to ignorance of native English rules

The Universal Tag-Related Peculiarity
Question tag in native English is a component that basically involves helping verbs. For example,
>   I am not going, am I?
>   You are not going, are you?
>   He is not going, is he?

In Krio, however, these tags have been simplified by using the tag 'nɔ to so' for all situations. It is probably this invariant pattern that has been transferred to English usage. This peculiarity-type can therefore be first language-induced (see 141a-143a of p. 75).

The Reduplication-Related Peculiarity

The tendency to use reduplicated words is typical of Sierra Leonean languages. Examples of this feature include the following:

i)   Limba: yako (quick) = yako-yako
          (quick-quick, very quickly)
       wunthe (one)   =   wunthe-wunthe
          (one-one, one after the other)

ii)   Mende flo (quick) = floflo (quick, quick, very quickly)

iii)   Krio fayn (beautiful)   fayn fayn (very beautiful)
       wɔwɔ (ugly)   wɔwɔ wɔwɔ (very ugly)

One can use the above examples to assert that this peculiarity-type is L_1-induced (see 144a-146a in p. 75).

The Responses to Negative Yes/No Question/Statement-Related Peculiarity

In native English, the response to yes/no questions is contingent upon the facts surrounding a given situation. This means that if the situation is positive, the answer will be yes; if it is negative, the answer will be no. This tendency is different from what obtains in the Sierra Leonean languages where the response to the question depends on the form and not the content of the question. An example of this tendency can be seen in Krio as follows:

Question: yu mama nɔ kam yɛstade?
Translation: Didn't your mother come yesterday?

Answer: yɛs i nɔ kam yɛstade?
Meaning: Yes, she did not come yesterday.

One can thus attribute this peculiarity-type (see 147a-148a in pp. 75 - 76) to the influence of Sierra Leonean languages.

Conclusion

One can deduce from the above discussion that the causes of these grammatical peculiarities can be broadly categorised into two. These include the L_1 and the learning-induced peculiarities. The learning-induced factors include the over-generalisation of native English rules, ignorance and the incomplete application of these rules.

The Causes of the Discoursal-Related Preculiarity

This section comprises forms of address, riddles/proverbs, phatic communion and style.

The Form of Address-Related Peculiarity

Sierra Leoneans' cultural backgrounds probably account for this peculiarity-type. In Sierra Leone, there is reverence for people who hold positions of trust and for the elderly. Therefore, someone who has become a parliamentarian even once in his life time seems to carry the title of 'honourable' for life. That is, he is called honourable even when he is no longer a parliamentarian. This is shown in 1 and 5 of pp. 76 - 77. This title is also extended to presidents and vice-presidents as indicated in 3 and 4 of this section. Similarly, honorary doctoral degree holders are accorded doctoral titles for life (see 6 of the same reference). The same is also the case with people who carry ambassadorial, judicial and academic titles. That is, they are still addressed by such titles even though they may no longer be engaged in activities relating to those titles. This is respectively shown in 10, 8 and 9 of the same reference. This is a mark of respect for the elderly. This situation is different from what obtains in native English where, for example, a parliamentarian is referred to as 'honourable' only when he is in a parliamentary session and where a professor can still be addressed as such if he is attached to the academic field. Sierra Leoneans' cultural background can therefore be attributed to this peculiarity-type.

The Proverb/Riddle-Related Peculiarity

The proverbs cited in pp 77 - 78 are borrowed from Krio and they help to illustrate the cultural values of the society. The first proverb for example hinges on the acceptance of destiny while the second example highlights the need for unity. The peculiarity-type relating to riddles involves traditional beliefs and practices in Sierra Leone. For example, in Sierra Leone there are certain items and/or activities that are associated with witchcraft (see 14-15 of this section). Also, touching someone's feet is a sincere mark of repentance for wrong doing (see 18). Furthermore, the husband is shown to be the head of the matrimonial home since he has 'bought' the wife who eventually becomes his 'commodity' (see 20); a child is owned by the husband and not the wife (see 21); male children are preferred to female children (see 25); the husband starts to show his responsibility to and eventual ownership of the child when it is in the mother's womb (see 22) and oath-taking (if done falsely) can lead to the termination of one's life within a short period (see 19). It is probably in recognition of the existence of such cultural structures and ideas in areas where the English language has emerged that prompts Gyening to remark that:

> ... as English spreads to all parts of the world, it has become necessary for its non-native speakers to fashion out for themselves words which are in their indigenous languages and cultures but which are absent from the English language and culture (Gyening, 1997:1).

It goes without saying therefore that these cultural beliefs and practices are expressed in the local languages. One can therefore view this peculiarity-type as L_1 transfer.

The Phatic Communion-Related Peculiarity

Malinowski (1923) investigates the tendency among native English speakers to use empty expressions as a way of initiating conversations. This is illustrated among others in greetings and expressions such as 'how do you do? and 'how are you?' In Sierra Leone, such questions are viewed as enquiries after someone's health and are responded to accordingly. In fact, it is considered impolite for two or more people to engage in an important discussion without first employing some opening courtesies. There is the interesting story, for example, of someone who visited a friend mainly to borrow something from him. However, because he spent some time talking about unrelated issues, another less evasive friend who came in later to make a similar request succeeded in his venture to the detriment of the first visitor. This cultural practice of using opening courtesies before discussing important issues is reflected in the local languages and can thus account for the feature in 26 and 27, p. 78.

The Style-Related Peculiarity

Speakers and writers of native English have a wide range of style to choose from depending on the context. This choice can be determined for example by whether they speak/write in a formal or informal situation. It can also be determined by the relationship between the speaker/writer and the addressee. On the other hand, English is taught and learnt in Sierra Leone as a second language. In this regard, Sierra Leoneans do not seem to have developed a wide range of styles of English to meet different contexts. Therefore, the formal literary variety to which they are exposed does not constitute the colourful English idiomatic expressions which characterise the casual use of the language. (see 28-31 in p. 79). This can thus be attributed to the methodology involved in teaching English.

Conclusion

It can be observed that the cultural milieu in which the English language finds itself accounts for the Sierra Leoneans' discoursal tendencies. That is, the cultural beliefs and practices are expressed in their local languages and these, in turn, have found their way into the English language. On the other hand, the impact of the methods of teaching English during colonialism is such that it has a mark on their English usage in relation to style.

Summary
The peculiarities that have been identified among Sierra Leoneans have also been noted in varieties that exist in other parts of the world enjoying some amount of legitimacy. It is also observed that these

peculiarities can be generally attributed to first language transfer and learning-induced factors. These are factors that are evident in all second language environments

CHAPTER FIVE
TESTS AND TEST RESULTS

Introduction
As mentioned in the Preface, lecturers of English and final year students of English were selected to verify the acceptability or otherwise of the observed features. These features include phonology, lexis and grammar. The discoursal features have not been involved because providing the contexts in which the structures are used would have proved to be taxing. Ten students and five lecturers from each of the institutions (that is Nothern Polytechnic (NP), Eastern Polytechnic (EP), Milton Margai College of Education and Technology (MMCET) and Njala University (NU)) were provided with questionnaires and later interviewed in this regard. The results are given below:

The Phonological Peculiarities
This section deals with tests and results relating to the segmental (that is the vowel and consonant-related features) and the suprasegmental features which include syllable timing, downdrift, tonality, intonation and stress.

Test on the Acceptability Level Relating to the Examples of the Vowel-Related Peculiarity

In order to test the level of acceptability of the vowel-related peculiarities, the respondents were asked to express their attitudes towards the production of the following words:
i) 'live' pronounced as / liv /
    (merging of front close and front half-close vowels)
ii) 'sit' produced as / sit /
    (merging of front close and front half-close vowels)
iii) 'ship' pronounced as / ʃip /
    (merging of front close and front half close vowels)
iv) 'give' rendered as / giv /

(merging of front close and front half-close vowels)
v) 'baton' produced as / batɔn /
(merging of back open and back half-open vowels)
vi) 'profit' produced as / prɔfit /
(merging of back open and back half-open vowels)
vii) 'college' rendered as / kɔlɛdʒ /
(merging of back open and back half-open vowels)
viii) 'pot' pronounced as / pɔt /
(merging of back open and back half-open vowels)
ix) 'class' rendered as / klas /
(merging of front open and central back open vowels)
x) 'sergeant' produced as / sadʒɛnt /
(merging of front open and central back open vowels)
xi) 'rather' produced as / rada /
(merging of front open and central back open vowels)
xii) 'branch' produced as / brantʃ /
(merging of front open and central back open vowels)
xiii) 'natural' produced as / natʃɔral /
(merging of front open and central open vowels)
xiv) 'man' produced as / man /
(merging of front open and central open vowels)
xv) 'push' pronounced as / puʃ /
(merging of back close and back half-close vowels)
xvi) 'could' rendered as / kuld /
(merging of back close and back half-close vowels)
xvii) 'would' pronounced as / wuld /
(merging of back close and back half-close vowels)
xviii) 'number' rendered as / nɔmba /
(substituting the central half-open vowel with the back half-open vowels)
xix) 'flood' pronounced as / flɔd /
(substituting the central half-open vowel with the back half-open vowel)
xx) 'does' pronounced as / dɔz /
(substituting the central half-open vowel with the back half-open vowel)
xxi) 'girl' pronounced as / ga l /

(substituting the central half-close vowel with the central open vowel)
xxii) 'learnt' rendered as / lant /
(substituting the central half-close vowel with the central open vowel)

xxiii) 'bird' produced as / bad /
(substituting the central half-close vowel with the central open vowel)
xxiv) 'turn' produced as / tɔn /
(substituting the central half-close vowel with the back half-open vowel)
xxv) 'first' pronounced as / fɔst /
(substituting the central half-close vowel with the back half-open vowel)
xxvi) 'journey' produced as / dʒɔni /
(substituting the central half-close vowel with the back half-open vowel)
xxvii) 'church' rendered as / tʃɔtʃ /
(substituting the central half-close vowel with the back half-open vowel)
xxviii) 'err' pronounced as / a /
(substituting the central half-close vowel with the central open vowel)
xxix) 'search' rendered as / sa tʃ /
(substituting the central half-close vowel with the central open vowel)
xxx) 'skirt' pronounced as / skat /
(substituting the central half-close vowel with the central open vowel)
xxxi) 'surgical' produced as / sɔdʒikal /
(substituting the mid central vowel with the central open vowel)
xxxii) 'journalist' produced as / dʒɔnalist /
(substituting the mid central vowel with the central open vowel)
xxxiii) 'teacher' pronounced as / titʃa /

(substituting the mid central vowel with the central open vowel)
xxxiv) 'parliament' produced as / palimɛnt /
(spelling-induced peculiarity)
xxxv) 'quality' pronounced as / kwaliti /
(spelling-induced peculiarity)
xxxvi) 'privilege' rendered as / privilɛdʒ /
(spelling-induced peculiarity)
xxxvii) 'monitor' produced as / mɔnitɔ /
(spelling-induced peculiarity)
xxxviii) 'want' rendered as / want /
(spelling-induced peculiarity)
xxxix) 'mayor' produced as / mejɔ /
(spelling-induced peculiarity)
xxxx) 'science' produced as / saĩs /
(nasalising the front-closing diphthong)
xxxxi) 'responsibility' produced as / rɛspɔ̃sibillti /
(nasalising the back half-open vowel)
xxxxii) 'hungry' pronounced as / hɔ̃ngri /
(nasalising the back half-open vowel)
xxxxiii) 'farewell' rendered as / fiawɛl /
(merging the front half-open centering and the front half-close centering diphthongs)
xxxxiv) 'share' pronounced as / ʃia /
(merging the front half-open centering and the front half-close centering diphthongs)
xxxxv) 'hair' produced as / hia /
(merging the front half-open centering and the front half-close centering diphthongs)
xxxxvi) 'major' produced as / medʒɔ /
(substituting the front closing diphthong with the cardinal front half-close vowel)
xxxvii) 'tail' rendered as / tel /
(substituting the front closing diphthong with the cardinal front half-close vowel)
xxxxviii) 'hold' pronounced as / hold /

(substituting the back closing diphthong with the cardinal back half-close vowel)

xxxxix)   'coat' pronounced as / kot /
(substituting the back closing diphthong with the cardinal back half-close vowel)

The Results of the Responses Relating to the Examples of the Vowel-Related Peculiarity

The average mean responses to the vowel-related peculiarity are illustrated in Table 1 (see p. 168). This Table shows that 92 percent of the students and about 90 percent of the lecturers are in agreement with the examples relating to this type of peculiarity. This result is reflected in Graph 1 (see p. 167). Importantly, this result is reflected in all the four institutions. For example, the students' responses are respectively recorded at 95 percent, 93 percent, 90 percent and about 91 percent in NP, EP, MMCET and NU. Also, the lecturers' responses are estimated at 93 percent, 87 percent, 92 percent and about 87 percent in NP, EP, MMCET and NU respectively. (see Graph 2 p. 168) One may use this result to infer that this peculiarity type is evident in the English usage of educated Sierra Leoneans.

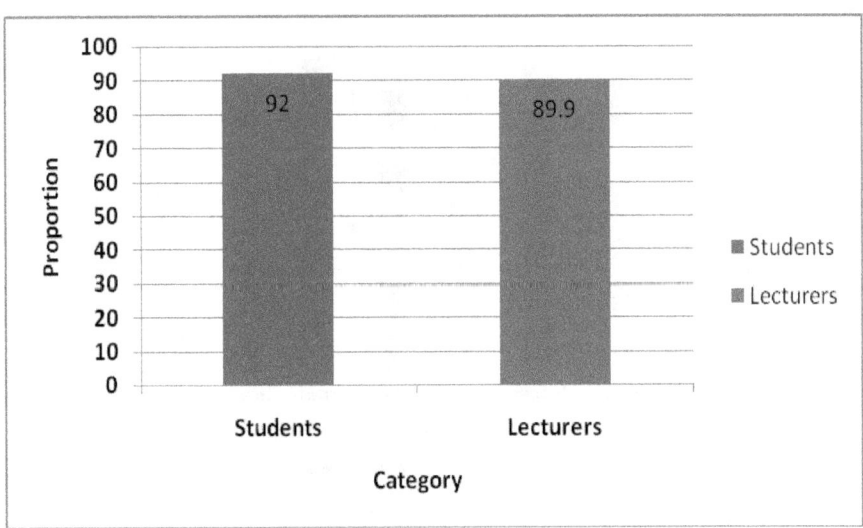

Graph 1: Summary of the responses relating to the examples of the vowel-related peculiarity

Table 1: Summary of the responses to the vowel-related peculiarity in the four institution

Category	NP		EP		MMCET		NU		Mean	
	Students	Lecturers	Students	Lecturers	Students	Lecturers	Students	Lecturers	Students	Lecturers
Vowel related peculiarities	94.7	93.3	92.5	87.2	90.3	92.2	90.6	86.8	92	89.9
Merging of vowels	95	97	98	97	93	98	95	94	95.3	96.5
Vowel substitution	97.2	93.8	86	72.2	86.8	85.2	93.6	80.8	90.9	83
Spelling induced	97	97	94	92	90	92	91	84	93	91.3
Nasalisation	97	88	95	93	90	96	88	88	92.5	91.3
Merging of diphthongs	93	92	85	86	88	86	92	78	89.5	85.5
Diphthong substitution	89	92	97	83	94	96	84	96	91	91.8

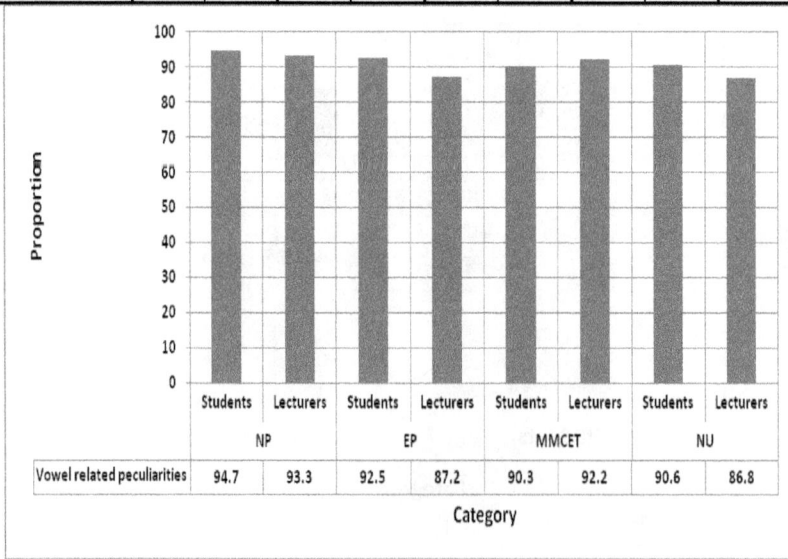

Graph 2: Summary of the responses relating to the examples of the vowel-related peculiarity in the four institutions

Test on the Acceptability Level Relating to the Examples of the Consonant-Related Peculiarity

To test the level of acceptability of the consonant-related peculiarities, the respondents were asked to express their attitudes towards the production of the words below:

i) 'three' pronounced as / tri /
(substituting the voiceless dental fricative with the voiceless alveolar plosive)

ii) 'thirty' pronounced as / tati /
(substituting the voiceless dental fricative with the voiceless alveolar plosive)

iii) 'there' rendered as / dia /
(substituting the voiced dental fricative with the voiced alveolar plosive)

iv) 'writhe' produced as / raid /
(substituting the voiced dental fricative with the voiced alveolar plosive)

v) 'nursing' pronounced as / nɔsin /
(substituting the velar nasal with the alveolar nasal)

vi) 'morning' rendered as / mɔnin /
(substituting the velar nasal with the alveolar nasal)

vii) 'among' pronounced as / amɔŋg /
(substituting the velar nasal with the velar nasal and the voiced velar plosive)

viii) 'sing' produced as / siŋg /
(substituting the velar nasal with the velar nasal and the voiced velar plosive)

ix) 'noise' rendered as / nɔis /
(Spelling-induced peculiarity)

x) 'is' pronounced as / is /
(Spelling-induced peculiarity)

xi) 'because' rendered as / bikɔs /
(Spelling-induced peculiarity)

xii) 'of' produced as / ɔf /
(Spelling-induced peculiarity)

xiii) 'Beware of the people who pretend to like you' rendered as
/ bi wia ɔf di pipul hu pritɛn to laik ju /
(omission of the linking 'r' in 'beware of')

xiv) 'His doctor is at the meeting' produced as
/ his dɔktɔ is at di mitin /
(omission of the linking 'r' in 'doctor is')

xv) 'I cannot entertain the idea of condoning criminals' produced as
/ ai kanɔt ɛntaten di aidia ɔf kɔndonin kriminals /
(omission of the intrusive 'r' in 'idea of')

xvi) 'It is better to jaw and jaw than to shoot and shoot' produced as
/ it is bɛta to dʒɔ an dʒɔ dan to ʃut an ʃut /
(omission of the intrusive 'r' in 'jaw and jaw')

xvii) 'particles' pronounced as / patikuls /
(omission of the syllabic consonant)

xviii) 'bottle' rendered as / bɔtul /
(omission of the syllabic consonant)

xix) 'understand' in 'understand me' produced as / ɔndastan /
(omission of the voiced alveolar plosive)

xx) 'criticized' in 'criticized the government' pronounced as
/ kritisaiz /
(omission of the voiced alveolar plosive)

xxi) 'explained' in 'explained my plight' produced as / ɛksplen /
(omission of the voiced alveolar plosive)

The Results of the Responses Relating to the Examples of the Consonant-Related Peculiarity

Table 2 (see p. 171) illustrates inter alia the average mean responses to the consonant-related peculiarity. In this Table, about 94 percent of both the students and the lecturers consider this peculiarity-type acceptable. Graph 3 (see p. 172) shows a similar result. This result is also shown in each of the four institutions. In other words, the students' responses are estimated at 96 percent, about 94 percent, about 92 percent and 93 percent in NP, EP, MMCET and NU respectively. Moreover, the lecturers' responses are respectively recorded at about 95 percent, 94 percent, 92 percent and about 94 percent in NP, EP, MMCET and NU. (See Graph 4 p. 172). One may use this result to infer that this peculiarity type is evident in the English usage of educated Sierra Leoneans.

Table 2: Summary of the responses relating to the examples of the consonant-related peculiarity in the four institutions

Category	NP		EP		MMCET		NU		Mean	
	Students	Lecturers	Students	Lecturers	Students	Lecturers	Students	Lecturers	Students	Lecturers
Consonant related peculiarities	96.1	94.9	93.8	94.1	91.9	92.3	93	93.8	93.7	93.8
Consonant substitution	93.8	95	96.3	90	90	92.5	87.5	87.5	91.9	91.3
Spelling induced	98	96	95	92	91	86	92	94	94	92
Omission of syllabic consonant	97.5	97.5	95	95	93.8	97.5	97.5	97.5	95.9	96.9
Omission of the linking and intrusive 'r'	97.4	94.7	99	98	95.4	96	99	94.7	97.7	95.9
Consonant deletion	92.9	91.4	78.6	91.4	85.7	85.7	82.9	94.3	85	90.7

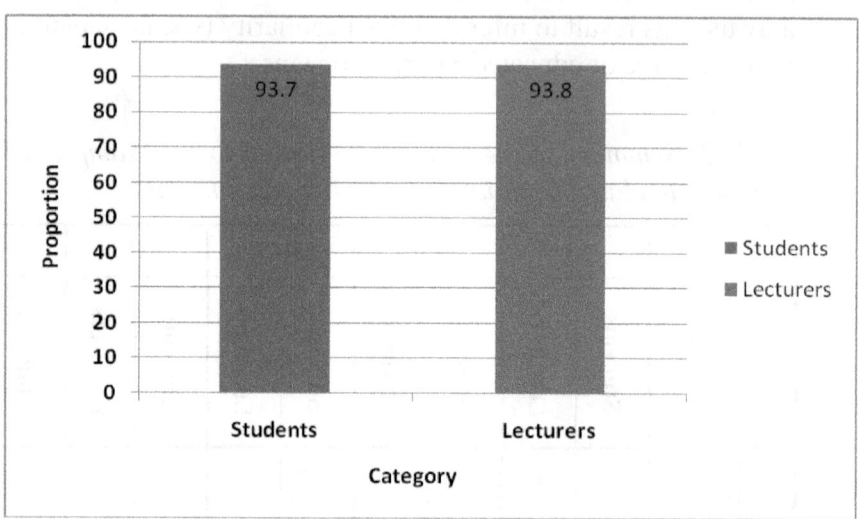

Graph 3: Summary of the responses relating to the examples of the consonant-related peculiarity

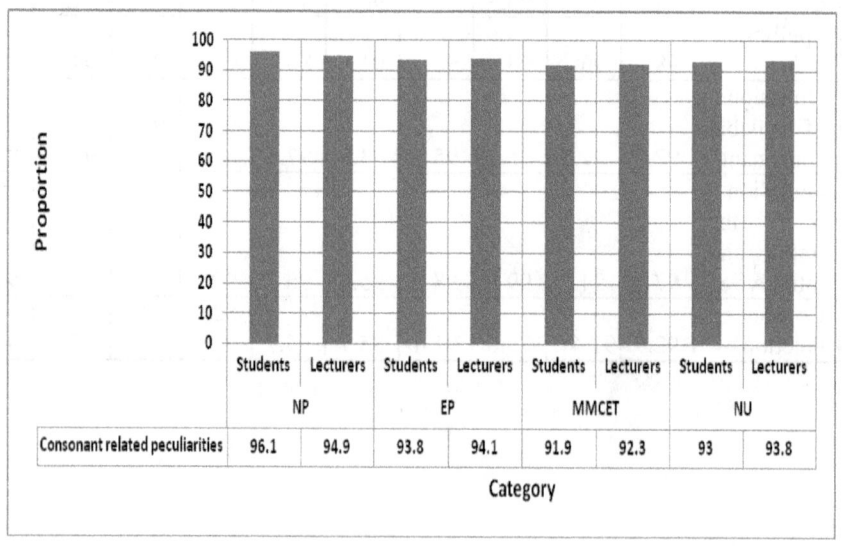

Graph 4: Summary of the responses to the consonant-related peculiarity in the four institutions

Test on the Acceptability Level Relating to the Examples of the Suprasegmental Peculiarity

In order to test the level of acceptability of the suprasegmental related peculiarities, the respondents were asked to express their attitudes towards the following words or structures:

i) 'He said in a letter to judges that he did not believe he would have a fair hearing' produced as:
/ hi / 'sɛd / in / e / 'lɛ / ta /to / dʒɔ / 'dʒis / dat / hi /did / nɔt / bi / liv / hi / wuld / hav / e / fi / a / 'hia / r ĩ /
(syllable-time related peculiarity)

ii) 'You cannot judge a man going to heaven by the amount of people following the corpse'.
rendered as:
/ ju / ka / nɔt / 'dʒɔdʒ / e / man / go / in/ to / 'hɛ / vin / bai / di / a/ maunt / ɔf / pi/ pul / fɔ/ lo / in / di / kɔps /.
(syllable-time related peculiarity)

iii) 'Some can give birth to the young alive as mammals and humans do'
rendered as:
/ sɔm / kan / giv / 'bat / to / di / 'jɔng / a / 'laiv / as / ma / mals / an / 'hu / mans / du /
(syllable-time related peculiarity)

iv) 'They go house to house to collect these taxes' produced as:

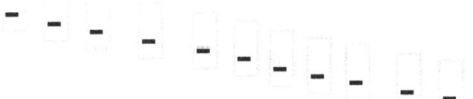

de go haus to haus to kɔlɛkt diz taksis
(downdrift-related peculiarity)

v) 'When you do not receive God's favour, it is very hard for you to succeed in the long term'
produced as:

wɛn ju du nɔt risiv gɔds fevɔ it is vɛri had to sɔksid in di lɔng tam (downdrift-related peculiarity)

vi) 'Every citizen in this country has a role to play'
rendered as:

/ ɛvri sitizin in dis kɔntri haz e rol to ple /
(downdrift-related peculiarity)

vii) 'What message do you want to send to people all around the world?' rendered as:

/ wat mɛsedʒ du ju want to sɛn to pipul ɔl araund di wɔld
(downdrift-related peculiarity)

viii) 'What exactly are you talking about?'
produced as:

wat ɛgz'aktli a ju 'tɔkin abaut
(downdrift-related peculiarity)

ix) 'cement' pronounced as / 'simɛnt /
(tonality-related peculiarity)
x) 'career' rendered as / 'keria /

(tonality-related peculiarity)

xi) 'invalid' (adjective) pronounced as / 'invalid /
(tonality-related peculiarity)

xii) 'participate' produced as / patisi'pet /
(tonality-related peculiarity)

xiii) 'maximise' pronounced as / magzi'maiz /
(tonality related peculiarity)

xiv) Question: So you believe everything on earth is the creation of God?
Response: Indeed, indeed Allah is the originator of everything. We have no doubt in that.
produced as:
Question: /so ju biliv ɛvri θin ɔn aθ is di krieʃɔn ɔf gɔd?/

Response: /<u>indid indid</u> ala is di ɔridʒinetɔ ɔf ɛvritin. <u>wi hav no daut in dat</u>/ (intonation-related peculiarity)

xv) Question: Are you the only first born son?
Response: Yes, yes I am the first born son.
rendered as:
Question: /a ju di ɔnli fɔs bɔn sɔn?/
Response: /<u>jɛs jɛs</u> ai am di ɔnli fɔst bɔn sɔn /
(intonation-related peculiarity)

xvi) Question: Are you sure of winning?
Response: Yes if the police live up to their task which appears doubtful.
produced as:
Question: /a ju ʃɔ ɔf winin/
Response: / <u>jɛs</u> if di polis liv ɔp to dia task <u>witʃ apiaz dautful</u>/
(intonation-related peculiarity)

xvii) 'We were saved because our trust is not in man but in God'.
produced as:

/wi wia sevd bikɔs aua trɔst is nɔt in man bɔt in gɔd./
(stress-related peculiarity)

xviii) 'He was the one who took the responsibility to educate me' produced as:
/hi wɔz di wan hu tuk di rspɔnsibiliti to ɛdjuket mi/
(stress-related peculiarity)

xix) 'It is the police alone that should be blamed for this problem' produced as:
/it is di polis elon dat ʃuld bi blemd fɔ dis prɔblɛm/
(stress-related peculiarity)

The Results of the Responses Relating to the Examples of the Suprasegmental-Related Peculiarity

Table 3 (see p. 177) deals with the average mean responses to the suprasegmental-related peculiarity. This Table shows that 94 percent of the students and 92 percent of the lecturers consider the examples relating to this peculiarity acceptable. This result is reflected in Graph 5 (see p. 177). It is important to note that the above result cuts across each of the four institutions. For instance, the students' responses are recorded at about 96 percent, about 95 percent, 94 percent and 90 percent in NP, EP, MMCET and NU respectively. In the same vein, the lecturers' responses are respectively recorded at 92 percent, 94 percent, 94 percent and 86 percent in NP, EP, MMCET and NU (see Graph 6 p. 178). Because of the high rate of acceptance of this peculiarity, one would venture to state that it is typical of the English usage of educated Sierra Leoneans.

Table 3: Summary of the responses relating to the examples of the suprasegmental-related peculiarity in the four institutions

Category	NP		EP		MMCET		NU		Mean	
	Students	Lecturers	Students	Lecturers	Students	Lecturers	Students	Lecturers	Students	Lecturers
Supra Segmental	95.5	92.3	94.7	94.3	94.3	94.3	90.3	86	93.7	91.7
Syllable timing	97	92	92	94	96	95	89	83	93.5	91
Down drift	96	95	99	94	95	96	96	90	96.5	93.8
Tonality	95	93	94	96	95	96	94	91	94.5	94
Inadequate intonation	95	93	95	93.5	95	94	87	85	93	91.4
Contrastive stress	94.5	88.5	93.5	94	90.5	90.5	85.5	81	91	88.5

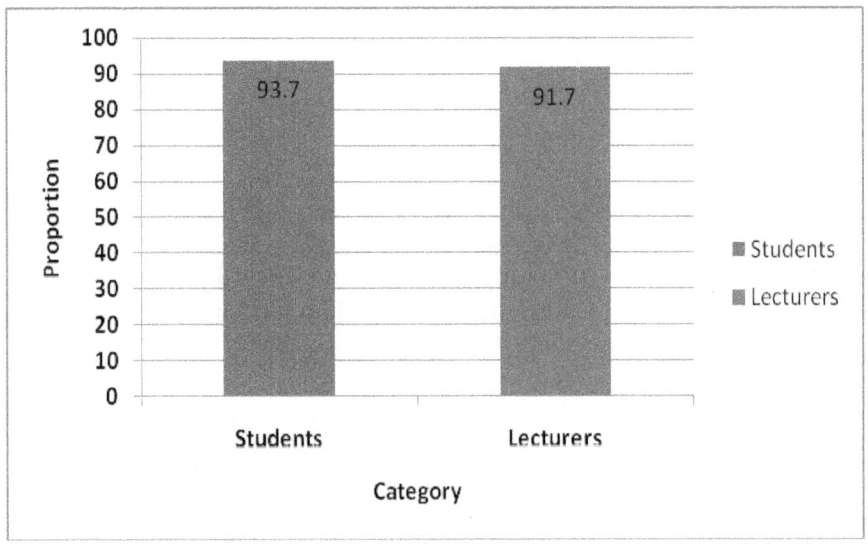

Graph 5: Summary of the responses to the suprasegmental-related peculiarity

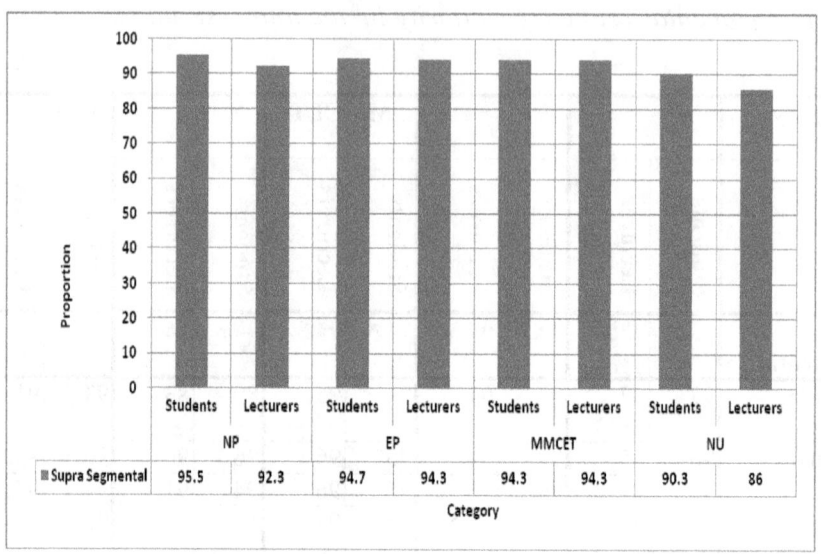

Graph 6: Summary of the responses to the suprasegmental-related peculiarity in the four institutions

The Lexical Peculiarities

This section involves tests and results on collocation, word modification, idiom, innovation and aboriginal-related peculiarities

Test on the Acceptability Level Relating to the Examples of the Collocation-Related Peculiarity

To guage the level of acceptability of this peculiarity – type, the respondents were asked to express their attitudes towards the underlined words in the following sentences:

i) How do you hope to <u>ameliorate</u> the suffering?
(native English collocation-related peculiarity)

ii) TAJCO is very notorious of selling <u>rotten</u> rice to market women.
(native English collocation-related peculiarity)

iii)   … he/she is employed because he/she is capable and <u>addicted</u> to duty. (native English collocation-related peculiarity)

iv)   It is comprised of sharp bends <u>to</u> which most visitors are not conversant. (native English collocation-related peculiarity)

v)   Such information should be put in the press and even <u>over</u> the various community radios now operating.
(native English collocation-related peculiarity)

vi)   Our leaders say we have not yet lost the election but I <u>denied</u> them.
(first language collocation-induced peculiarity)

vii)   My Aunty was a business woman. She would go to Banjul, Dakar and Lagos to buy <u>things</u> and sell.
(first language collocation-induced peculiarity)

viii)   I consulted my other cousin who said I was pregnant. I became worried over the issue and thought of <u>spoiling</u> it.
(first language collocation-induced peculiarity) see p vii

ix)   I too felt <u>bad</u> that I was not there.
(first language collocation-induced peculiarity)

x)   There are other <u>powerful</u> tracks in the album…
(first language collocation-induced peculiarity)

xi)   Nobody can challenge my personality and character as a true APC <u>man</u>.
(first language collocation-induced peculiarity)

xii)   It came to an extend that she took advantage of my submissiveness, call me a fool, <u>bush girl</u> and a rustic.
(first language collocation-induced peculiarity)

xiii) Reports reaching the African Champion from inside the SLPP are that there is great terror and panic among the <u>big men</u>.
(first language collocation-induced peculiarity)

xiv) One evening, Sergeant Major Aruna Sesay who had isolated himself from his <u>palm wine</u> drinking friends for…
(culturally-induced collocation)

xv) … you could boast of only one wrapper and a <u>head tie</u>.
(culturally-induced collocation)

xvi) One morning, Mamy Fatu was busy digging <u>bush yams</u> in the forest when…
(culturally-induced collocation)

The Results of the Responses Relating to the Examples of the Collocation-Related Peculiarity

Table 4 (see p. 181) shows the average mean responses to the collocation-related peculiarity. In this Table, about 86 percent of the students and about 70 percent of the lecturers view this peculiarity-type as acceptable. This result is reflected in Graph 7 (see p. 181). The above result is similar to what obtains in each of the four institutions. The students' responses for instance are estimated at 79 percent, 93 percent, 86 percent and 85 percent in NP, EP, MMCET and NU respectively. Furthermore, the lecturers' responses are respectively estimated at 63 percent, about 73 percent, 69 percent and 79 percent in NP, EP, MMCET and NU (see Graph 8 p. 182). One may use this result to infer that this peculiarity type is evident in the English usage of educated Sierra Leoneans.

Table 4: Summary of the responses relating to the examples of the collocation-related peculiarity in the four institutions

Category	NP Students	NP Lecturers	EP Students	EP Lecturers	MMCET Students	MMCET Lecturers	NU Students	NU Lecturers	Mean Students	Mean Lecturers
Collocation	78.8	60	93	72.5	86.3	69	85	79	85.8	70.1
Native English Collocation	77.5	60	90	65.5	82.8	70	81	71	82.8	66.6
Krio Collocation	80.8	60	95	80	89	68	90	88	88.7	74
Culturally Induced Collocation	78	60	94	72	87	69	84	78	85.8	69.8

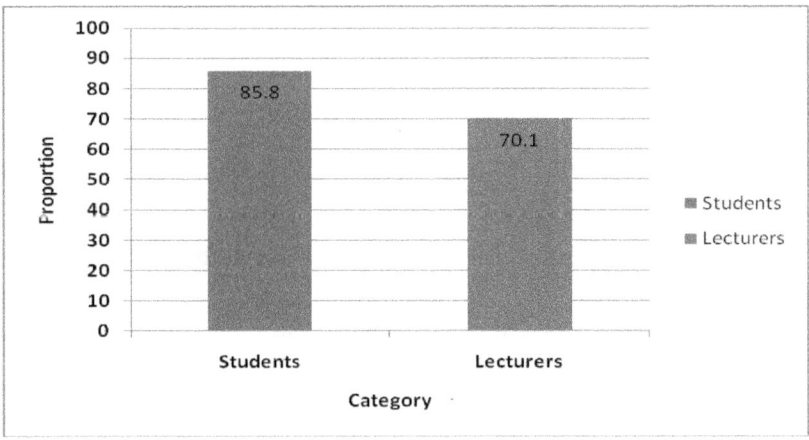

Graph 7: Summary of the responses relating to the examples of the collocation-related peculiarity

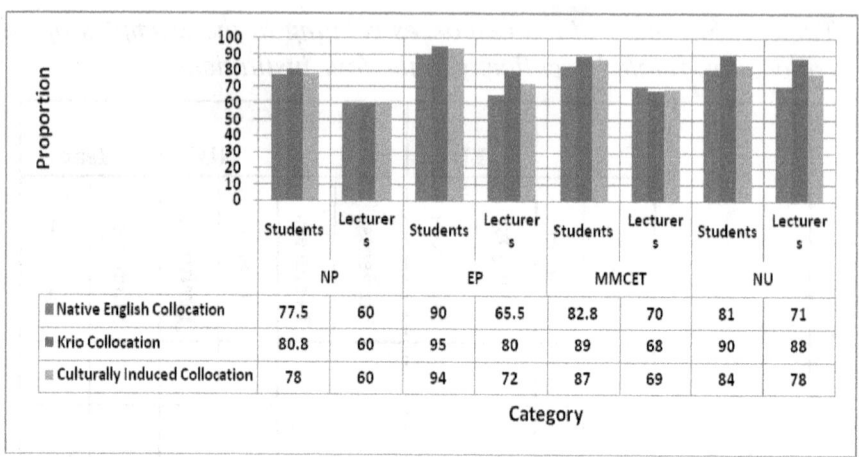

Graph 8: Summary of the responses relating to the examples of the collocation-related peculiarity in the four institutions

Test on the Acceptability Level Relating to the Examples of the Word Modification-Related Peculiarity

To test the level of acceptance of the word modification-related peculiarity, the respondents were asked to express their attitudes towards the underlined words in the following structures:

i) It is also believed that children's sense of reasoning is very small.
(extension of word meaning related peculiarity)

ii) Meanwhile, Awareness Times has five correspondents scattered all over...
(extension of word meaning related peculiarity)

iii) The referee should have called the two captains before taking the decision...
(extension of word meaning related peculiarity)

iv) It is this smell which principally leads to their being ostracised by their husbands, family and friends.
(extension of word meaning related peculiarity)

v)   ... create the chaotic traffic gush for which Dan Street has become <u>renowned</u>
(extension of word meaning related peculiarity)

vi) Whatever job I am fortunate to have, I will <u>manage</u>.
(extension of word meaning related peculiarity)

vii) ... I would call my friend, Olu Gordon of Peep Newspaper to <u>provoke</u> him after we would have swept the votes in Freetown.
(extension of word meaning related peculiarity)

ix) One morning they got her up and ordered her to pack her things out of his house. Sao was too stupefied and when she hestitated, he <u>pulled</u> out his belt and lashed at her.
(extension of word meaning related peculiarity)

x)   She will accuse me today of X, tomorrow Y and the <u>other</u> day Z.
(extension of word meaning related peculiarity)

xi) ...and to their <u>colleague</u> students in other institutions across the country.
(extension of word meaning related peculiarity)

xii) Who told you that you were the only one <u>sleeping with</u> that brat?
(restriction of word meaning related peculiarity)

xiii) They both began <u>to see each other</u> and after about two months, she accepted to date him.
(restriction of word meaning related peculiarity)

xiv) The driver made a fake attempt to <u>dull</u> the music.
(change of word meaning related peculiarity)

xv)   Mr. De'souza George strongly noted that the need to give women equal opportunities to <u>partake</u> in state governance... (change of word meaning related peculiarity)

The Results of the Responses Relating to the Examples of the Word Modification-Related Peculiarity

Table 5 (see p. 184) shows the average mean responses to the word modification -related peculiarity. In this Table, 87 percent of the students and about 69 percent of the lecturers view this peculiarity type as acceptable. This result is reflected in Graph 9 (see p. 185). The above result is similar to what obtains in each of the four institutions. The students' responses for instance are estimated at 82 percent, 91 percent, 88 percent and 87 percent in NP, EP, MMCET and NU respectively. Furthermore, the lecturers' responses are respectively estimated at 73 percent, 70 percent, about 71 percent and 61 percent in NP, EP, MMCET and NU (see Graph 10 p. 185). One may use this result to infer that this peculiarity type is evident in the English usage of educated Sierra Leoneans.

Table 5: Summary of the responses relating to the examples of the word modification-related peculiarity in the four institutions

Category	NP Students	NP Lecturers	EP Students	EP Lecturers	MMCET Students	MMCET Lecturers	NU Students	NU Lecturers	Mean Students	Mean Lecturers
Word Modification	81.8	73.1	91.1	70.2	88.3	70.9	86.9	61.1	87	68.8
Extension	85.3	69.3	93.3	70.7	93.3	62.7	84	66.7	89	67.3
Restriction	80	70	90	80	85	70	80	50	83.8	67.5
Meaning Change	80	80	90	60	86.7	80	96.7	66.7	88.3	71.7

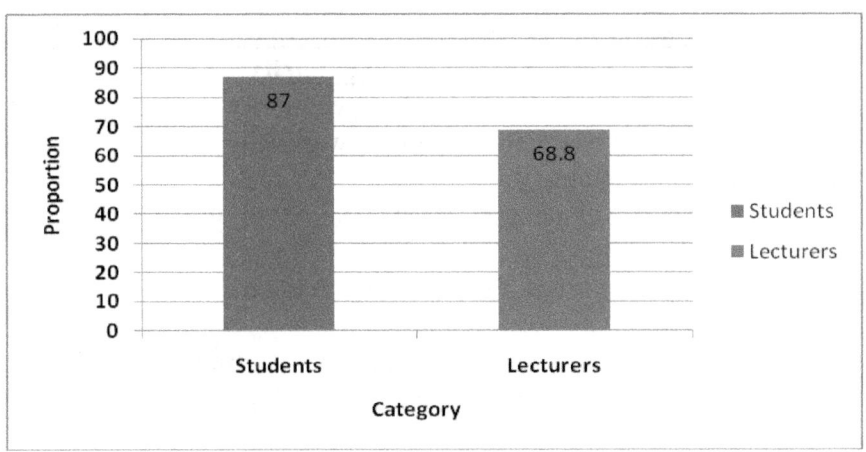

Graph 9: Summary of the responses relating to the examples of the word modification-related peculiarity

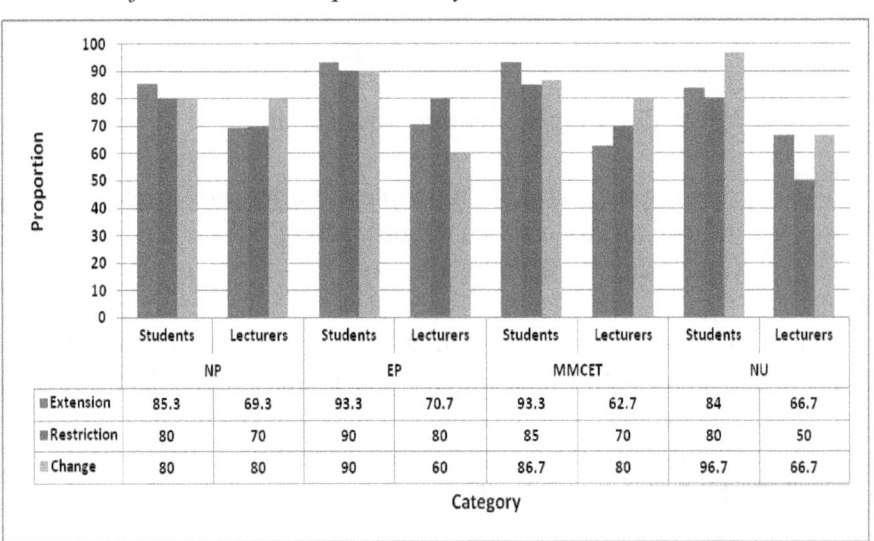

Graph 10: Summary of the responses to the word modification-related peculiarity in the four institutions

Test on the Acceptability Level Relating to the Examples of the Idiom-Related Peculiarity

To test the level of acceptance of this peculiarity-type, the subjects were asked to express their attitudes towards the underlined words in the following sentences:

i) ... the previous government failed to give <u>ear</u> to their concerns.
      (the different use of native English idioms)

ii) ... and anything he said seemed to be getting on her <u>nerve</u>.
      (the different use of native English idioms)

iii) Sulie replied as best as he could without going into <u>details</u>.
      (the different use of native English idioms)

iv) ... they went <u>on</u> blows after unprintable words ignited the duel...
      (the different use of native English idioms)

v) ... alleging that certain people are <u>after their blood</u> in order to have an easy ride in the up coming polls.
      (local idiom related peculiarity)

vi) The new Sierra Leone rulers greedily consumed the <u>national cake</u>, and it went so quickly that in no less than 10 years after indepedence our national treasury was declared empty.
      (local idiom related peculiarity) see p. v

vii) He said he would not <u>clock</u> me any longer but...
      (local idiom related peculiarity)

The Results of the Responses Relating to the Examples of the Idiom-Related Peculiarity

Table 6 (see p. 187) shows the average mean responses to the idiom-related peculiarity. According to this Table, about 82 percent of the students and about 67 percent of the lecturers considered the examples related to this feature as acceptable. This result is also reflected in Graph 11 (see p. 188). Significantly, this overall result is reflected in the four institutions that were involved. For example, with regard to the students' responses, 83 percent, 80 percent, 83 percent and 80 percent were recorded in NP, EP, MMCET and NU respectively. Similarly, the lecturers' responses in NP, EP, MMCET and NU are shown to be 68 percent in each case (see Graph 12 p. 188). This high level of response to this peculiarity type illustrates that the feature is evident in the English usage of educated Sierra Leoneans.

Table 6: Summary of the responses relating to the examples of the idiom-related peculiarity in the four institutions

Category	NP		EP		MMCET		NU		Mean	
	Students	Lecturers	Students	Lecturers	Students	Lecturers	Students	Lecturers	Students	Lecturers
Idiom	83.3	66.7	80	66.7	83.3	66.7	80	66.7	81.7	66.7
Local Idioms	88.2	44.4	58.8	44.4	82.4	55.6	88.2	55.6	79.4	50
English Idioms	76.9	100	92.3	100	84.6	83.3	53.8	83.3	76.9	91.7

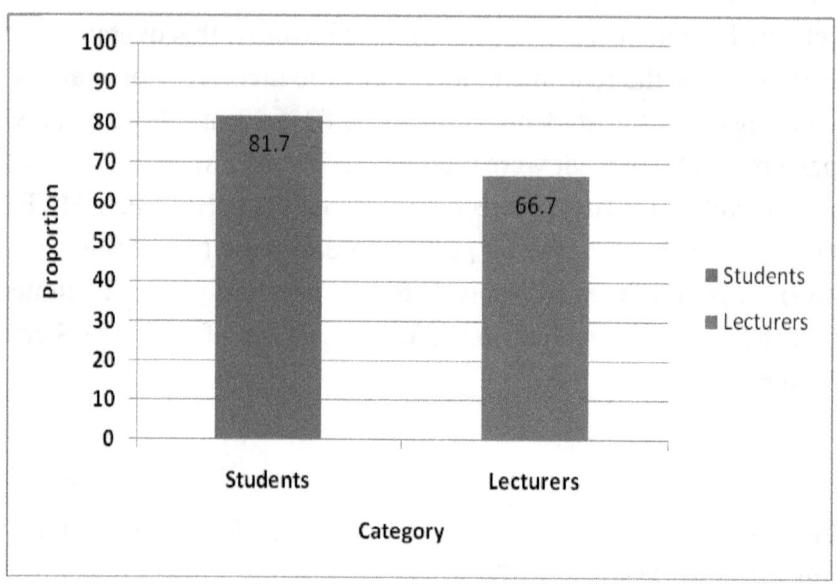

Graph 11: Summary of the responses relating to the examples of the idiom-related peculiarity

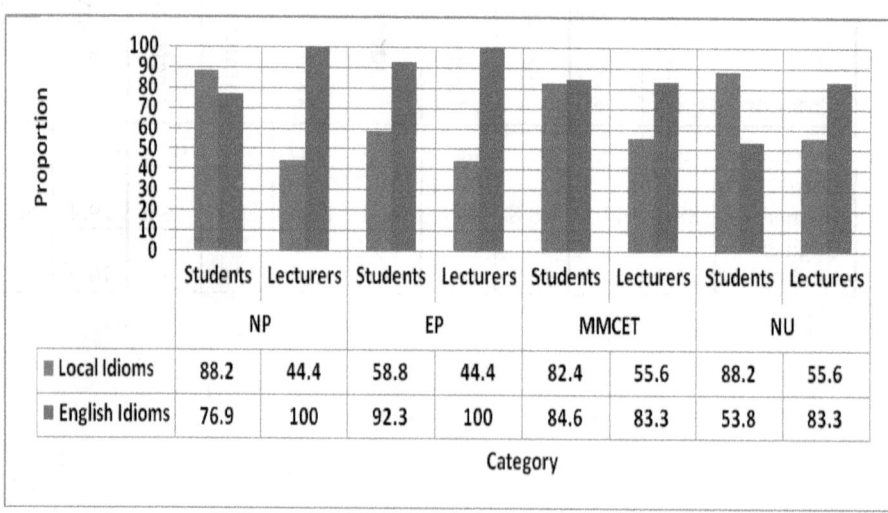

Graph 12: Summary of the responses relating to the examples of the idiom-related peculiarity in the four institutions

Test on the Acceptability Level Relating to the Examples of the Innovation-Related Peculiarity

To gauge the level of acceptability of this peculiarity – type, the respondents were asked to express their attitudes towards the underlined words in the following sentences:

i) The search for children had taken Biareh far and wide, first in his search for the right woman who would deliver his sons primarily and daughters <u>secondarily</u>.
(innovation-related peculiarity)

ii) ... before the second <u>rounds</u> of the league commence.
(innovation-related peculiarity)

iii) ... the people have the <u>unalienable</u> right to vote.
(innovation-related peculiarity)

iv) From this the people of this country will be able to make a firm judgement on whether to choose what is on offer – peace of mind and tranquility – or go for the past <u>troublous</u> years of APC's brutality.
(innovation-related peculiarity)

The Results of the Responses Relating to Examples of the Innovation-Related Peculiarity

Table 7 (see p. 190) shows the average mean responses to the innovation-related peculiarity. In other words, this Table indicates that 86 percent of the students and 58 percent of the lecturers view the examples related to this peculiarity as acceptable. A similar result is shown in Graph 13 (see p. 190). One can deduce from the above that both the students and the lecturers are in accord with the examples under reference presented to them. This result is reflected in all the four institutions. For example, in terms of the students' responses, 83 percent, 93 percent, 88 percent and 83 percent were indicated in NP, EP, MMCET and NU respectively. Also, the lecturers' responses are estimated at 55 percent, 65 percent, 60 percent and 50 percent in NP, EP, MMCET and NU respectively (see Graph 14 p. 191). It can be inferred from the above that the innovation-related peculiarity is typical of educated Sierra Leonean English usage.

Table 7: Summary of the responses relating to the examples of the innovation-related peculiarity in the four institutions

Category	NP		EP		MMCET		NU		Mean	
	Students	Lecturers	Students	Lecturers	Students	Lecturers	Students	Lecturers	Students	Lecturers
Innovation	82.5	55	92.5	65	87.5	60	82.5	50	86.3	57.5

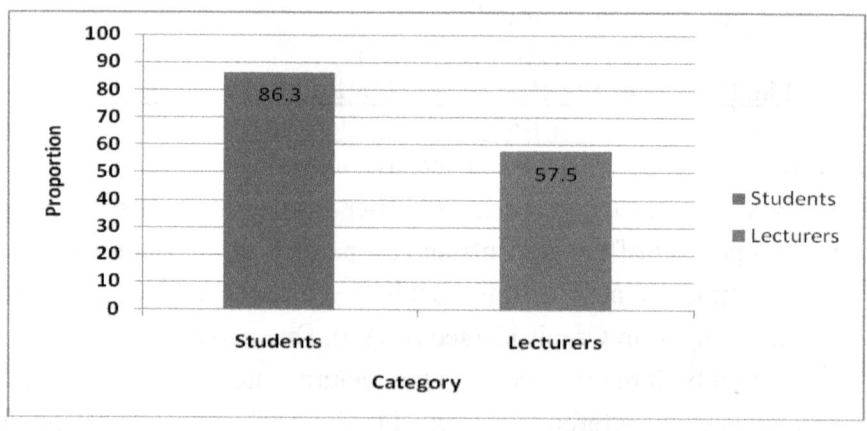

Graph 13: Summary of the responses relating to the examples of the innovation-related peculiarity

Graph 14: Summary of the responses relating to the examples of the innovation-related peculiarity in the four institutions

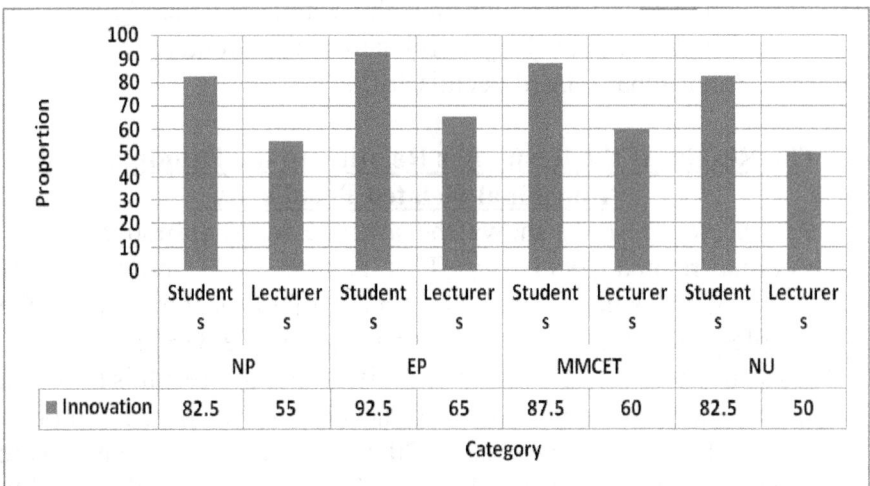

Test on the Acceptability Level Relating to the Examples of the Aboriginal-Related Peculiarity

To test the level of acceptance of this peculiarity – type, the respondents were asked to express their attitudes towards the underlined words in the following sentences:

i) ... the husband apologised to her openly in the chief's court <u>barrie</u>
(aboriginal related peculiarity)

ii) ... the livelihood of many people depends on the marketing of cassava, <u>gari</u> and <u>foo foo</u>.
(aboriginal related peculiarity)

iii) APC <u>Ariogbos</u> terrorise Mambolo
(aboriginal related peculiarity) see p. iii

iv) Paramount Chiefs from the eight chiefdoms arrived in their flowing gowns, many of them chewing <u>kola nuts</u>...
(aboriginal related peculiarity)

v) In all cases the country also witnessed the proliferation of small arms and light weapons, the emergence of civil defence organisations like the <u>Kamajors</u>, the <u>Donsos</u>, the <u>Gbethis</u> and the <u>Tamaboroh</u> across the country.
(aboriginal related peculiarity)

The Results of the Responses Relating to the Examples of the Aboriginal-Related Peculiarity

Table 8 (see p. 193) shows the average mean responses to the aboriginal-related peculiarity. That is, the Table shows that 71 percent of the students and 54 percent of the lecturers view the examples related to this peculiarity as acceptable. Graph 15 (see p. 193) also shows the same result. Significantly, this result is reflected in all the institutions in relation to the students' responses. In other words, 80 percent, 74 percent, 70 percent and 60 percent were recorded in NP, EP, MMCET and NU respectively. With regard to the lecturers' responses, the results are not as uniform as those of the students because while those in NP and MMCET are estimated at 72 percent and 60 percent respectively, those from EP and NU are respectively estimated at 44 percent and 40 percent (see Graph 16 p. 194). However, since the overall result is not affected by the relatively low responses from EP and NU, one could venture to assert that the aboriginal-related peculiarity is evident in educated Sierra Leonean English usage.

Table 8: Summary of the responses relating to the examples of the aboriginal-related peculiarity in the four institutions

Category	NP		EP		MMCET		NU		Mean	
	Students	Lecturers	Students	Lecturers	Students	Lecturers	Students	Lecturers	Students	Lecturers
Aboriginal	80	72	74	44	70	60	60	40	71	54

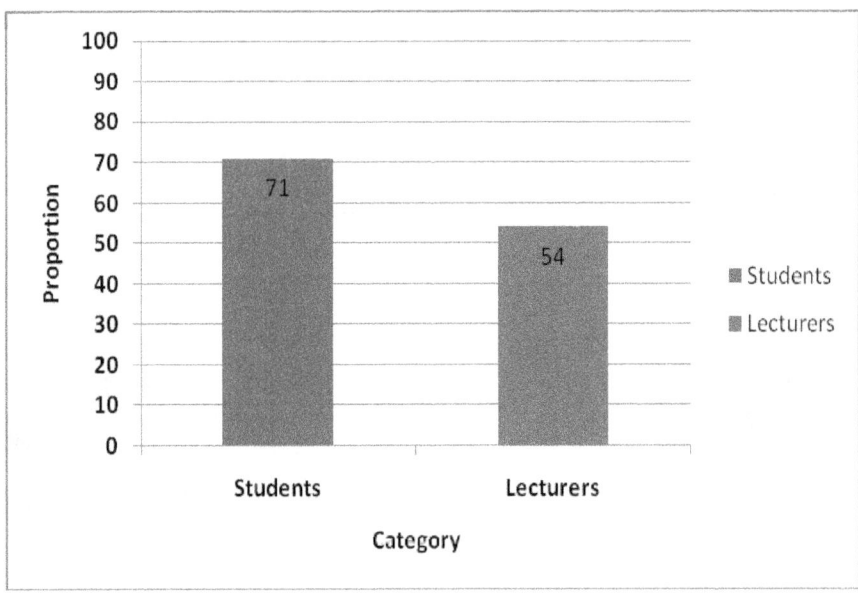

Graph 15: Summary of the responses relating to the examples of the aboriginal-related peculiarity

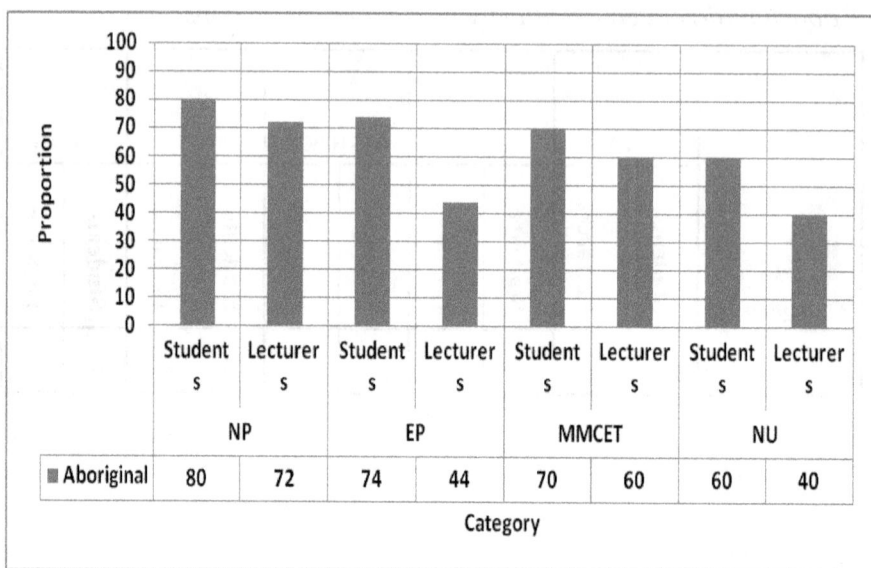

Graph 16: Summary of the responses relating to the examples of the aboriginal-related peculiarity in the four institutions

The Grammatical Peculiarities

This section is concerned with tests and results on noun, pronoun, verb, determiner, adjective, preposition, word class and syntax related peculiarities.

Test on the Acceptability Level Relating to the Examples of the Noun-Related Peculiarity

To test the level of acceptability of this peculiarity–type, the respondents were asked to express their attitudes towards the underlined words in the following sentences:

i)   ... success in life did not only depend on book learning but also on sound moral principles that entailed good <u>characters</u> and discipline.

    (pluralisation with respect to count and non-count nouns)

ii) She however cautioned the students to take their academic <u>works</u> seriously (pluralisation with respect to count and non-count nouns)

iii) ... they have been assigned by the government to sell those <u>lands</u> in that area.
(pluralisation with respect to count and non-count nouns)

iv) They say the reason for the strike is because the management failed to seek the welfare of <u>staffs</u> ...
(pluralisation with respect to count and non-count nouns)

v) ... for the joy of producing healthy and strong <u>off-springs</u>.
(pluralisation with respect to count and non-count nouns)

The Results of the Responses Relating to the Examples of the Noun-Related Peculiarity

Table 9 (see p. 196) indicates the average mean responses to the noun-related peculiarity. That is, 87 percent of the students and 62 percent of the lecturers consider the examples relating to this peculiarity as acceptable. Graph 17 (see p. 196) shows a similar result. It can be discerned that this general result is reflected in the four institutions that are involved in this study. That is, the students' responses are on the average estimated at 80 percent, 92 percent, 86 percent and 90 percent of the students in NP, EP, MMCET and NU respectively. On the other hand, the lecturers' responses are on the average shown to be 68 percent, 72 percent, 48 percent and 60 percent in NP, EP, MMCET and NU respectively (see Graph 18 p. 197). One can deduce from this result that, apart from the unique case of MMCET, the lecturers in the institutions are generally in agreement with this peculiarity type. This relative uniformity in the high level of acceptance rate from both the students and lecturers indicates that the noun related peculiarity is acceptable in educated Sierra Leonean English usage.

Table 9: Summary of the responses relating to the examples of the noun-related peculiarity in the four institutions

Category	NP Students	NP Lecturer	EP Students	EP Lecturer	MMCET Students	MMCET Lecturer	NU Students	NU Lecturer	Mean Students	Mean Lecturer
Noun (Pluralisation)	80	68	92	72	86	48	90	60	87	62

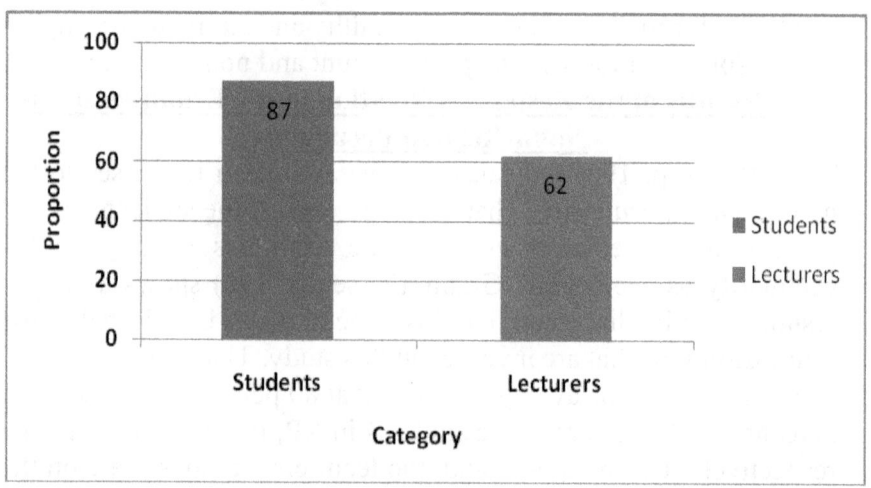

Graph 17: Summary of the responses to the noun-related peculiarity

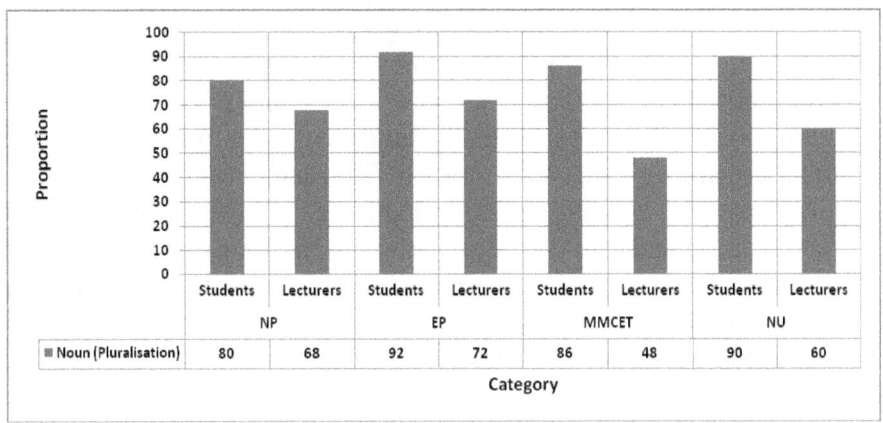

Graph 18: Summary of the responses relating to the examples of the noun-related peculiarity in the four institutions

Test on the Acceptability Level Relating to the Examples of the Pronoun-Related Peculiarity

To gauge the level of acceptance of this peculiarity-type, the subjects were requested to express their views towards the underlined words in the following sentences:

i) ... their long standing differences over <u>who</u> they should support between two aspirants for the APC Symbol.
(difference in pronoun usage)

ii) ... and since he was older than <u>her</u> he didn't see a reason why he should greet her first...
(difference in pronoun usage)

iii) Sadly, even as the two men were hugging <u>themselves</u>, their supporters were engaging <u>themselves</u> along...
(difference in pronoun usage)

iv) He said even though his life and <u>that</u> of his family were...
(difference in pronoun usage)

The Results of the Responses Relating to the Examples of the Pronoun-Related Peculiarity

Table 10 (see p. 198) indicates the average mean responses to the pronoun-related peculiarity. In other words, about 82 percent of the students and 67 percent of the lecturers view the examples relating to this peculiarity type as acceptable. This same result is reflected in Graph 19 (see p. 199). An examination of the results reveals that there is uniformity in the responses in all the four institutions. That is, the students' average mean responses are estimated at 87 percent, 80 percent, 83 percent and 72 percent in NP, EP, MMCET and NU respectively. Also, the lecturers' average mean responses are respectively estimated at 67 percent, 73 percent, 67 percent and 60 percent in NP, EP, MMCET and NU (see Graph 20 p. 199). In view of this high level of acceptance rate of this peculiarity type, one can infer that it is typical of educated Sierra Leonean English usage.

Table 10: Summary of the responses relating to the examples of the pronoun-related peculiarity in the four institutions

Category	NP Students	NP Lecturers	EP Students	EP Lecturers	MMCET Students	MMCET Lecturers	NU Students	NU Lecturers	Mean Students	Mean Lecturers
Pronoun (Usage)	86.7	66.7	80	73.3	83.3	66.7	76.7	60	81.7	66.7

A Survey of Sierra Leonean English *Momodu Turay*

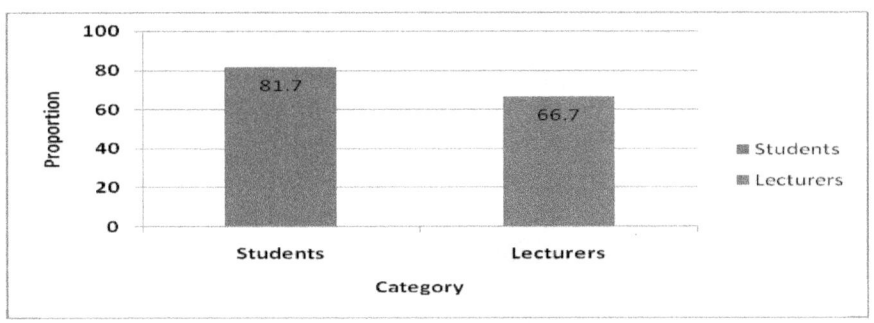

Graph 19: Summary of the responses relating to the examples of the pronoun-related peculiarity

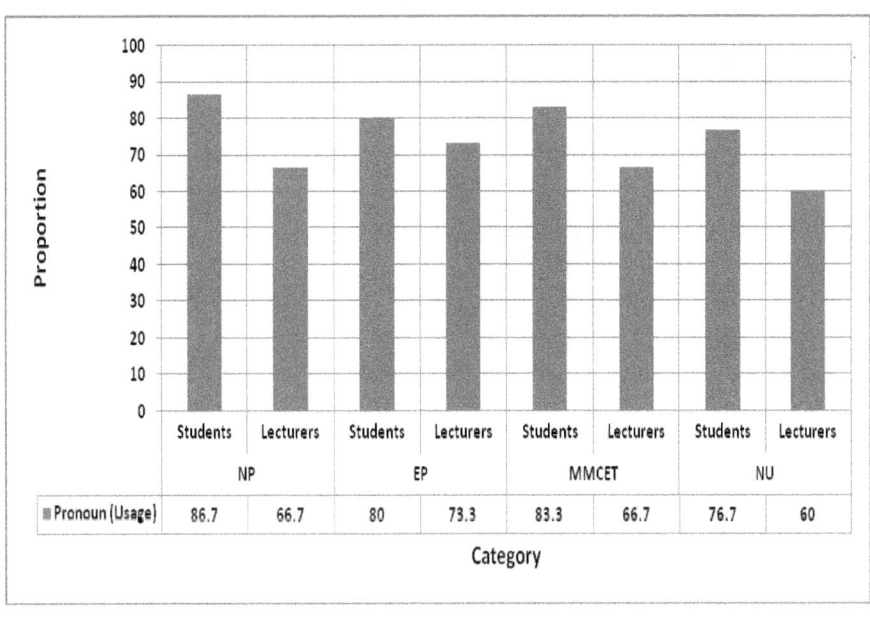

Graph 20: Summary of the responses relating to the examples of the pronoun-related peculiarity in the four Institutions

Test on the Acceptability Level Relating to the Examples of the Verb-Related Peculiarity

To gauge the level of acceptance of this peculiarity-type, the respondents were asked to express their attitudes towards the underlined words in the following sentences:

i) In Koroma's entourage was the familiar face of failed presidential hopeful Charles Francis Margai and the ever loyal Victor Foh...
(concordial-related peculiarity)

ii) The number of rape cases are rising to the skies.
(concordial-related peculiarity)

iii) Secretary General of RUFP Jonathan Kposowa said that Fatou Sankoh together with other members have visited the...
(concordial-related peculiarity)

iv) Motuba was one of those that was strongly against giving an...
(concordial-related peculiarity)

v) This is one of the areas of the country's life that was severely impaired by our fellow Sierra Leoneans
(concordial-related peculiarity)

vi) ... a complete overhauling by government if the will and readiness are there. (concordial-related peculiarity)

vii) It is against this backdrop that the current violence of arson, looting, rapes and antagonism in particularly the southern towns of Moyamba and Pujehun are very worrisome.
(concordial-related peculiarity)

viii) ... asking the District Commissioner Peter Warren to intervene in an effort to restore peace in the township of Rolama.
(infinitive/participle-related peculiarity)

ix) Chief Bai Maka convened a meeting of his elders in an effort to <u>take</u> action against ...
(infinitive/participle-related peculiarity)

x) ... with a view to <u>purchase</u> two generators they claimed they had   for sale.(infinitive/participle-related peculiarity)

xi) I began <u>playing</u> Indian music at anytime they would leave for their night performance.
(infinitive/participle-related peculiarity)

xii) In-service training should also be adequately sponsored to enable teachers <u>develop</u> their capacity.
(infinitive/participle-related peculiarity)

xiii) The Network Movement in support of Solomon Berewa <u>has</u> past Saturday denoted huge quantity of...
(tense/aspect-related peculiarity)

xiv) The indicators are clear and many people <u>are seeing</u> the writings on...
(tense/aspect-related peculiarity)

xv) ... it's high time we <u>take</u> the advantage of the available opportunities and <u>see</u> how we can contribute towards...
(tense/aspect-related peculiarity)

xvi) John saw his father <u>removed</u> from a sack a long knife...
(tense/aspect-related peculiarity)

xvii) When the corpse was laid out at their Block N6 Grafton barracks on Wednesday, they (the family) noticed that he <u>was having</u> whip marks on his face...
(tense/aspect-related peculiarity)

xviii) If I were you, I <u>will</u> be...

(tense/aspect-related peculiarity)
xix) Because I know the SLPP <u>has started</u> campaigning some three years ago.
(tense/aspect-related peculiarity)
xx) The government of Sierra Leone <u>has</u> last Friday reportedly <u>signed</u> a trade agreement with...
(tense/aspect-related peculiarity)
xxi) This statement made those in the gathering including the jurors <u>to laugh</u>
(tense/aspect-related peculiarity)

The Results of the Responses Relating to the Examples of the Verb-Related Peculiarity

The average mean responses to the verb-related peculiarity are indicated in Table 11 (see p. 203). The Table shows that 84 percent of the students and 70 percent of the lecturers are in accord with this type of peculiarity. This result is reflected in Graph 21 (see p. 203). Significantly, the above result is also evident in each of the four institutions. The responses of the students for instance are estimated at 82 percent, 86 percent, about 82 percent and about 87 percent in NP, EP, MMCET and NU respectively. Also, the lecturers' responses are recorded at 62 percent, about 76 percent, 68 percent and 76 percent in NP, EP, MMCET and NU respectively (see Graph 22 p. 204). It can be deduced from these results that the peculiarity under reference is common in educated Sierra Leonean English usage.

Table 11: Summary of the responses relating to the examples of the verb-related peculiarity in the four institutions

Category	NP Students	NP Lecturers	EP Students	EP Lecturers	MMCET Students	MMCET Lecturers	NU Students	NU Lecturers	Mean Students	Mean Lecturers
Verbs	**82.2**	**62**	**86.2**	**75.7**	**81.8**	**68**	**86.8**	**76**	**84.3**	**70.4**
Concord	95	60	77.5	75	67.5	75	85	80	81.3	72.5
Infinitive/Participle	76.7	73.3	96.7	93.3	96.7	76	93.3	93.3	90.8	84
Tense/Aspect	74.9	52.7	84.4	58.8	81.2	53	82.1	54.7	80.7	54.8
(a) Uninflected Verb	86.7	53.3	66.7	66.7	60	46.7	70	56.7	70.9	55.9
(b) Different Inflection	72.5	53	90	50	85	45	84	51	82.9	49.8
(c) Aspectual Usage	74	52.2	84.9	57	83.2	52.4	80	54.3	80.5	54
(d) Inclusion of the to-infinitive	66.4	52.3	96	61.5	96.6	67.9	94.4	56.8	88.4	59.6

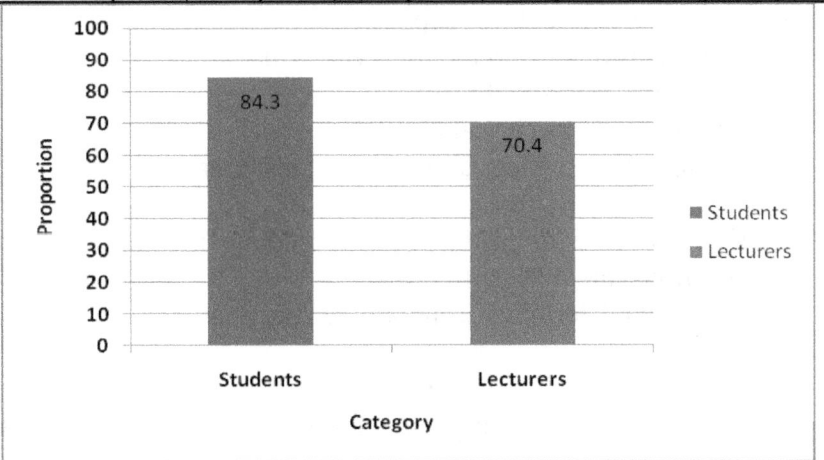

Graph 21: Summary of the responses relating to the examples of the verb-related peculiarity

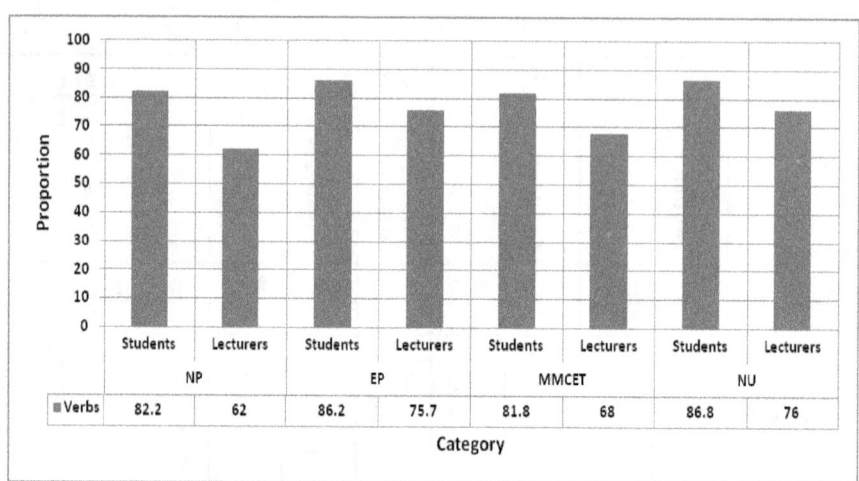

Graph 22: Summary of the responses relating to the examples of the verb-related peculiarity in the four institutions

Test on the Acceptability Level Relating to the Examples of the Determiner Related-Peculiarity

To test the level of acceptance of this peculiarity-type, the respondents were asked to express their attitudes towards the underlined words or gaps in the following sentences:

i) This time they should work as a block to seek their interests and to get as <u>much</u> seats in...
(different determiner usage-related peculiarity)

ii) Because if with just <u>a little</u> over three months away to elections, the APC still...
(different determiner usage-related peculiarity)

iii) ... he won the hearts of the leadership which gave him the opportunity of stepping into the shoes of the vice presidency on <u>few</u> occasions.
(different determiner usage-related peculiarity)

iv) ... as <u>less</u> members of Clearing and Forwarding Agents attended with very short notice
(different determiner usage-related peculiarity)

v) What do you expect of <u>a</u> HTC holder like Hilary Kanu as Head at the Police Media Unit?
(different determiner usage-related peculiarity)

vi) ... who had expressed <u>an</u> interest in the running mate issue.
(article inclusion-related peculiarity)

vii) ... if divulging <u>an</u> information will jeopardise public safety, it should not be done.
(article inclusion-related peculiarity)

viii) ... he said among other things that the statement from Obasanjo was <u>an</u> advice for Sierra Leoneans.
(article inclusion-related peculiarity)

xi) He was responding to ø series of allegations we have previously published about SLRA...
(article omission-related peculiarity)

x) Indeed, this is a moment in our history when women are needed ø most in the area of nation building.
(article omission-related peculiarity)

xi) Drumming and dancing commenced and lasted for <u>one</u> full week.
(article omission-related peculiarity)

xii) At that meeting, the chief spoke for <u>one</u> full hour...
(article omission-related peculiarity)

The Results of the Responses Relating to the Examples of the Determiner-Related Peculiarity

Table 12 (see p. 206) shows the average mean responses to the determiner-related peculiarity. According to this Table, 91 percent of the students and about 80 percent of the lecturers view the examples relating to this feature as acceptable. Graph 23 (see p. 207) shows a similar result. Significantly, the overall result is in consonance with what obtains in all the four institutions. For instance, the students' responses are on the average estimated at 92 percent, 93 percent, 84 percent and 94 percent in NP, EP, MMCET, and NU respectively. Similarly, the lecturers' average responses are recorded at 78 percent, 90 percent, 77 percent and 75 percent in NP, EP, MMCET and NU respectively (see Graph 24 p. 207). This uniformity in the high level of acceptance rate observed from both the students and the lecturers indicates that the determiner-related peculiarity is common in educated Sierra Leonean usage.

Table 12: Summary of the responses relating to the examples of the determiner-related peculiarity in the four institutions

Category	NP Students	NP Lecturer	EP Students	EP Lecturer	MMCET Students	MMCET Lecturer	NU Students	NU Lecturer	Mean Students	Mean Lecturer
Determiner	92	78.2	92.7	88.9	84.4	77.3	93.6	74.7	90.7	79.8
Different use	96	88	88	80	90	72	94	64	92	76
Inclusion	93.3	66.7	93.3	100	70	86.7	100	73.3	89.2	81.7
Omission	86.7	80	96.7	86.7	93.3	73.3	86.7	86.7	90.8	81.7

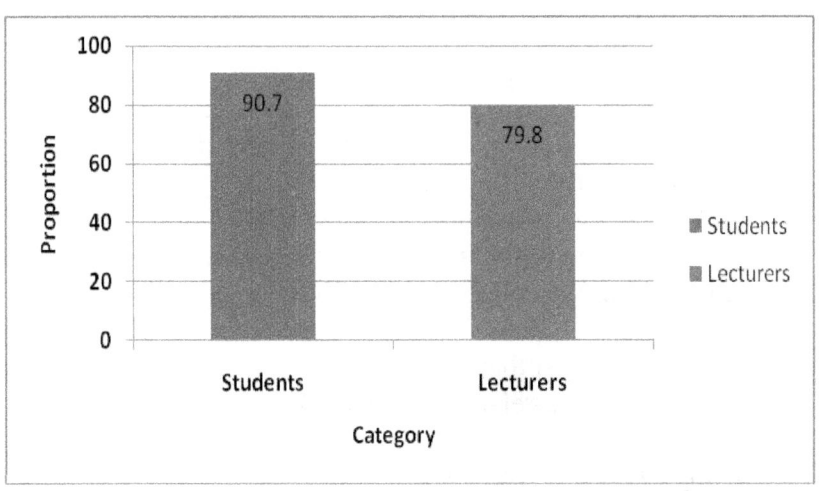

Graph 23: Summary of the responses relating to the examples of the determiner-related peculiarity

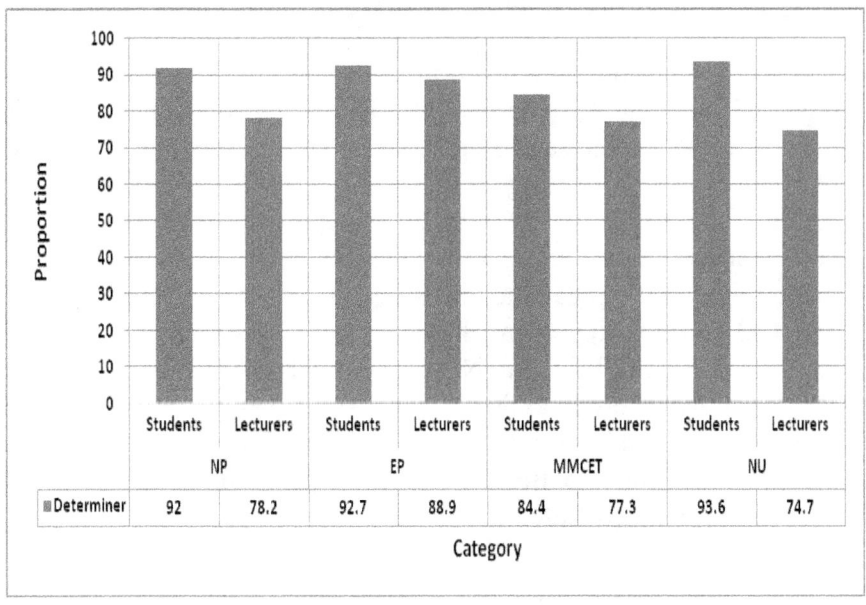

Graph 24: Summary of the responses relating to the examples of the determiner-related peculiarity in the four institutions

Test on the Acceptability Level Relating to the Examples of the Adjective-Related Peculiarity

To test the level of acceptance of this peculiarity-type, the respondents were asked to express their attitudes towards the underlined words in the following sentences:

i) ... Mr. Berewa's running mate seems to have just made things even <u>worst</u> for an already dying political dispensation. (adjective usage-related peculiarity)

ii) ... are even <u>worst</u> than the sinners who go to them to repent. (adjective usage-related peculiarity)

iii) Things became <u>worst</u> when it was announced that Chief Hinga Norman had died...
(adjective usage-related peculiarity)

The Results of the Responses Relating to the Examples of the Adjective-Related Peculiarity

The average mean responses to the adjective-related peculiarity are recorded in Table 13 (see p. 209). This Table indicates about 79 percent of the students and 76 percent of the lecturers are of the view that the examples relating to this peculiarity are acceptable. This result is also reflected in Graph 25 (see p. 209). It is important to note that the above result is similar to that of each of the four institutions. With regard to the students' responses, for instance, about 83 percent, 78 percent, 80 percent and 70 percent are recorded in NP, EP, MMCET, and NU respectively. Also, the lecturers' responses are recorded at 80 percent, 70 percent, 80 percent and 75 percent respectively (see Graph 26 p. 210). The uniformity in the high response rate to this peculiarity type lends credence to its existence among educated Sierra Leoneans.

Table 13: Summary of the responses relating to the examples of the adjective-related peculiarity in the four institutions

Category	NP		EP		MMCE T		NU		Mean	
	Students	Lecturer	Students	Lecturer	Students	Lecturer	Students	Lecturer	Students	Lecturer
Adjectives (Usage)	82.5	80	77.5	70	80	80	75	75	78.8	76.3

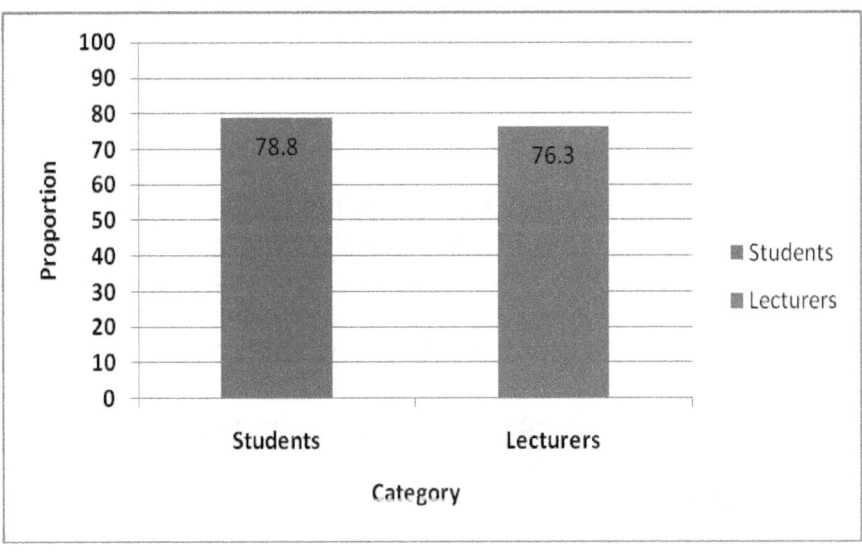

Graph 25: Summary of the responses relating to the examples of the adjective-related peculiarity

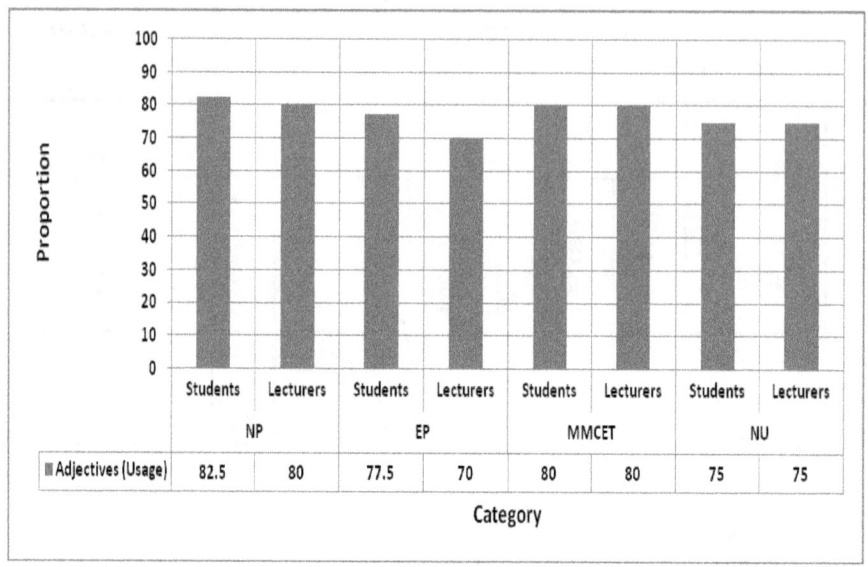

Graph 26: Summary of the responses relating to the examples of the adjective-related peculiarity in the four institutions

Test on the Acceptability Level Relating to the Examples of the Preposition-Related Peculiarity

To gauge the level of acceptance of this peculiarity-type, the respondents were asked to express their attitudes towards the underlined words or gaps in the following sentences:

i) M. L. Bangura went on to state he bears no grudge <u>for</u> Ernest Koroma. (see p iv)
(prepositional usage)

ii) ... as most players threatened to quit the club if the executive reneged <u>from</u> their promise.
(prepositional usage)

iii) Eastend Lions <u>during</u> the weekend registered their first victory in...
(prepositional usage)

iv) The only advantage I would look up to was to produce a child <u>for</u> RSM Sankoh Kamara...
(prepositional usage)

v) TAJCO is very notorious <u>of</u> selling rotten rice to...
(prepositional usage)

vi) ... the professor seems very clearly harboring grievances <u>for</u> the SLPP and Vice President Berewa
(prepositional usage)

vii) Central Parade's Foday Turay and Foday Kargbo alias 'double chair' will contest <u>for</u> the Vice Chairperson position.
(prepositional inclusion)

viii) Dr. Santigie Sesay advocated <u>for</u> the urgent posting of...
(prepositional inclusion)

ix) He said the album comprises <u>of</u> 16 songs...
(prepositional inclusion)

x) I want us to discuss <u>about</u> the lies put out at FM 103.7
(prepositional inclusion)

xi) ... commercial vehicle with registration number ADB 721 which plies the Wellington route dropped ø passengers half way at Ferry junction.
(prepositional omission)

xii) ... and that is the area we must concentrate our effort ø.
(prepositional omission)

xiii) He said the police is not interested in knowing which political party the suspect belong ø ...
(prepositional omission)

The Results of the Responses Relating to the Examples of the Preposition-Related Peculiarity

The average mean responses to the preposition-related peculiarity are shown in Table 14 (see p. 212). According to this Table, about 87 percent of the students and 83 percent of the lecturers considered the examples that illustrate this peculiarity as acceptable. The same result is reflected in Graph 27 (see p. 213). Significantly, this result is similar to those that are observed in the four institutions. For instance, as regards the students, the results are 87 percent, 85 percent, about 88 percent and about 86 percent in NP, EP, MMCET and NU respectively. Similarly, the lecturers' responses are estimated at about 84 percent, 85 percent, 78 percent and 85 percent in NP, EP, MMCET and NU respectively (see Graph 28 p. 213). On the whole, this result shows that the peculiarity type under reference is now part of educated Sierra Leonean English usage.

Table 14: Summary of the responses relating to the examples of the preposition-related peculiarity in the four institutions

Category	NP Students	NP Lecturer	EP Students	EP Lecturer	MMCET Students	MMCET Lecturer	NU Students	NU Lecturer	Mean Students	Mean Lecturer
Preposition	87.4	83.5	85.3	85.4	87.7	77.8	85.6	85.4	86.5	83
Different use	87.1	77.1	74.3	82.9	81.4	80	88.6	82.9	82.9	80.7
Inclusion	85	86.7	88.3	80	88.3	73.3	81.7	86.7	85.8	81.7
Omission	90	86.7	93.3	93.3	93.3	80	86.7	86.7	90.8	86.7

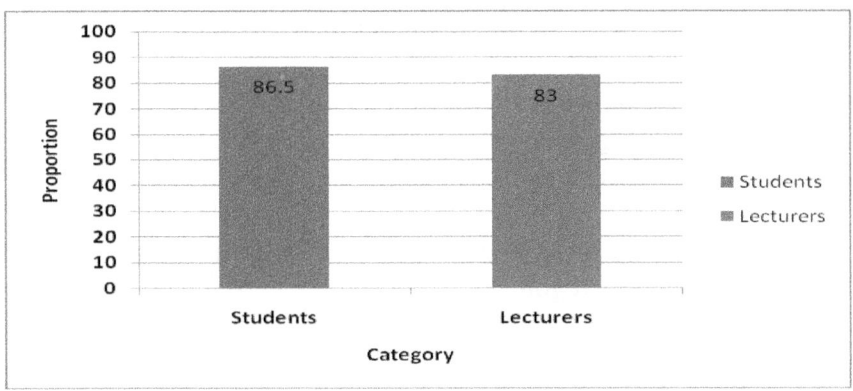

Graph 27: Summary of the responses relating to the examples of the preposition-related peculiarity

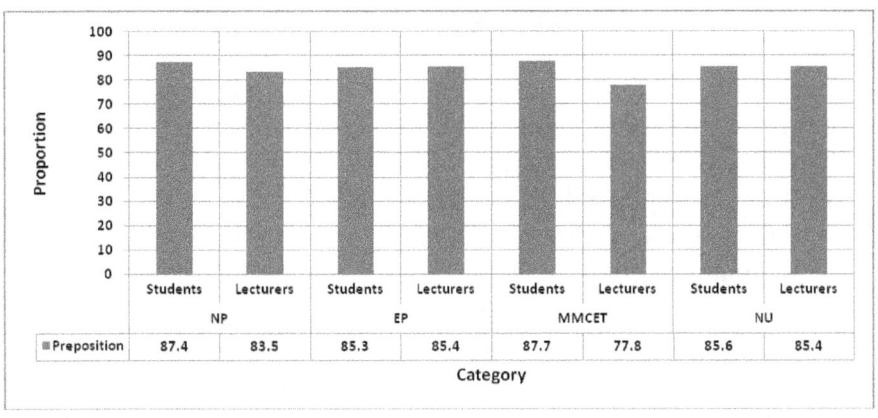

Graph 28: Summary of the responses relating to the examples of the preposition-related peculiarity in the four institutions

Test on the Acceptability Level Relating to the Examples of the Word Class-Related Peculiarity

To test the level of acceptance of this peculiarity-type, the respondents were asked to express their attitudes towards the underlined words in the following sentences:

i) We were so <u>closed</u> that we sometimes sleep together on the same bed.

(word-class related peculiarity)

ii) She added that, at this stage they should be in the position to make <u>matured</u> decisions that...
(word-class related peculiarity)

iii) We have seen how powerful FM 98.1 was during the nine <u>months</u> interregnum
(word-class related peculiarity)

iv) He was my personal <u>assistance</u> when I was ...
(word-class related peculiarity)

The Results of the Responses Relating to the Examples of the Word Class-Related Peculiarity

The average mean responses to the word class-related peculiarity are indicated in Table 15 (see p. 215). In other words, the Table shows that 86 percent of the students and about 78 percent of the lecturers view the examples relating to this type of peculiarity as acceptable. A similar result is shown in Graph 29 (see p. 215). This high level of acceptance rate of the word class-related peculiarity is illustrated in each of the four institutions. That is, among the students, 85 percent, about 88 percent, 88 percent and 85 percent are respectively recorded in NP, EP, MMCET and NU. In a similar vein, the lecturers' responses are respectively estimated at 65 percent, 75 percent, 90 percent and 80 percent in NP, EP, MMCET and NU (see Graph 30 p. 216). One can deduce from the above that this peculiarity is part of the English usage of educated Sierra Leoneans.

Table 15: Summary of the responses relating to the examples of the word class-related peculiarity in the four institutions

Category	NP		EP		MMCET		NU		Mean	
	Students	Lecturers	Students	Lecturers	Students	Lecturers	Students	Lecturers	Students	Lecturers
Word Class	85	65	87.5	75	87.5	90	85	80	86.3	77.5

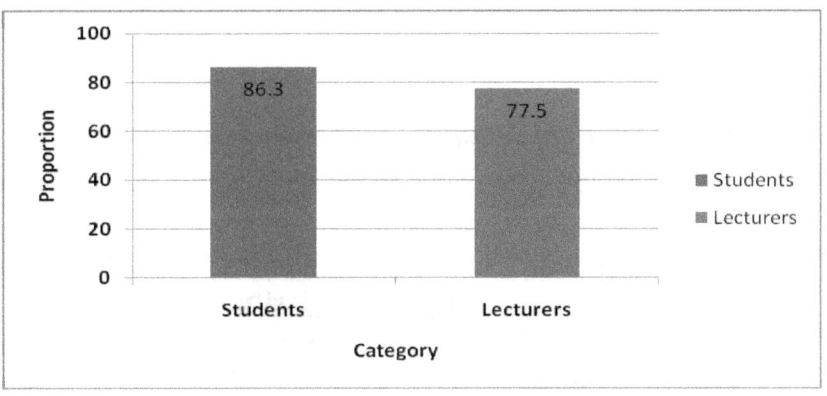

Graph 29: Summary of the responses relating to the examples of the word class-related peculiarity

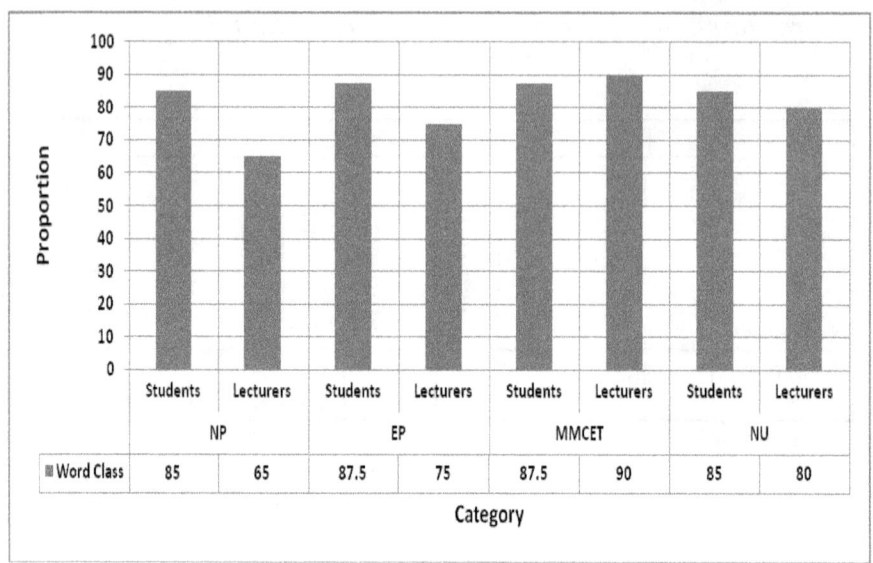

Graph 30: Summary of the responses relating to the examples of the word class-related peculiarity in the four institutions

Test on the Acceptability Level Relating to the Examples of the Syntax-Related Peculiarity

In order to test the level of acceptance of this peculiarity-type, the respondents were asked to express their attitudes towards the following:

i) ... and end up abusing their positions either by perpetrating criminal activities or <u>condoning criminals</u>.
(imbalance-related peculiarity)

ii) ... and it would be judged illogical, counter-productive and <u>an exercise in futility</u>.
(imbalance-related peculiarity)

iii) ... but people should do their jobs competently and <u>with fairness</u>.
(imbalance-related peculiarity)

iv) Neighbours poured water over her head and <u>a tin of milk was given to her</u>.
(imbalance-related peculiarity)

v) The people of this country will be put in a position <u>to be able to make up</u> their minds rationally instead <u>of relying</u> on APC's criticism of the good things SLPP had achieved for this country.
(imbalance-related peculiarity)

vi) As a <u>surveyor</u> by <u>profession</u>, he has only helped many students in…(repetition-related peculiarity)

vii) Bangura said the only <u>reason</u> for the postponement of the elections date was only <u>because</u> the ruling party has…
(repetition-related peculiarity)

viii) Justifying the need of the twin taps, the Chairman of De Humanitarian Organisation, Muctarr Daramy said <u>because</u> of the scarcity of pipe borne water and the difficulty in fetching water <u>prompted</u> them to re-erect them.
(repetition-related peculiarity)

ix) … the utmost <u>reason</u> for such an evil plan is <u>due to the fact</u> that Kenema district is the party's strong hold.
(repetition-related peculiarity)

x) … we will carry our leader shoulder high and <u>walk</u> <u>on foot</u> to the NEC office
(repetition-related peculiarity)

xi) <u>Let</u> him <u>don't</u> confuse voters.
(repetition-related peculiarity)

xii) The idea of instituting a commission of inquiry is not a witch hunting venture but rather a system of transparency which

will ensure there is a clean slate <u>from</u> which the government can operate <u>from</u>.
(repetition-related peculiarity)

xiii) No sooner the boy opened the letter ø he got blind.
(structural omission-related peculiarity)

xiv) Aunty Mary's devotion ø and interest in our family is second to none.
(structural omission-related peculiarity)

xv) She will accuse me today of X, tomorrow of Y and the other day ø Z.
(structural omission-related peculiarity)

xvi) While John Conteh refused to hand over the money, he was then invited to the Shell Police Post. <u>Whilst ø at the station</u>, the leader of the team H. S. Kargbo went back to the shop to forcefully take the money from Conteh's wife.
(structural omission-related peculiarity)

xvii) Our locally based footballers should be given appropriate training and support so that they could do better ø than relying on 'professionals'
(structural omission-related peculiarity)

xviii) Who else has the power to rig elections ø than the incumbent?
(structural omission-related peculiarity)

xix) … it makes no ø news when people move back to SLPP than it makes when an individual moves from the SLPP to the PDMC.
(structural omission-related peculiarity)

xx) <u>ø Standing in the dock before Magistrate Sam Margai</u>, the statement of offence was read to him through an interpreter
(structural omission-related peculiarity)

xxi) Nanny Tenneh said what had happened between <u>me and Sheriff</u> had brought a case…
(structural difference-related peculiarity)

xxii) … and told me that she heard what happened between <u>me and Andrew</u>
(structural difference-related peculiarity)

xxiii) Speaking to this press, the principal, Mr. Domonic T. G. Gogra on Monday 5th November at his school office <u>he</u> explained that he would first and foremost like to…
(structural difference-related peculiarity)

xxiv) On the other hand, Wusum Stars have played five matches and <u>only</u> lost to FC Kallon.
(modifier placement-related peculiarity)

xxv) … ordered the suspension of Prince Harding, pending the outcome of investigations into the course of the crash <u>by a panel of aviation specialists</u>.
(modifier placement-related peculiarity)

xxvi) … regional and unit commanders of the police have been directed to arrest and prosecute anyone committing an offence liable to breach the peace security of the state before, during and after elections <u>without fear or favour</u>.
(modifier placement-related peculiarity)

xxvii) Every day these boys harass local and international guests who visit our beaches <u>with impunity</u>.
(modifier placement-related peculiarity)

xxviii) … are the only countries that have so far met all the four primary convergence criteria while Sierra Leone has <u>only</u> met three.
(modifier placement-related peculiarity)

xxixi) The next morning VP Berewa visited the NDA and PLP offices where he addressed these two parties' supporters together with Baba Conteh and Amadu Jalloh.
(modifier placement-related peculiarity)

xxx) In other words, if one fails to adhere to the law, that person also is corrupt not so?
(universal tag-related peculiarity)

xxxi) I will advise people to play and play.
(reduplication-related peculiarity)

xxxii) So so suffering
(reduplication-related peculiarity)

xxxiii) Sir Albert said, "gentlemen, you need not tell me any longer that after the bomb was dropped the meeting suddenly came to an abrupt end".

Marah observed, "certainly. Well, Sir Albert, Johnny Paul was now in a state of dilemma as he held the belief that whenever he was in public or even if he hid himself in the most secured place he could be the target of a bomb attack".
(responses to negative yes/no statements/questions)

The Results of the Responses Relating to the Examples of the Syntax-Related Peculiarity

Table 16 (see p. 221) expresses the average mean responses to the syntax-related peculiarity. In this Table, about 83 percent of the students and about 77 percent of the lecturers considered the examples relating to this peculiarity type acceptable. This result is reflected in Graph 31 (see p. 222). In specific terms, the above result is reflected in each of the four institutions. That is, with regard to the students' responses, 77 percent, 87 percent, 87 percent and 80 percent are recorded in NP, EP, MMCET and NU respectively. Moreover, the lecturers' responses are respectively estimated at 68 percent, 86 percent, 69 percent and about 83 percent in NP, EP, MMCET and NU (see Graph 32 p. 222). This high level of acceptance rate can be used to assert that the peculiarity under review is evident in the English usage of educated Sierra Leoneans.

Table 16: Summary of the responses relating to the examples of the syntax-related peculiarity in the four institutions

Category	NP Students	NP Lecturers	EP Students	EP Lecturers	MMCET Students	MMCET Lecturers	NU Students	NU Lecturers	Mean Students	Mean Lecturers
Syntax	77.2	67.6	87	86.1	87.1	69.3	79.8	82.8	82.8	76.5
1. Imbalance	77.1	71.4	82.9	71.4	85.7	77.1	78.6	82.9	81.1	75.7
2. Redundancy	73.8	75	81.3	85	78.8	60	78.8	72.5	78.1	73.1
3. Structural Omission	78	64	94	88	84	80	92	76	87	77
(a) Omission of the comparative word	72.7	54	92	96	71.3	90	96	85.3	83	81.3
(b) Omission of content and function words	83.3	74	96	80	96.7	70	88	66.7	91	72.7
4. Universal Tag	80	60	90	100	100	60	70	100	85	80
5. Structural Diff	71.7	71.7	91.7	80	90	68.3	92.5	70	86.5	72.5
(a) Order of Pronouns	60	70	90	80	90	70	95	60	83.8	70
(b) Pronoun Inclusion	83.3	73.3	93.3	80	90	66.7	90	80	89.2	75
6. Placement of Modifiers	70	86.7	88.9	71.1	83.3	73.3	90	64.4	83.1	73.9
7. Reduplication	70	80	90	60	70	60	60	60	72.5	65
8. Responses to Yes/No question	60	60	100	80	80	80	90	80	82.5	75

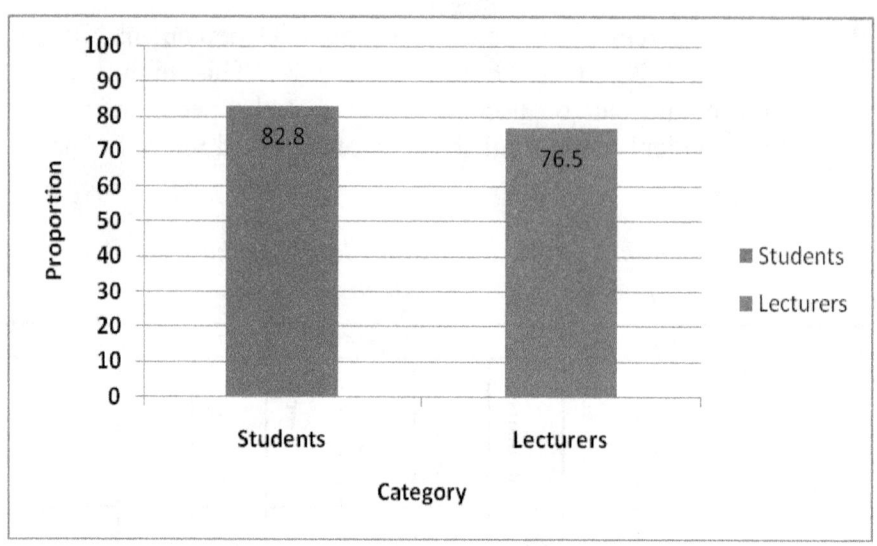

Graph 31: Summary of the responses relating to the examples of the syntax-related peculiarity

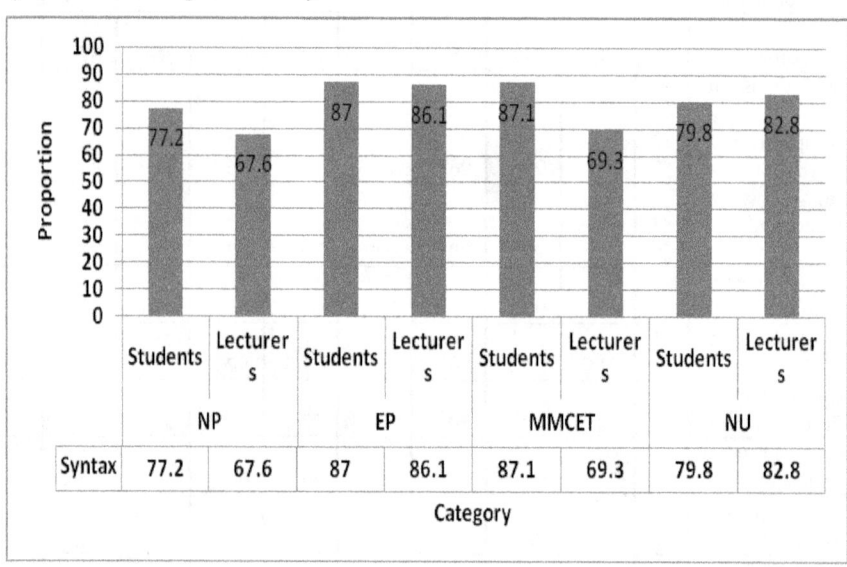

Graph 32: Summary of the responses relating to the examples of the syntax-related peculiarity in the four institutions

Conclusion

The phonological, lexical, and grammatical peculiarities highlighted in this study have been shown to have a high level of acceptance among the respondents. This reflects their wide-spread acceptance in the nation at large. They are therefore now part of the Eglish usage of educated Sierra Leoneans. Against this background, is it not necessary for these peculiarities to be recognised in order to save ourselves from the foolhardiness of "[seeming] to be running away from something that is already part of [us]?" (Pemagbi, 1989:22).

CHAPTER SIX

SUMMARY, CONCLUSIONS, RECOMMENDATIONS AND THE FUTURE OF ENGLISH AND ITS IMPLICATIONS FOR THE SIERRA LEONEAN VARIETY

Introduction
This chapter is concerned with the summary of the findings of this study, its conclusions, recommendations and projections about the future of English with respect to the emerging Sierra Leonean variety.

Summary
The findings of this study include the following:

i) The majority of the respondents view the examples relating to the highlighted features as acceptable. For example, Table 17 (see p. 226) provides a summary of the responses to the phonological, lexical and grammatical peculiarities. According to this Table, about 87% of the students and about 76% of the lecturers regard the examples representing these peculiarity-types as acceptable. This result is reflected in Graph 33 (see p. 226). It can also be observed that this result is reflected in all the four institutions. That is, according to Graph 34 (see p. 227) about 87%, 88%, about 87% and about 85% of the students in NP, EP, MMCET and NU respectively consider these peculiarity-types as acceptable. Similarly, the lecturers' responses are estimated at about 76%, 78%, 76% and about 74% in NP, EP, MMCET and NU respectively. These results further confirm that there is a variety of English in Sierra Leone.

ii) It is also discerned that the highlighted tendencies are not restricted to the Sierra Leonean English variety. That is, many non-native varieties and a few native varieties are shown to exhibit the tendencies under review. This indicates that these tendencies have led to the emergence of legitimate English varieties across the globe.

ii) With respect to the causes of the features, this study considers but goes beyond the over-used theory of mother-tongue transfer. This means that first-language transfer is not advanced as the only possible cause of the highlighted features. Instead, the researcher also considers the likelihood of the subjects' (as L_2 learners) unfamiliarity with the rules of the target language. In this regard, in addition to the influence of language teaching methods in the colonial days, learning-induced factors which include the over-generalisation of target language rules (also referred to as analogy), ignorance of native English rules, incomplete application of target language rules and the influence of culture are also considered. This finding lends credence to that of Mesthrie who, in discussing the implausibility of exclusively adducing first language transfer to the development of African, South and Southeast Asian English features, observes that such a view implies that "all languages of Africa-Asia are the same in structure, united in their differences from English" (Mesthrie, 2006: 1141).

Table 17: *Summary of the responses relating to the total peculiarities in the four institutions*

Category	NP		EP		MMCET		NU		Mean	
	Students	Lecturers	Students	Lecturers	Students	Lecturers	Students	Lecturers	Students	Lecturers
PHONOLOGICAL	95.5	93.2	93.9	92.5	92.7	93.3	91.1	88.2	93.3	91.8
LEXICAL	81.3	65.4	86.1	63.7	83.1	65.3	78.9	59.4	82.4	63.4
GRAMMATICAL	84.1	71.4	86	78.3	84.7	72.1	84.1	74.2	84.8	74
TOTAL	87.0	76.7	88.7	78.2	86.8	76.9	84.7	73.9	86.8	76.4

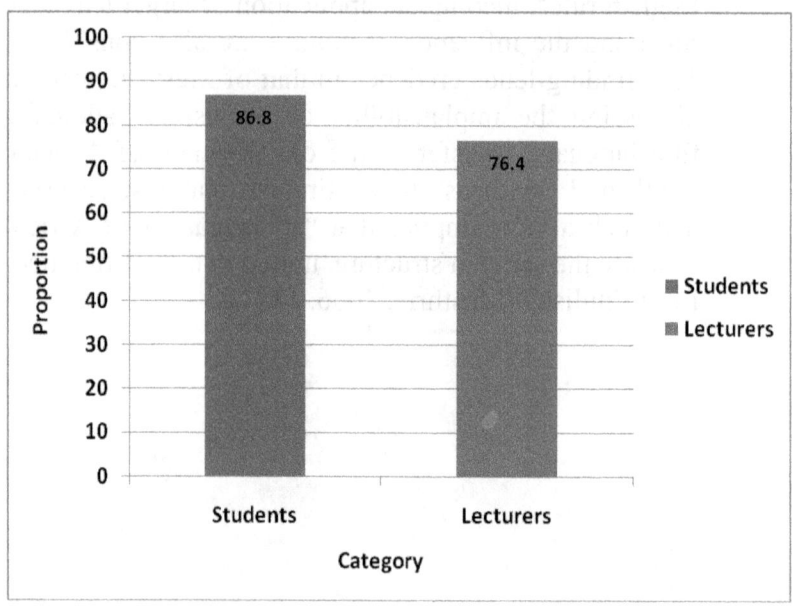

Graph 33: *Summary of the responses relating to the total peculiarities*

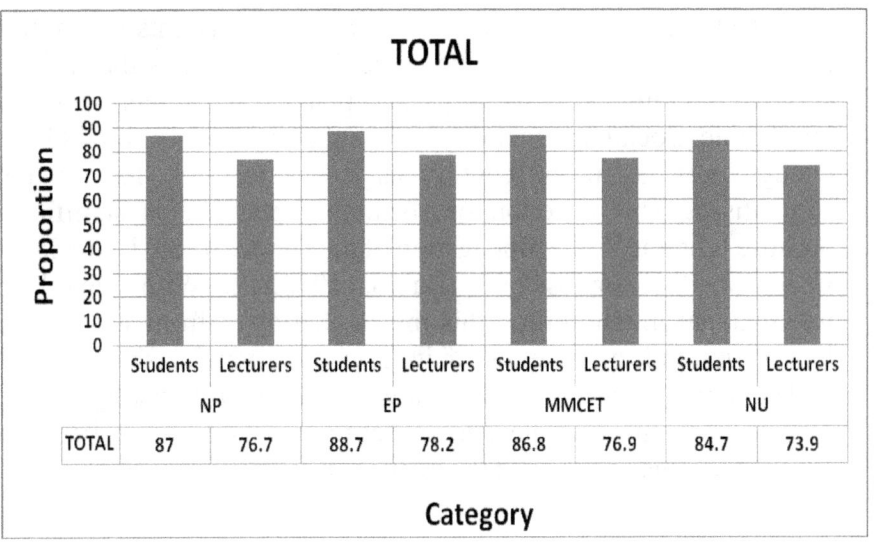

Graph 34: Summary of the responses to the total peculiarities in the four institutions

Conclusions
This study has attempted to demonstrate that identifiable forms of English usage peculiar to Sierra Leone are evident. These forms are not haphazard in nature since they appear to show some level of systematicity. A new English variety has therefore emerged in Sierra Leone. Will it be wrong to give this variety a name? After all, such a variety can provide a background which, an 'alien' English – something from abroad-never could. Native as well as non-native varieties are being labelled for identification purpose. Examples include British English, American English, Australian English, Malaysian English, Ghanaian English and Nigerian English. So why not Sierra Leonean English?

A significant step in this direction is the codification of the features that are typical of this variety which identify its users and distinguish them from those of other varieties. Such a step should involve important stakeholders including teachers and students of English across the country. It should be noted that the features that will be codified should be socially acceptable and internationally intelligible. Social acceptability means that the variety should have enough prestige in the country as it has features that are not stigmatised. This criterion of social acceptability is significant because 'without it, the propagation of the variety would be difficult, if not in fact impossible' (Banjo, 1996:82). With regard to international intelligibility, this means that apart from serving the local communication needs of its users, the variety should serve wider communication needs within the English-speaking world. This is to ensure that there is no communication barrier between speakers of this variety and those of other English varieties.

The responses to the highlighted features in the fifth chapter reveal that they have gained widespread acceptability in the country. Also, in spite of the differences between the variety and native English or any other variety for that matter, they are not significant enough to lead to communication breakdown. It is therefore hoped that this study can make a meaningful contribution towards the codification process.

Recommendations for Further Research
This study cannot claim to have comprehensively investigated the English usage of educated Sierra Leoneans. There are a few areas which require further research. These include:

i) A longitudinal study involving a group of educated Sierra Leoneans to investigate their usage at intervals with a view to identifying tendencies that characterise their English usage. This may indicate how 'fossilised' these tendencies have become in the subjects' usage.

ii) An investigation into the features of groups of educated Sierra Leoneans of different academic levels can also be carried out. That is, like Sey (1973), Banjo (1971) and

Conteh-Morgan (1997), subjects of different academic backgrounds can be engaged in order to identify the common features that typify each group. This can be done against the numerical strength of each group in the country and the level of prestige associated with it. Also, features that cut across all the groups can be identified. These considerations may influence the variety and features that will be selected for the country.

iii) An investigation involving wider sources of the discoursal features in the country may also be considered. For example, in relation to phatic communion, Sierra Leoneans tend to express politeness by mentioning the main issue(s) in a conversation only after some opening courtesies. It is likely that this tendency can be elicited if the subjects are requested to write letters on specific topics or to engage in similar modes of communication.

The Future of English and Its Implications for the Sierra Leonean Variety

In view of the pluricentricity of the English language, there have been concerns about what the future holds for the world's most powerful language. The English language has so far survived and still survives in spite of its fragmentation into different varieties. To explain this phenomenon, we have to consider two concepts which are of comparatively recent origins in Socio-linguistics and which relate to language functions. These are nationality (giving rise to nationalism) and nation (giving rise to nationism).

Simply and briefly, "a nationality is a group of people who think of themselves as a social unit different from other groups but not just on a purely local scale" (Fishman, 1984:2). In this respect, a nationality should be distinguished from an ethnic group which is like a nationality but whose socio-cultural organisation is smaller, more particularistic and more localistic. Also, a nationality does not necessarily have an independent territory of its own. That is, the term 'nationality' is neutral with respect to the existence or non-existence of a political boundary. A nation, on the other hand, is "any political-territorial unit which is largely or increasingly under the control of a particular nationality" (Fishman, 1972: 5) cited in Fasold (1984: 2). These two concepts have respectively given rise to the terms nationality and nationism. Nationalism refers to the feelings that develop from and support nationalities, while nationism is concerned with the political problems of governing.

The function of language in nationism is in the area of general government administration and education; that is, it serves the purpose of communication within the governing institutions, and between government and the people, and as a medium of instruction that effectively transmits knowledge to school children. In respect to nationalism, language together with culture, religion and history is a major component. Language serves as a link with the glorious past. That is, language is part of the history itself; and it is advantageous to the nationality to have a language of its own. Also, for nationalism, language serves the purpose of contrastive self-identification (Fishman, 1972). That is, they refer to the feelings of members of a nationality that they are united and identified with others who speak the same language, and that they contrast with and are separated from those who do not speak that language. This distinction between nationism and nationalism borders on two distinct functions of language; namely the official (or nationist) function and the nationalist function.

Now, with this distinction in mind, we can turn our attention to the survival of the English language. There is no doubt that where the English language is spoken and used as a native language, it is serving, both the nationist and the nationalist functions. There is then no threat of its becoming obsolete or eliminated in the near future. Therefore, when we talk about the survival of the English language, we are thinking mainly of the continued existence of the non-native varieties and their continued functions in non-native English communities. The survival of these varieties will, to a great extent, depend on government language policies in general and on education policies in particular. It will also depend on the attitudes which the non-native users have to particular policies. Consequent on such policies and attitudes, some of these varieties will develop further, fulfiling more and more functions. For others, their range of functions may diminish and they may gradually become less institutionalised.

There seem to be various possibilities in policy which may lead to differing effects. For example, one possibility is where a local language performs both official or nationist and nationalist functions. This would leave English with no function or very little function. This is the case with Tanzania, where English has given place to Kiswahili, which now functions as the national and official language, as distinct from the international language. Similarly, before Bahasa Malaysia became the national and official language in Malaysia, a strongly developing non-native variety of English existed there. With the conversion process from English to Bahasa Malaysia throughout the education system which is now complete, the range of functions for English has diminished and the type of English used has changed considerably, particularly among the speakers of the younger generation.

Another possibility is where a local language is used as the national language and English as the official language. This would leave English with some, often quite important functions. This would appear to be the case in, for example, Kenya and Uganda. While Kenya and, to some extent, Uganda have opted for Kiswahili as a national language, the functions of English in these countries are slightly different. Whereas in Kenya you may have overlapping roles in certain official domains, such domains are purely the preserve of English in Uganda. While English is the official language in these countries and still has important functions, it is believed by some scholars that the importance of English is manifested more in the rural areas. It is felt in this regard that while English will be widely used by an educated elite, its functions may even decrease for the rest of the community, particularly in the rural areas.

A third possibility is where English is the official language, and no local language is raised to the status of a national language, thus giving English a wide range of functions. Some functions may be given to the local languages. This would appear to be the case in Ghana, Nigeria and so on. In these countries, English is used as the medium of instruction in the education system and for many functions in the community. It often enjoys a high status as against the local languages. Although the importance of English is recognised, there have been moves not only to have local languages used for instruction in the early years of primary school, but also to extend their range as school subjects and subjects at colleges and universities.

There are of course variations within these possibilities. For example, in Singapore, English shares the official status with Mandarin, Tamil and Malay, with Malay designated as the national language. Also, in the Southern African region, while English is predominantly the official language, its status and functions vary from nation to nation. In addition to the growing awareness of nationalism in the political arena, there is the call not only to use the local languages creatively in literature but also to reject the use of English for the preservation of non-native English cultures (Wa Thiong'o, 1986). Although the enthusiasm in this regard is yet to be tested, one wonders what the effect will be in the range of functions and the development of non-native varieties of English.

Whatever the future holds, there are two reasons why English will continue to be needed by non-native English nations. One is its use as an international language all over the world, and the other is its function as a neutral language of wider communication within a country.

This view is similar to Crystal's in his discussion of English as an international language. He states that:

> We may, in due course, all need to be in control of two standard Englishes – the one which gives us our national and local identity and the other which puts us in touch with the rest of the human race (Crystal, 1988:265).

Significantly, these two factors are shown to be evident in Sierra Leone. With regard to the use of English as an international language, Fyle (1968), for example, observes that in Sierra Leone "English is the country's official language and the language of foreign communication, and also a vehicle of world culture (Fyle, 1968: 8). Also, in addition to Krio which is the contry's lingua franca, English serves as a neutral language of wider communication among the educated elites from different regions of Sierra Leone. In fact, this neutralist function coupled with the relatively negligible number of native speakers at its disposal is a redeeming quality in Sierra Leone in relation to its position as a possible contender for the choice of a national language in the country. English thus falls into the third category of the possibilities highlighted above which involves the use of English to perform a wide range of functions. One could therefore deduce that the English language has a place in Sierra Leone for a long time to come.

However, what perhaps needs to be done in order to preserve the language as it is spoken and written in the country is a change of attitude towards it involving both native and non-native speakers. What Kachru (1982) refers to as "attitudinal readjustment" includes the following admonitions for non-native speakers:

i) non-native users must now dissociate English from the colonial past, and not treat it as a coloniser's tool;

ii) they must avoid regarding English as an evil influence which necessarily leads to westernisation;

iii) non-native users should accept the large body of English literature written by local creative writers as part of the native literary tradition. In addition to interpreting national traditions and aspirations to readers across linguistically and culturally pluralistic areas, these literatures have an international reading public;
iv) it is important to distinguish between the national and international use of English. It is primarily the national uses of the institutionalised varieties which contribute towards the nativisation of these varieties.

v) non-native users ought to develop and identify with the local model of English without feeling that it is a 'deficient' model. The local (non-native) models of English are functionally as much a part of the linguistic repertoire of people as are the indigenous languages.
(Kachru, 1982: 51-2).

It would appear that many Sierra Leoneans are yet to come to terms with Kachru's admonitions. For example, features that are used by educated Sierra Leoneans are still being rated as deficient if they deviate from native English usage. For example, in a letter to the Deputy Vice Chancellor of Fourah Bay College, one of the constitutent colleges of the University of Sierra Leone, expressing the need for the strengthening of the English language component of Foundation Studies (a module offered by all first year students), the Head of the Language Studies Department of that institution had this to say:

> I find it difficult to sleep easily when I look back at what I see as the deterioration in competence of our students and children in our school system in Englist usage.
> (Osho, Language Studies Department, Fourah Bay College; 20th November, 2007:1)

He recommended the suspension of other components of the Foundation Studies module on the grounds that: 'The situation of

English usage is all but catastrophic, and delay might be fatal to our efforts to revive this crucial discipline.' (Osho, Language Studies Department, Fourah Bay College 20th November, 2007:3)

Pitt (1973) expressed a similar concern involving secondary pupils over thirty years earlier:
> One of the thorniest problems the language teacher has to face is how to get the students to express themselves well on paper, not only using English idiomatically and accurately, but also by avoiding stereotyped ideas.
> (Pitt, 1973: 3)

What can be observed is that in spite of these ceaseless complaints, that has not in any way minimised the differences between the English usage in Sierra Leone and that of native English; instead, these differences appear to continue to widen. This indicates the futility of reversing what would appear to be an unstoppable trend. English lecturers at Fourah Bay College are among others apparently aware of this existential reality as is shown in their use of lexemes (in passages set for their students) that reflect the country's social milieu:

I served them and each, with relative ease, voraciously reduced the mountain of foofoo with assorted meats in bitter leaf soup set before them. (Fourah Bay College, First Semester Examinations for the Diploma in Mass Communication, Communication Skills, February/March 2010, p. 2)

Ruru was soon restrained by the strong men who overpowered him and carried him, screaming and kicking in hysteria to the hut of the village's famous medicine man who alone knew how to cure mad people. (Fourah Bay College, Second Semester Examinations Foundation Studies, July 2008, p. 2) (emphasis mine)

It is interesting to note that in spite of her long years of western exposure, Forna (2002) – a Sierra Leonean – fully recognises the significance of the language that can capture the Sierra Leonean experience. This can be seen in the following examples, among others:

The massive hulk of the truck might easily crush the flimsy panbody of rusting corrugated iron...
> (The Devil that Danced on the Water, 2002: 3 emphacis mine)

> Empty by day, it serves as an illicit drinking den at night where men and women from the low-cost houses gather and drink omole, a twice-distilled palm wine...
> (The Devil that Danced on the Water, 2002: 4 emphacis mine)

> Against the metronome of cracking rocks I can hear car horns and the poda podas on Kissy Bye-Pass Road revving their engines...
> (The Devil that Danced on the Water, 2002: 5 emphacis mine)

> There were the tarnarind trees, black tombla.
> (The Devil that Danced on the Water, 2002: 6 emphacis mine)
> At the weekends my stepmother supervises in the kitchen and we have akara...
> (The Devil that Danced on the Water, 2002: 9 emphacis mine)

Significantly, Fyle (1968) earlier warned that "[the] attitude of 'British' and 'best' may be desirable for the patriotic Britisher; but it is narrowing and limiting for the Sierra Leonean" (Fyle, 1968: 9).

In this regard, English should be used in the country in ways that reflect the needs and aspirations of the locales of the country and at the same time be used for wider communication in the English-speaking world. This means that the emergence of a new variety should not trigger any fear that trends towards fragmentation will likely threaten the role of English as a lingua franca. Smith's research (1992), for example, has put this fear to rest. This research involves speakers of nine national varieties of English which are China, India, Indonesia, Japan, Papua New Guinea, the Philippines, Taiwan, the United Kingdom and the United States. Smith's aim is to show whether the fragmentation of the English language can lead to intelligibility problems across cultures. His findings indicate that English still functions as a lingua franca as there is no breakdown in communication among the subjects and that 'native speakers (from Britain and the US) were not found to be the most easily understood, nor were they, as subjects, found to be the best able to understand the different varieties of English' (Smith, 1992:88). One can therefore infer that the emergence of this new variety will add to the richness of the English language and leave it as unmistakably one language.

BIBLIOGRAPHY

Abott, G. (1991) "English Across Cultures: The Kachru Catch." In: <u>English Today</u> 7 (4), pp. 55-57.

Achebe, C. (1965) "English and the African Writer, Transition" In: <u>A Journal of the Arts, Culture and Society</u>, Vol. 4, No. 18.

– (1977) <u>Morning Yet on Creation Day</u>; London: Heinemann.

– (1958) <u>Things Fall Apart</u>; London: Heinemann.

– (1966) <u>Arrow of God</u>; London: Heinemann.

– (1966) <u>A Man of the People</u>; London: Heinemann.

Adichie, C. N. (2006) <u>Purple Hibiscus</u>; Nigeria: Farafina.

Adjaye, A. S. (1987) "English Pronunciation in Ghana". (Unpublished Ph.D Thesis, University of London).

Ahmar, M. (2006) "Pakistani English: Morphology and Syntax" In: Kortmann, B. et al. (eds.) (2006) <u>A Handbook of Varieties of English Vol. 1, Phonology</u>; Berlin and New York: Mouton de Gruyt pp. 1045-1057.

Ahulu, S. (1994) "How Ghanaian is Ghanaian English?" In: <u>English Today</u>, 38, 10.2 pp. 25-29.

Ajani, T.T. (2007) "Is There Indeed A "Nigerian Englsih?" In: <u>Journal of Humanities and Social Sciences</u> Vol. 1 issue 1. pp. 1-14.

Alo, M.A. and Mesthrie, R. (2006) "Nigerian English: Morphology and Syntax" In: Kortmann B. et al. (eds.) (2006) <u>A Handbook of Varieties of English Vol. 2, Morphology and Syntax</u>; Berlin and New York: Mouton de Gruyter pp. 813-827.

Anderwald, L. (2006) "The Varieties of English Spoken in the Southeast of England: Morphology and Syntax" In: Kortmann, B. et al. (eds.) (2006) <u>A Handbook of Varieties of English Vol. 2: Morphology and Syntax</u>; Berlin and New York: Mouton de Gruyter pp. 175-195.

Atechi, S. N. (2004) "The Intelligibility of Native and Non-Native English Speech: A Comparative Analysis of Cameroon English and American and British English" (Unpublished PhD. Thesis, Technischen Universität Chemnitz).

Awobuluyi, O. (1998)   "Language Education in Nigeria: Theory, Policy and Practice" In: <u>Internal Journal of Education</u>, Fafunwa Foundation
pp. 1-6.

Awonusi, V. (1987)   "The Identification of Standards within Institutionalised Non-Native Englishes: The Nigerian Experience" In: <u>Lares</u> IX, 47-63.

Bailey, R.W. and J. L. Robinson (1973)
<u>Varieties of Present Day English</u>; New York: Macmillan.

Bamgbose, A. (1971)   'The English Language in Nigeria' In: J. Spencer (ed.) (1971) <u>The English Language in West Africa</u>; London: Longman
pp. 35-48.

– (1976)   "Language in National Integration: Nigeria as a Case Study", read at the 12th West African Languages Congress,
University of Ife, Nigeria, March 15-20.

– (1982)   'Standard Nigerian English: Issues of Identification' In: B. B. Kachru (ed.) (1982)
<u>The Other Tongue: English across Cultures</u>;
Oxford: Pergamon Press
pp. 99-111.

– (1991) Language and the Nation, The Language Question in Sub-Saharan Africa;
Edinburgh: Edinburgh University Press.

Banjo, A. (1971) "Towards a Definition of 'Standard Nigerian Spoken English" Actes da 8a Congress de la Societe Linguistique
de l'Afrique
Occidental, Abidjan.

Baskaran, L. (2006) "Malaysian English: Phonology" In: Schneider, E. W. et al. (eds.) (2006) A Handbook of Varieties of English Vol. 1, Phonoloy;
Berlin and New York: Mouton de Gruyter
pp. 1034-1046.

Barber, C. L. (1977) The Story of Language;
London: Longamn.

Bartsch, R. (1987) Norms of Language;
London: Longman.

Baumgardner, Robert J. (1993)
"The Indigenisation of English in Pakistan" In: Robert J. Baumgardner (ed.) (1993) The English Language in Pakistan;
Karachi: Oxford University Press.
pp. 41-54.

Beal, J. (2006) "English Dialects in the North of England: Morphology and Syntax" In: Kortmann, B. et al. (eds.), (2006) <u>A Handbook of Varieties of English Vol. 2: Morphology and Syntax</u>; Berlin and New York: Mouton de Gruyter pp. 114-141.

Berman, R. A. Olshtain, E. (1983) "Features of First Language Transfer in Second Language Attrition" <u>Applied Linguistics</u> Vol. 4, No. 3, pp. 222-235.

Bex T. and Watts R. J. (1999) <u>Standard English: The Widening Debate</u>; New York: Routeledge.

Bhatt, Rakesh M. (2006) "Indian English: Syntax" In: Kortmann, B. et al. (eds.) (2006) <u>A Handbook of Varieties of English Vol. 2, Morphology and Syntax</u>; Berlin and New York: Mouton de Gruyter pp. 1016-1030.

Bobda, A. S. (1994) <u>Aspects of Cameroon English Phonology</u>; Peter Lang. Inc., European Academic Publishers: Bern.

– (1997) "Sociocultural Constraints in EFL Teaching in Cameroon". In: Pütz, Martin (ed.) <u>The Cultural Context in Foreign Language Teaching</u>;

Frankfurt a.m.: Lang. 221-240.

– (1999) "Pertinent, but not a Contradiction of Kachru" [Comment on Modiano [1999]. In: English Today 15/2 29

– (2000a) "Comparing Some Phonological Features across African Accents of English" In: English Studies (2000) pp. 249-266.

– (2000b) "Explicating the features of African English Pronunciation: Some Steps Further", Zeitschrift fur Afrikanistik (ZAA) (Tubingen, Germany) Vol. 48 (2), 123-136.

– (2000c) "Research on New Englishes: A Critical Review of Some Findings So Far, with Focus on Cameroon English." In: Arbeiten aus Anglistik und Amerikanistik (AAA), Austria, Vol. 25 (1) pp. 53-70.

– (2006) "Cameroon English: Phonology" In: Schneider, E. W. et al. (eds.) (2006) A Handbook of Varieties of English Vol. 1, Phonology; Berlin and New York: Mouton de Gruyter pp. 885-901.

– (2007) "Patterns of Segment Sequence Simplification in Some African

Englishes" In: World Englishes (2007) Vol. 26, No. 4, pp. 411-423.

Bokamba, Eyamba G. (1982) "The Africanisation of English" In: B. B. Kachru (ed.)
(1982) The Other Tongue, English Across Cultures; Oxford: Pergamon 77-98.

– (1991) "West Africa" (Overview article) In: Jenny Cheshire (ed.) (1991) English Around the World Sociolinguistic Perspectives;
Cambridge: Cambridge University Press.
pp. 493-508.

Brosnahan, L.F. (1958) "English in Southern Nigeria" In: English Studies. 39(3) pp. 97-110.

Brown, K. (1968) "Intelligibility", In: Davies, A, (ed.) (1968)
Language Testing Symposium; London: Oxford University Press. pp. 180-191.

Buyonge, C. (1968) "Presuppositions and Implicature in the Use of Ekegusii Modal Construction, Conditional and Honorifics".
(Unpublished M. A. Thesis, Egerton University).

Cheshire, J. (1991) (ed.) English Around the World: Sociolinguistics Perspectives;
Cambridge: Cambridge University Press.

Chevillet, F. (1993)   "English or Englishes?" In: English Today 36, Vol. 9 (4). Cambridge: Cambridge University Press. pp. 29-33

Chinebuah, Isaac K. (1976) "Grammatical Deviance and First Language Interference".
                            In: West African Journal of Modern Languages 1: 67-78.

Chisanga, T. (1989)   "Non-Problematic Zambianisms' and their Implications for the Teaching of English in Zambia" In: Schmied, J. (ed.) (1989) English in East and Central Africa; Bayreuth: Bayreuth University.
                            pp. 63-84.

Chomsky, N. (1986)   Knowledge of Language: its Nature, Origin and Uses;
                            New York: Praeger.

Christerphersen, P. (1973) Second Language Learning: Myth and Reality; Harmondsworth: Penguin.

– (1992)   "Native" Models and Foreign Learners"In: English Today 31, Vol. 8 (3).
                            Cambridge: Cambridge University Press.
                            pp. 16-18.

Clarke, S. (2006)   "New Foundland English: Morphology and Syntax"
                            In: Kortmann, B. et al. (eds.) (2006)

<u>A Handbook of Varieties of English Vol. 2, Morphology and Syntax</u>; Berlin and New York: Mouton de Gruyter
pp. 303-318.

Coomber, Melvin E. A. (1969) "A Descriptive Story of Krio Phonology"
(Unpublished Master of Science Thesis, Georgetown University).

– (1995) "Deviances in the English of Kenyan Newspapers?"
(Unpublished Article, Moi University).

Conteh, O. (2005) "An Investigation into the Lexical Errors in the Written English Composition of Junior Secondary School Three (JSS III) Krio Speaking Pupils: A Case Study of Ahmadiyya Muslim Secondary School, Freetown" (Unpublished B. A. Long Essay, Fourah Bay College).

Conteh-Morgan, M. (1997) "English in Sierra Leone: A Description of the Language as used in this West African Country and a Consideration of its Status There" In: <u>English Today</u> 13/3: 52-56.

Corder, S.P. (1971) "Idiosyncratic Dialects and Error Analysis" In: <u>IRAL</u> 9.
pp. 147-159.

Crystal, D. (1988) <u>The English Language</u>; Harmondsworth: Penguin.

– (1997) English as a Global Language; Cambridge: Cambridge University Press.

– (1999) "The Future of Englishes" In: English Today 15 (2), 10-20.

– (2003) English as a Global Language; 2nd ed. Cambridge: Cambridge University Press.

Dako, K. (2003) Ghanaianisms: A Glossary; Accra: Ghana Universities Press.

Davies, Alan (1989) "Is International English an Inter-language?" In: TESOL Quarterly 23/3 447-467.

Davies, Ruth M. (2006) "Socio-Economic Status and Performance in Language Arts in the Basic Cerfiticate Examination with Special Reference to Junior Secondary School Three (JSS III) at St. Joseph's Secondary School and Government Model Secondary School" (Unpublished B. A. Long Essay, Fourah Bay College).

De Kadt, Elisabeth (1993) "Attitudes towards English in South Africa" In: World Englishes 12/3 311-324.

Deneire, Mark (1998) "A Response to Widdowsons's EIL, ESL, EFL: Global Issues and Local Interests" In: <u>World Englishes</u> 17/3 393-395.

Department of Education (1993) <u>Source Book for Four Sierra Leonean Languages</u>; Freetown: The Government Printing Department

– (1995) <u>New Education Policy for Sierra Leone</u>; Freetown: The Government Printing Department

Derwing, T. and J. M. Munro (1997) "Acceptability, Intelligibility and Comprehensibility: Evidence From Four L_1s" In: Studies in Second Language Acquisition 19, 1-16.

Dundy, E. (2005) <u>The Old Man and Me</u>. London: Virago Press.

Ellis, R. (1985) <u>Understanding Second Language Acquisition</u>; Oxford: Oxford University Press.

Fakoya, A. H. (1989) "Describing Nigerian English Phonology: A Step Further". Paper presented at the XIXth Annual Conference of Nigerian English Studies Assocation (NESA).

Fasold, R. (1984) <u>The Sociolinguistics of Society</u>; Oxford: Basil Blackwell.

Feltz, V. (2007) "Don't Sentence Our Language to Death" In: <u>Daily Express</u> England, 30th October, 2007, p. 11.

Fergusson, C.A. (1982) (1982) 'Forward' In: Braj B. Kachru, (ed.) <u>The Other Tongue: English Across Cultures</u>; Oxford: Pergamon Press pp. vii-xi).

Filppula, M. (2006) "Irish English: Morphology and Syntax" In: Kortmann, B. et al. (eds.) (2006) <u>A Handbook of Varieties of English Vol. 2, Morphology and Syntax</u>; Berlin and New York: Mouton de Gruyter pp. 73-101.

Fishman, J. A. (1972) <u>The Sociology of Language: An Interdisciplinary Social Science Approach to Language in Society</u>; Rowley, Mass: Newbury House.

Flynn, S. and O'Neil W. (1988) <u>Lingusitic Theory in Second Language Acquisition</u>; Dordrecht.. Kluwer Academic Publishers.

Forna, A. (2002) <u>The Devil that Danced on the Water</u>; London: Flamingo.

Fyle, C. (1968) "The Local Languages and the Teacher of English in the Secondary School" In: <u>Journal of Education</u>,

	Ministry of Education, Sierra Leone, Vol. 3, no. 1, October 1968, pp. 8-13.
– (1975):	"A National languages Policy and the Teacher of English in Sierra Leone" In: <u>Journal of Education</u>, Ministry of Education, Sierra Leone, Vol. 10, no. 2, October 1975, pp. 6-11.
Fyle, C. and Jones, E. (1980)	<u>Krio – English Dictionary</u>; Oxford: Oxford University Press.
Gargesh, R. (2006)	"Indian English: Phonology" In: Schneider, E. W. et al. (eds.) (2006) <u>A Handbook of Varieties of English Vol. 1: Phonology</u>; Berlin and New York: Mouton de Gruyter pp. 992-1002.
Gill, S. K. (1993)	"Standards and Pedagogical Norms for Teaching English in Malaysia" In: <u>World Englishes</u> 12 (2) 223-238.
Gimson, A. C. (1989)	<u>An Introduction to the Pronunciation of English</u>; (fourth edition) London: Edward Arnold.
Görlach, M. (1997)	"Language and Nation: The Concept of Linguistic Identity in the History of Englsih" In: <u>English World-Wide</u> 18, 1-34.
Graddol, D. (1996)	"Global English, global Culture?" In: Groodman, S. and Graddol, D. (eds.)

(1996) <u>Redesigning English New Texts, New Identities</u>; London, Routledge pp. 181-217.

Gut, U. (2006)   "Nigerian English: Phonology" In: Schneider, E. W. (eds.) (2006) <u>A Handbook of Varieties of English Vol. 1, Phonology</u>; Berlin and New York: Mouton de Gruyter pp. 813-830.

Gyasi, I. K. (1990)   "The State of English in Ghana" In: <u>English Today</u> 6 (3), 24-26.

– (1991)   "Aspects of English in Ghana" In: <u>English Today</u> 26, pp. 26-31.

Honey, John (1997)   <u>Language is Power: The Story of Standard English and its Enemies</u>; London: Faber and Faber.

Hornby, A.S. (2005)   Oxford Advanced Learners' Dictionary; Oxford: Oxford University Press.

Huber, M. and Dako, K. (2006)
"Ghanaian English: Morphology and Syntax" In: Kortmann B. et al. (eds.) (2006) <u>A Handbook of Varieties of English Vol. 2: Morphology and Syntax</u>; Berlin and New York: Mouton de Gruyter pp. 854-865.

Huber, M. (2006) "Ghanaian English: Phonology" In: Schneider, E. W. et al. (eds.) (2006) <u>A Handbook of Varieties of English Vol. 1, Phonology</u>; Berlin and New York: Mouton de Gruyter pp. 842-865.

Hughes, A. and Trudgill, P. (1987) <u>English Accents and Dialects An Introduction to Social and Regional Varieties of British English</u>; (second edition) London: Edward Arnold.

Huang, Q. (2009) "Probe into the Internal Mechanism of Interlanguge Fossilisation" In: <u>English Language Teaching</u> Vol. 2, No. (2009) pp. 73-77.

Hung, T. (1995) "Some aspects of the Segmental Phonology of Singapore English" In: Teng Su Ching and Ho Mian Lian (eds.) (1995) <u>The English Language in Singapore: Implications for Teaching</u>. 29-41 Singapore: Singapore Association for Applied Linguistics.

Jenkins, J. (2000) <u>The Phonology of English as an International Language</u>; Oxford: Oxford University Press.

Jones, D. (2006) <u>Pronouncing English Dictionary</u>;

	Cambridge, Cambridge University Press.
Jowitt, D. (1991)	<u>Nigerian Usage: An Introduction</u>; Ikeja: Longman.
Kachru, Braj B. (1976)	"Indian English: A Sociolinguistic Profile of a Transplanted Language" In: <u>Dimensions of Bilingualism; Theory and Studies, Special Issue of Studies in Language Learning</u>, Unit for Foreign Language Study and Research, Urbana: University of Illinois. pp.139-189.
– (1982)	<u>The Other Tongue: English across Culltures</u>; Oxford: Pergamon Press.
– (1982)	"Models for Non-Native Varieties of English" In: Braj B. Kachru (ed.) (1982) <u>The Other Tongue: English across Culltures</u>; Oxford: Pergamon Press. pp. 31-57.
– (1985)	"Standards, Codification and Sociolinguistic Realism: The English Language in the Outer Circle" In: Quirk and Widdowson (eds.) (1985) <u>English in the World</u>; Cambridge: Cambridge University Press pp. 11-30.

– (1986)   The Alchemy of English: The Spread, Functions and Models of Non-Native Englishes; Oxford: Pergamon Press.

– (1988)   "The Sacred Cows of English" In: Englsih Today, The International review of the English Language, ET 16 Vol. IV No. 4 pp. 3-8.

– (1990)   "World Englishes and Applied Linguistics" In: World Englishes 9 (1), 3-30.

– (1991)   "Liberation Linguistics and the Quirk Concerns" In: English Today 25 7 (1), 3-13.

– (1992)   The Other Tongue: English across Cultures; (second edition) Urbana, University of Illnois Press.

Kallay, A. Y. (2006)   "Private Schools in Sierra Leone" In: Standard Times, 1st May 2006, p. 2.

Kasper, G. (1995)   "Inter-language Pragmatics" In: Jef Verschueren, Jan-Ola Ostman and Jan Blommaert (eds.) (1995) Handbook of Pragmatics; Amsterdam: John Benjamins.

Kershaw, George (1996)   "The Developing Roles of Native-Speakers and Non-native Speakers Teachers" In: Modern English Teacher 5/3 7-11.

Kingman, J. (1988)   "The Kingman report" In: Englsih Today, The International review of the English Language, ET 16 Vol. IV No. 4
pp. 15-29.

Labov, W. (1966)   The Social Stratification of English in New York City, Washington D.C.; Centre for Applied Linguistics.

Lardiere, D. (1988)   "Case and Tense in the 'Fossilised' State. Second Language Acquisition" In: Applied Linguistics 18.2 pp. 141-165.

Lardo, V. (2000)   McNally's Dilemma; The Berkley Publishing Group; New York

Lass, R. (1984)   Phonology: An Introduction to Basic Concepts;
Cambridge: Cambridge University Press.

Leith, D. (1983)   A Social History of English;
London: Routledge and Kegan Paul.

MacArthur, Tom (1998)   The English Language;
Cambridge: Cambridge University Press.

Mahboob, A. and Ahmar, N.H. (2006)
"Pakistani English: Phonology" In: Schneider, E. W. et al.
(eds.) (2006) A Handbook of Varieties of English Vol. 1, Phonology;

Berlin and New York: Mouton de Gruyter
pp. 1003-1016.

Maryns, K. (2000) English in Sierra Leone: Sociolinguistic Investigation; Studia Germanic Gandensia.

Mazrui, Ali A. (1975) The Political Sociology of the English Language: An African Perspective; The Hague, Mouton.

Mbangwana, P. (1987) "Some Characteristics of Sound Patterns of Cameroon Standard English" In: Multilingua 6 (4): pp. 411-424.

– (1992) "Some Grammatical Sign Posts in Cameroon Standard English" In: Schmied Josef J. (ed.) (1992) English in East and Central Africa. 11
pp. 93-102
Bayreuth: Bayreuth University.

– (1999) "The Linguistic Deculturation of English Usage in Cameroon," In: Echu, G; and Grundstrom, A. W. (eds.) (1999) Official Bilingualism and Linguisitc Commuication in Cameroon;
New York: Peter Lang.
pp. 87-102.

– (2006) "Cameroon English: Morphology and Sytax" In: Kortmann, B. et al. (eds.) (2006) A Handbook of Varieties of

English Vol. 2: Morphology and Syntax;
Berlin and New York: Mouton de Gruyter
pp. 898-908.

McCormick, L. (2006)   "Cape Flats English: Morphology and Syntax" In: Kortmann, B. et al. (eds.) (2006) A Handbook of Varieties of English Vol. 2, Morphology and Syntax;
Berlin and New York: Mouton de Gruyter
pp. 993-1005.

Mclaughlin, B. (1987)   Theories of Second Language Learning;
London: Edward Arnold.

Mesthrie, R. (2006)   "Synopsis: The Phonology of English in Africa and South and Southeast Asia" In: Schneider, E. W. et al. (eds.) (2006) A Handbook of Varieties of English Vol. 1, Phonology;
Berlin and New York: Mouton de Gruyter
pp. 1099-1110.

– (2006)   "Synopsis: morphological and syntactic variation in Africa and south and south east Asia" In: Kortmann, B. et al. (eds.) (2006) A Handbook of Varieties of English Vol. 2, Morphology and Syntax;
Berlin and New York: Mouton de Gruyter
pp. 1132-1141.

– (2006) "Black South African English: Morphology and Syntax" In: Kortmann, B. et al. (eds.) (2006) <u>A Handbook of Varieties of English Vol. 2: Morphology and Syntax</u>; Berlin and New York: Mouton de Gruyter pp. 962-973.

– (2006) "Indian South African English: Morphology and Syntax" In: Kortmann, B. et al. (eds) (2006) <u>A Handbook of Varieties of English Vol. 2, Morphology and Syntax</u>; Berlin and New York: Mouton de Gruyter pp. 974-992.

Mesthrie, R. and Bhatt, R. (2008) "World Englishes The Study of New Linguistic Varieties; Cambridge: Cambridge University Press

Mettle, E. E. D. (1984) "Error Analysis of Samples of Primary School English". (Unpublished B. A. Dissertation, Fourah Bay College).

Milroy, J. (1981) <u>Regional Accents of English</u>; Belfast: Blackstaff.

Milroy, J. and Milroy, L. (1985) Authority in Language Investigation

Language, Prescription and Standardisation; London: Routledge and Kegan Paul.

Ministry of Education (1970)   White Paper on Educational Policy; Freetown: The Government Printing Department.

– (1987)   "Policy and Strategies for Adult Education in Sierra Leone". Jointly Organised by the Ministry of Education, Cultural Affairs and Sports and the Sierra Leone Adult Education Association 10th – 13th March, 1987, Freetown, Sierra Leone.

– (1979)   Indigenous Languages Education Pilot Project; Freetown: The Government Printing Department.

Modiano, Marko (1999)   "International English in the Global Village" In:
English Today 15/2 22-27.

Mugler, F. & Tent J. (2006)   "Fiji English: Morphology and Syntax"
In: Kortmann, B. et al. (eds.) (2006) A Handbook of Varieties of English Vol. 2, Morphology and Syntax; Berlin and New York: Mouton de Gruyter
pp. 770-788.

Nimako, A. (2004)   Mind Your Language: Educated Ghanaian English;
Tema: Ronna Publishers.

Number 10 Gov. UK (2008) "English – The World's Language" In: The Official Site of the Prime Minister's Office; 17th January, 2008. pp. 1-3.

Okoro, O. (1986) "Standard Nigerian English vs Errors: Where to Draw the Line?" In: Wares VIII, 94-106.

Osho, K. O. (2007) "Proposal for the Expansion of the English Language Program, Foundation Studies" In Department of Language Studies Fourah Bay College 20th November, 2007.

Owu-Ewie, C. (2006) "The Language Policy of Eduction in Ghana: A Critical Look at the English – Only Language Policy of Education" In: Mugane J. et al. (eds.) (2006) Selected Proceedings of the 35th Annual Conference on African Linguistic;
Somervilles, M A: Cascadilla Proceedings Project. pp. 76-85.

Oyétádé B. A. and Fashole-Luke, V. (2007)
"Sierra Leone: Krio and the Quest for National Integration"
In: A. Simpson (ed.) (2007) Language and National Identity in Africa;
Oxford: Oxford University Press. pp. 122-140.

Palmer, G. 1996 "In-Service Education and Training of Secondary School Teachers of English: The Overseas Development

Administration (ODA) British Funded Key English Language Teaching (KELT) In-Service Courses for Secondary School Teachers of English" (Unpublished Masters of Education Thesis, Fourah Bay College, University of Sierra Leone).

Passe, H. A. (1947) "The English Language in Ceylon." (Unpublished PhD. Thesis, University of London).

Pemagbi, J. (1987) "Sierra Leone – A Multilingual Community." In: <u>Policy and Strategies for Adult Education</u>; Report of a National Conference jointly organised by the Ministry of Education, Cultural Affairs and Sports and the Sierra Leone Adult Education Association, 10th – 13th March, 1987, Freetown, Sierra Leone.
pp. 32-64.

– (1989) "Still a Deficient Language?"
- A Description and Glossary of the "New English" of Sierra Leone. In: <u>English Today</u> 5-17, 20-24.

– (1992) The Implications of the New English in Sierra Leone for the English Language Teacher" In: <u>Educational Research in Africa</u>:
<u>Journal of the Faculty of Education</u>, Njala University College, University of Sierra Leone, Vol. 2.
pp 23-37.

– (1995) "Using Newspapers and Radio in English Language Teaching: The Sierra Leone Experience." In: <u>English Teaching Forum: A Journal of English Otside the United States</u> Vol. 33 No. 3, July, 1995, pp. 53-55.

Penhallurick, Robert J. (1991) <u>The Anglo-Welsh Dialects of North Wales</u>; A Survey of <u>Conservative Rural Spoken English in the Countries of Gwynedd and Clwyd</u>; Frankfurt am Main: Lang.

– (2006) "Welsh English: Morphology and Syntax" In: Kortmann, B. et al. (eds.) (2006) <u>A Handbook of Varieties of English Vol. 2: Morphology and Syntax</u>; Berlin and New York: Mouton de Gruyter pp. 102-113.

Pennycook, A. (1994) <u>The Cultural Policies of English as an International Language</u>; London: Longman.

Phillipson, Robert (1996) "Realities and Myths of Linguistic Imperialism" In: <u>Journal of Multilingual and Multicultural Development</u> 18/3 238-247.

Platt, John, Heider, Weber and Ho, Mian Lian (1984)
<u>The New Englishes</u>;
London: Routledge and Kegan Paul.

Prator, C. (1968) "The British Heresy in TESL"
In: J. A. Fishman et al. (eds.) (1968) <u>Language Problems in Developing Nations</u>;
New York: John Wiley.
pp. 459-476.

Pulcini, Virginia (1997) "Attitude towards the Spread of English in Italy." In: <u>World Englishes</u> Vol. 16/1. 77-85.

Quirk, R. (1968) <u>The Use of English</u>;
London: Longman.

Quirk, R., Greenbaum, S., and Svartvik, J. (1972)
<u>A Grammar of Contemporary English</u>;
London: Longman.

Quirk, R. & Widdowson, H. G. (eds.) (1985)
<u>English in the World Teaching and Learning the Language and Literatures</u>;
The Press Syndicate of the University of Cambridge.

Quirk, Randolph (1985) "The English Language in a Global Context."
In: Randolph Quirk and H. G. Widdowson (eds.) (1985) <u>English in the World. Teaching and Learning the Language and Literatures</u>;

Rahman, T. (1990)   Cambridge: Cambridge University Press pp. 1-6.

Rahman, T. (1990)   <u>Pakistani English: The Linguistic Description of a Non- Native Variety of English</u>.
Islamabad: National Institute of Pakistan Studies
Quaid – I – Azan University.

Roach, P. (2000)   <u>English Phonetics and Phonology</u>; (Third Edition)
Cambridge: Cambridge University Press.

Rooy, B. V. (2006)   "Black South African English: Phonology" In: Schneider, E. W. et al. (eds.) (2006) <u>A Handbook of Varieties of English Vol. 1, Phonology</u>;
Berlin and New York: Mouton de Gruyter
pp. 943-952.

Sampson, G. P. and Richards, J. E. (1973)
         "Learner Language Systems." In: <u>Language Sciences</u> 19. pp. 18-25.

Schmied, J. (1985)   "Attitudes towards English in Tanzania." In: <u>English World-Wide</u> 6,
pp. 237-269.

– (1988)   "Recognising and Accepting East African English

	Grammar." In: Proceedings of the British Council Conference on the Place of Grammar in the Teching of English, Nairobi, April, 1988. pp. 94-101.
– (1989)	"Second-Language Varieties Across the Indian Ocean." In: Josef Schmied (ed.) (1989) English in East and Central Africa; Bayreuth: Bayreuth University. pp. 85-97.
– (1991)	English in Africa: An Introduction ; London: Longman.
– (1996)	"English in Zimbabwe, Zambia and Malawi." In: De Klerk, Vivian (ed.) (1996) Varieties of English Around the World: Focus on South Africa; Amsterdam: Benjamins. pp. 211-230.
– (2006)	"East African English (Kenya, Uganda, Tanzania): Morphology and Syntax" In: Kortmann, B. et al. (eds.) (2006) A Handbook of varieties of English Vol. 2, Morphology and Syntax; Berlin and New York: Mouton de Gruyter pp. 929-947.
Seidlhofer, B. (2004)	"Research Perspectives on teaching English as a Lingua Franca" In :

	Annual Review of Applied Linguistics; 24, pp. 209-239.
– (1999)	"Double Standards. Teacher Education in the Expanding Circle." In: *World Englishes* 18/2 pp. 233-245.
Sekyi-Baidro, Y. and Koranteng L. A. (2008)	"English General Greetings in the Ghanaian Sociolinguistic Context" In: Thao Lõ LE and Quynh Lã (eds.) (1989) *The International Journal of Language Society and Culture*; Issue 26 pp. 113-125.
Selinker, L. (1972)	"Inter-language" In: *International Review of Applied Linguistics* 10.3:209-31.
– (1974)	"Inter-language" In: Richards J. (eds.) (1974) *Error Analysis: Perspectives on Second Language Acquisition*; London: Longman. pp. 31-54.
– (1992)	*Rediscovering Inter-language*; London: Longman.
Sesay, K. (1982)	"An Analysis of Grammatical and Lexical NP Errors in the Written English of University Students in Sierra Leone and their Pedagogical Implications."

	(Unpublished Ph.D thesis, University of London).
Sey, K. (1973)	<u>Ghanaian English: An Exploratory Survey</u>; London: Macmillan
Shaw, W. D. (1981)	"Asian Student, Attitudes Towards English" In: L. E. Smith (ed.) (1983) (sic) <u>Readings in English as an International Language</u>; Oxford: Pergamon pp. 21-33.
Shorrocks, G. (1999)	<u>A Grammar of the Dialect of the Bolton Area</u>; Frankfurt am Main: Lang.
Smith, L. E. (1976)	"English as an International Auxiliary Language." In: Smith (ed.) (1983) (sic) <u>Readings in English as an International Language</u>; Oxford: Pergamon, pp. 1-6.
– (1983)	<u>Readings in English as an International Language</u>; Oxford: Pergamon.
– (1992)	"Spread of English and Matters of Intelligibility" In: B. B. Kachru (ed.) (1992), <u>The Other Tongue: English across Cultures</u>; (second edition) Urbana: University of Illinois Press pp. 75-90.

Sorance, A. (1996) "Permanent Optionality as Divergence in Non-native Grammars". Paper presented at EUROSLA6, Nijmegen.

Soyinka, W. (1973) <u>Collected Plays 2</u>;
Oxford: Oxford University Press.

Spencer, J. (1971) <u>The English Language in West Africa</u>;
London: Longman.

Sridhar, K. K. & Sridhar, S. N. 1992
"Bridging the Paradigm Gap: Second-language acquisition theory and indigenised varieties of English" In: B. B. Kachru, (ed), 1992, <u>The Other Tongue: English Across Cultures</u>; (second edition)
Urbana, Illinois: University of Illinois Press.
pp 91-107.

Strevens, P. (1983) "What is Standard English?" In: Larry Smith (ed.) (1983)
<u>Readings in English as an International Language</u>;
Oxford: Pergamon Press.
pp. 87-93.

Sumner, D. L. (1963) <u>Education in Sierra Leone</u>; Freetown, Sierra Leone
The Government of Sierra Leone.

Sure, K. (1996)   "Expression of National Ethos in a Non-Native Language." In: <u>Journal of Third World Studies Vol. XIII</u> New Columbus, Georgia: Georgia Printing Service Inc.
pp. 189-208.

Thullah, A. (2009)   "An Examination of the Lexical Deviations in the English Usage of Senior Secondary School Pupils of the Methodist Boys' High School." (Unpublished B.A. dissertation, Fourah Bay College).

Todd, L. (1982)   "The English Language in West Africa" In: Bailey and Gorleach (eds.) (1982) <u>English as a World Language</u>;
Cambridge: Cambridge University Press,
pp. 282-305.

– (1986)   <u>International English Usage</u>;
London: Routledge.

– (1989)   "Languages in Conflict: Varieties of English in Northern Ireland." In: Ofelia Garcia, Richardo Otherguy (eds.) (1989) <u>English Across Cultures</u>: <u>Cultures across English</u>;
Berlin: de Gruyter
pp. 335-355.

Trudgill, P. (1974)   <u>The Social Differentiation of English in Norwich</u>; Cambridge: Cambridge University Press.

– (1986)   <u>Dialects in Contact</u>;

Oxford: Basil Blackwell.

Trudgill, P. and Hannah J. (1985)
<u>International English: A Guide to Varieties of Standard English</u>;
(Second Edition)
London: Edward Arnold.

Udofot, I. (2003)
"Stress and Rhythm in the Nigerian Accent of English." In:
<u>English World-Wide</u> 24, pp. 201-220

Vavrus, Francess (1991)
"When Paradigms Clash: The Role of Institutionalised Varieties in Language Teacher Education." In: <u>World Englishes</u> 10/2, pp. 181-196.

Vincent, I. (1974)
"Registers in Achebe."
In: <u>INESK</u>,
pp. 95-106.

Walsh, N. (1967)
"Distinguishing Types and Varieties of English in Nigeria" In: <u>Journal of the Nigerian English Studies Association</u> 2:2, pp. 47-55.

Wa Thiong'o, N. (1964)
<u>Weep Not Child</u>;
London: Heinemann.

– (1977)
<u>Petals of Blood</u>;
London: Heinemann.

– (1981)
<u>A Writer's Prison Diary</u>;
Nairobi: Heinemann Kenya.

– (1986)
<u>Decolonising the Mind</u>;
London: James Curry.

Wee, I. (2006) "Singapore English: Phonology" In: Schneider, E. W. et al. (eds.) (2006) *A Handbook of Varieties of English Vol. 1, Phonology*; Berlin and New York: Mouton de Gruyter pp. 1017-1033. Widdowson, Henry G.

- (1993) "Proper Words in Proper Places." In: *ELT Journal* 47/4 pp. 317-329.

– (1994) "The Ownership of English." In: *TESOL Quarterly* 28/2 pp. 377-389.

– (1997) "EIL, ESL, EFL. Global Issues and Local Interests" In: *World Englishes* 16/1 pp. 146-153.

– (1998) "EIL: Squaring the Circles: A Reply." In: *World Englishes* 17/3 pp. 397-401.

Wilkins, D. (1974) *Second Language Learning and Teaching*; London: Edward Arnold.

INDEX
Aboriginal Words, 54, 99, 100, 142, 191, 192.
Adjective, 64, 110, 208, 209, 210.
Collocation, 46, 47, 48, 92, 93, 94, 95, 138, 139, 178, 179, 180.

Consonants
Deletion/omission, 38, 87, 88, 133, 134, 170, 171, 172.
Intrusive r, 36, 37, 86, 133, 170, 171, 172.
Linking r, 36, 37, 86, 133, 170, 171, 172.
Spelling-induced, 31, 32, 83, 84, 132, 168, 169, 170.
Substitution, 34, 35, 85, 86, 131, 132, 169, 170, 171, 172.
Syllabic Consonant, 37, 81, 133, 170, 171, 172.

Determiner
Determiner usage, 61, 62, 106, 107, 149, 150, 204, 205, 206, 207.
Article inclusion, 63, 107, 108, 150, 204, 205, 206, 207.
Article omission, 63, 64, 109, 110, 150, 151, 205, 206, 207.

Discourse
Form of address, 76, 122, 159.
Phatic communion, 78, 125, 160.
Proverb/riddle, 77, 123, 160.
Style, 79, 126, 161.

Downdrift, 39, 89, 134, 177.

Idiomaticity
Local idioms, 52, 98, 141, 186, 187, 188.
Native English idioms, 51, 97, 141, 186, 187, 188.

Intonation, 42, 90, 135, 175, 176, 177.
Nasalization, 32, 84, 130.
Nationalism, 229, 230.
Nationality, 229.
Noun, 55, 101, 143, 195.

Preposition

Prepositional usage, 65, 110, 151, 210, 211, 212.
Prepositional inclusion, 66, 112, 153, 211, 212, 213.
Prepositional omission, 65, 112, 153, 211, 212, 213.

Pronoun
Pronoun usage, 50, 101, 144, 197, 198, 119.
Resumptive pronoun/ pronoun copying, 72, 118, 156, 219.

Spelling, 31, 35, 83, 130, 132, 166, 169.
Stress, 44, 91, 136, 176, 177, 178.
Syllable timing, 38, 39, 134, 173.

Syntax
Comparison, 71, 116, 155, 173, 218, 221.
Function and content words, 71, 117, 155, 219, 221.
Imbalance, 68, 114, 154, 216, 217, 221.
Placement of modifiers, 73, 119, 157, 219, 220, 221.
Reduplication, 69, 115, 154, 217, 221.
Repetition, 69, 115, 154, 217, 221.
Universal tag, 75, 157, 220, 221.
Yes/no questions/statements, 75, 122, 158, 220, 221.

Tonality, 42, 90, 135, 175, 177.

Verb
Concord, 57, 103, 145, 200, 203.
Infinitive/participle, 58, 104, 146, 201, 203.
Tense/aspect, 59, 105, 147, 201, 202, 203.

Vowel
Vowel margin, 27, 51, 128, 163, 164, 168.
Vowel substitution, 29, 82, 129, 165, 168.
Dipthong margin, 33, 131, 166, 167, 168.
Dipthong substitution, 131, 166, 167, 168.

Word class, 67, 113, 153, 213, 214, 215.
Word meaning, 51, 96, 140, 184.

Meaning change, 51, 96, 140, 184.
Restriction of word meaning, 50, 95, 140, 183, 184.
Extension of word meaning, 49, 95, 139, 182, 183, 184.

www.ingramcontent.com/pod-product-compliance
Lightning Source LLC
Chambersburg PA
CBHW050133170426
43197CB00011B/1821